Form
and
History
in
American
Literary
Naturalism

June
Howard

Form
and
History
in
American
Literary
Naturalism

The
University
of
North
Carolina
Press

Chapel
Hill
and
London

The publication of this work was made
possible in part through a grant from the
National Endowment for the Humanities,
a federal agency whose mission is to
award grants to support education, schol-
arship, media programming, libraries,
and museums, in order to bring the results of cultural activities to a broad, general public.

Manufactured in the United States of America

Library of Congress Cataloging in Publication Data
Howard, June.
    Form and history in American literary naturalism.

    Includes index.
    1. American fiction—History and criticism.
2. Naturalism in literature. I. Title.
PS374.N29H68 1985   813'.009'12   85-1005
ISBN 0-8078-1650-7

Part of Chapter 1 appeared in somewhat
different form in *Critical Exchange*,
no. 14 (Fall 1983): 70–80, and was
reprinted in *The New Orleans Review*
11, no. 1 (Spring 1984): 52–58.

For my fathers

Contents

Preface

The present study is a detailed reading of a single literary genre, American literary naturalism, as a distinctive response to its historical moment. As I make that statement its implications clamor for annotation—I may not mean exactly what the reader expects when I speak of genre, of history, or of literary texts as responses to history. The chapters that follow make those discriminations; they proceed more or less inductively, working from within familiar formulations to reconstruct our ideas of genre criticism, of the relation between literary form and history, and of naturalism and American naturalism. Let me here suggest more summarily just where those arguments will lead us.

When Americans of the late nineteenth and early twentieth centuries voiced their thoughts for contemporaries or recorded them for posterity they often reported that they felt themselves living in a perilous time, a period of change and uncertainty, of dislocations and disorders. Naturalism is a literary form that struggles to accommodate that sense of discomfort and danger, a form that unremittingly attends to the large social questions of its period. An investigation of naturalism thus doubly entails an investigation of its historical moment—as the condition of its production and as the source of discourses embedded within the works. I will sketch a range of historical and cultural reference for the ideas and images we encounter in the pages of American naturalist novels; in this matrix, narrative strategies, literary conventions, and passing references to concepts or stereotypes take on significances unsuspected when one is reading only in terms of a single text. I conceive my task to be reading across the texts not to uncover but to construct an object of study: naturalism as a literary form. My contention will not be that naturalism has an ideology or reflects an ideology, but that the form itself *is* an immanent ideology. It is a way of imagining the world and the relation of the self to the world, a way of making sense—and making narrative—out of the comforts and discomforts of the historical moment. Those reports of disorder and that narrative sense express, we should note, not "America" but some Americans. Our generalizing habit of speech, embodied in so many discussions of American literature, is itself continuous with the assumption that certain points of view matter more than others, with a systematic forgetfulness organized along the lines of class, race, and gender. To elicit the voices of nonhegemonic groups from the historical record is not the task I have taken on here. But naturalism does bear within itself the memory of that forgetfulness, for silenced (but not silent) masses are one of its most urgent concerns. In today's public language social class is often deeply encoded, even disguised, while the naturalists remind us of a world in which actions and meanings are constantly seen in terms of class, in which omnipresent class conflict is virtually assumed.

Social class is a crucial, although it is certainly not the only, concern focused in American naturalism's notion of the "brute," which I will examine as a conceptual category, a register of characterization, a pressure on plot. The brutal, doomed characters of naturalism have greatly interested literary critics, and the determined world they inhabit is indeed the best-known aspect of the genre. I will argue, however, that one cannot appreciate the significance of naturalism's philosophical determinism without also recognizing the perspective from which those characters are viewed, that of the observant and articulate naturalist in close conference with his reader. That perspective is often revealingly inscribed within the narrative itself in the form of observant and articulate characters who explore and deplore the terrain of cause and effect. The author and reader and the characters who represent them inhabit a privileged location, assuming a kind of control over forces and events through their power to comprehend them. Yet the privilege of the spectator, constructed by contrast, is necessarily vulnerable; fear and desire—sexual passion and violence, the fatal spell of the commodity, the fascination of the Other—constantly disrupt the design of safety. To venture any dealings with the powers that inhabit causality proves hazardous; characters who go slumming in the realm of determinism risk their freedom and expose themselves to the dangers of paralysis and proletarianization. Acting on the assumption of control and attempting to translate knowledge to power, they reveal the crucial difference between omniscience and omnipotence.

The structure I adumbrate here is, I will suggest, characteristic of naturalism, and within literary forms it uniquely distinguishes that genre. But I will also suggest that this immanent ideology shares its imaginative horizons with roughly contemporary formations such as criminal anthropology and political progressivism. And although naturalism can be characterized by this gesture toward control, it cannot be reduced to it. I assume that genres are not static entities or even stable structures but distinctive concatenations of aesthetic imperatives and formal choices that weave, dynamically and unevenly, through literary texts; I will examine the heterogeneous conventions and narrative strategies—melodramatic, sentimental, documentary—to be found in naturalist novels. An understanding of the traces of other genres embedded in these works is indispensable to understanding them, for naturalism is strongly marked by such internal difference.

Naturalism is not a fashionable genre; the efflorescence of critical publication by American academics has produced only a relatively small body of work dealing with this group of writers. I suspect that many critics find naturalist novels somehow scandalous. They fail signally to be well-made novels; they insist tactlessly upon a relation between literature and reality; they traffic brazenly with the formulas of popular literature and journalism; and they are obsessed with class and commodities in a most embarrassing fashion. Aesthetic judgments and generic standards themselves of course embody values and are ideological; the nature and significance of critics' judgments of naturalism will also enter into my analysis. American naturalism was formed in the formative period of our own time, and the questions that absorb the naturalists will prove not so very distant from those of the latter twentieth century.

The naturalists and their contemporaries were scarcely alone in feeling that they lived in a peculiarly difficult period—in every modern period some have voiced this complaint. But to immerse oneself in the documents of the period is gradually to come to recognize the depth of their sense of confusion and danger and to respect the historical specificity of their reported discomfort. The naturalists imagined their situation in genuinely *different* terms from those in which we imagine ours. Whatever we have in common with them, they were not merely people like us wearing different clothes, characters in one of the costume dramas with which the mass media surround us. For the naturalists the world we live in now was not a foregone conclusion; the history they knew did not inevitably lead to the present state of American society. Their choices were real choices. It is my hope that this study will bring my readers, as it has me, to a recognition of the irrevocable openness of any historical moment and an apprehension of naturalism not as an exhibit in a gallery of literary types but as a dynamic solution to the problem of generating narrative out of the particular historical and cultural materials that offered themselves to these writers. This recognition is in some sense the discovery that our own history is contingent, that our world really was not a foregone conclusion. That discovery may perhaps produce not only a renewed sense of historical difference but a renewed sense of historical possibility.

These are ambitious aims for a work of genre criticism. I would suggest not only that genre criticism and historical analysis are compatible, but that they can complete each other in a literary history of unique flexibility and power. I propose this study as a contribution to a revitalized literary history that simultaneously attempts to do justice to the historical specificity of the given moment and attempts to imagine how human history might be one narrative, one adventure in which transformations of both literary and social forms play their parts. The theoretical grounds for such a literary history, as well as for my reading of American literary naturalism, are to be found in the first chapter.

The University of California at San Diego and the University of Michigan Department of English provided research leaves during crucial periods of my work on this project, and I am grateful for their assistance. I would like to thank Fredric Jameson, Roy Harvey Pearce, and Andrew Wright for guiding my research in its early stages and supporting my work over the course of a number of years. I would also like to thank Margot Norris and Martha Vicinus for their support during my work on the later versions of this study. The comments of Michael Davitt Bell and Eric J. Sundquist on the manuscript were very helpful; I owe much, as well, to Iris Tillman Hill and Sandra Eisdorfer of the University of North Carolina Press. Laynie Deutsch assisted me by checking quotations and references. Finally, Jim Dean has lent his aid at all stages of this project, and I would like to thank him here.

Form
and
History
in
American
Literary
Naturalism

1 Conceptual Combinatory: The Nature of Genre and the History of Realism, the Genre of Nature and the Reality of History

It is almost impossible to read any work of literary criticism without encountering some generic term, whether one as specific as "sonnet" or "bildungsroman" or one as broad as "poem" or "novel." Yet more often than not the content of such generic ascriptions remains implicit, and even when they do define a genre critics rarely state the theoretical assumptions governing their use of generic categories. Genre criticism is a great deal more common than genre theory, and theorists tend to find critics' use of generic concepts and the concept of genre deplorably lacking in rigor. This study is in fact a work of genre criticism rather than theory: my central concern is the nature and significance of American literary naturalism, not the uses and abuses of literary classification. But genre itself is an important topic, and in order to make it clear why I proceed as I do I will begin by making some observations about genre theory and the place of genre in this study. Although these remarks are not a systematic exposition of literary theory, they will serve to suggest the more general assumptions underlying my work. Similarly, the discussion of received notions of naturalism and realism that follows will lay the groundwork for my own reconstruction of those generic concepts and for my analyses of American naturalist novels.

Even among advocates of genre criticism it is common, if not uncontroversial, to admit that the approach is in some disrepute and that it is not easy to articulate a coherent genre theory.[1] Yet as I have indicated literary critics seem unable to do without generic classifications. As an editor of the journal *Genre* put it recently, "certitude about genre has now all but vanished, and we are left with a concept which, like Henry James' description of the novel *as a genre*, is a baggy monster. We, like James, know that the genre monster is out there, but we can never seem to describe it adequately or confine it."[2] One can, certainly, find a multitude of articles and books that argue for a meaningful continuity among a

4
Form
and
History
in
American
Literary
Naturalism

group of works, explicitly or implicitly constituting them as a genre
—or mode, or type, for it is the operation of classification and
not its vocabulary that is in question here. Often when one begins
to examine the assumptions informing such analyses, one finds
that they not only contradict other genre criticism (which is, however, rarely confronted as incompatible—the pages of *Genre* often
exemplify this disorder), but that they mobilize different ideas
about what constitutes a genre at different moments in the same
discussion.

There are as well many attempts at wider, more consistent classificatory systems; one can choose among a dizzying variety of taxonomies, each incommensurable with the others. For that matter,
one can choose among different schemes genre theorists have proposed for classifying generic systems into *their* kinds. We begin to
understand why Derrida writes, in disingenuous bemusement, of
the "terminological luxury or rapture" and "taxonomic exuberance"
of generic debates.[3] Ten years ago Paul Hernadi (actually one of the
more optimistic genre theorists) acknowledged the field's lack of
rigor, writing that "most critics propounding new generic concepts
or endorsing old ones show little awareness of the full theoretical
horizon against which recent genre criticism operates."[4] Despite
Hernadi's own useful survey and his proposed synthesis, the situation he described has not changed significantly. The theoretical
confusion that characterizes so much genre criticism is in fact per-
petuated by the disrepute of genre criticism and genre theory—
critics write in an atmosphere that discourages examination of
categories that nevertheless continue, unexamined, in use.

A strategic document with which to begin an exploration of the
debates over genre is Tzvetan Todorov's *The Fantastic*, the subject
of which is indicated by its subtitle, *A Structural Approach to a
Literary Genre*. In recent years Todorov's generic model has been
more widely discussed than any other critic's but Northrop Frye's.
Todorov in fact begins his own discussion of genre by summarizing
and critiquing the "preeminent" and "remarkable" Frye, in the process touching on a wide range of problems.[5] He finds the sets of
classifications proposed in *The Anatomy of Criticism* "not logically
coherent, either among themselves or individually" (p. 12). Sepa-
rately, he argues, they are incoherent and unjustifiable because the
categories on which they are based are arbitrary; Todorov states
directly and simply what is perhaps the most basic objection to a
systematic generic typology: "why are these categories and not others useful in describing a literary text?" (p. 16). I suspect that when
confronted by generic systems (especially the more elaborate ones)
many of us have shared his skepticism—why *should* this particular
order somehow inhere in the tremendous diversity of actually existing literary works? Todorov finds Frye's categories particularly un-

acceptable because they are not literary categories; they are, he accuses, "all borrowed from philosophy, from psychology, or from a social ethic" (p. 16). In raising the question of the source and justification of generic systems, Todorov poses a problem that goes far beyond the critique he makes of Frye and that is not fully resolved in his own theory. Todorov's own proposed generic model draws its categories from linguistics, which, given his assumptions, seems to him more legitimate, but which we will want to acknowledge as another borrowing. Indeed, it is difficult to imagine any defense of an ideal classification system that would not rely on nonliterary justifications. *Pace* Todorov, that does not necessarily invalidate such systems. We will find some justifications, those that draw on the explanatory systems we prefer, more persuasive than others. But surely no argument can demonstrate conclusively that literary kinds *must* derive from a particular cause; the ontological status of an ideal generic typology must always remain questionable, must always to some degree rely on our acceptance of arbitrary, a priori categories.

5
The
Nature
of
Genre,
the
Genre
of
Nature

Todorov argues that Frye's sets of classifications are not coherent as a group because they are not logically coordinated and because "many possible combinations are missing from Frye's enumeration" (p. 13). I would suggest, however, that one of the attractive features of Frye's system is that it offers multiple descriptive categories and thus accommodates our intuitive sense that generic expectations and recognitions are extremely complicated and, in fact, function in a rather untidy and unsymmetrical fashion. But the systematizing impulse of genre criticism persistently seems to do away with such multiplicity. Even Paul Hernadi, who attempts to incorporate the explanatory powers of the many generic systems he describes by proposing a "polycentric" genre theory, ends by suggesting a single, symmetrical—though extremely elaborate—chart of the modes of discourse.[6]

Todorov does accept that genres "exist at different levels of generality," depending upon the point of view chosen (p. 5), and that we tend to use the term to identify both "elementary" genres, defined by the presence or absence of one trait, and "complex" genres, defined by the coexistence of several (p. 15). He attempts to legitimate Frye's incomplete *combinatoire* by proposing a distinction between "historical" and "theoretical" genres, that is, between genres that "result from an observation of literary reality" and those that result from "a deduction of a theoretical order" (pp. 13–14); the missing terms become theoretical possibilities Frye omits because they have not come into actual, historical existence. Thus Todorov subsumes historical genres into his abstract system by construing them as "a part of the complex theoretical genres" (p. 15). Actually existing genres animate preexisting possibilities established by the

6

Form
and
History
in
American
Literary
Naturalism

abstract potential of language, and multiple methods and levels of generality once again disappear into an ideal order that is unified if perhaps not fully describable.

From this perspective, then, the task of genre criticism is to describe what is visible and deducible of the system of literature, articulating the criteria for accurate classification in a structure in which "a genre is always defined in relation to the genres adjacent to it" (p. 27). Thus *The Fantastic* would seem to equip us to decide whether or not a given work properly "belongs" to the genre. Such claims, so characteristic of genre criticism, open Todorov's theory to a host of serious theoretical questions. If generic order is immanent in literature, does that not mean a genre is immanent in the works that constitute it, that it exists somehow "in" the literary text? And if the work belongs to a genre, is it not in turn contained by it, and must not its every feature be generically bound?[7] Can we credit such homogeneous belonging after recognizing that, as Derrida argues, the very codes by which a text declares its genre simultaneously mark its participation in a system defined by difference?[8] Once we have classified a work, have we somehow "accounted for" and explained it, or is this a purely tautological operation since the traits that placed the text in a given class are by definition those that characterize the class? Are particular interpretive procedures prescribed and others proscribed by a classification—is it necessary, is it legitimate, to limit a work's meaning to what is evoked by the procedures specified for a particular genre? Does the value of a work depend on its conformity to norms established for the genre?[9]

Todorov attempts to avoid at least the prescriptive implications of a taxonomic approach, asserting that the significance of the concept of a genre or species in literary criticism differs decisively from its significance in, for example, botany and zoology because in literature "*every* work modifies the sum of possible works" (p. 6). A literary text "is not only the product of a pre-existing combinatorial system (constituted by all that is literature *in posse*); it is also a transformation of that system" (p. 7). Yet such statements make it still more apparent that Todorov views literature as an ideal system of works deployed in orderly fashion in some mysterious, closed realm and capable of shifting instantaneously to accommodate new contributions.

Even if we choose to read Todorov as referring not to an a priori typology but to mental codes and generic *expectations*, as Claudio Guillén proposes in a related theory of literature as system, such a model depends on a concept of static structure and an image of literature scarcely viable in the climate of contemporary critical theory.[10] In work later than *The Fantastic* Todorov himself begins to lose faith in that closed realm of literature; the effort to isolate something that is uniquely *literary* in literature and thus define and delimit the category seems, more and more, doomed to failure.[11]

We are perhaps most familiar with this question as it is put to us by
works that blur or even deny the boundary between literature and
literary criticism, but its consequences are potentially still more far-
reaching. Not only structuralist poetics but poetics itself assumes
an object of study defined by "literariness" and is put in question by
a challenge to the specificity and privilege of literature. Meanwhile,
the assumption that discrete works constitute integral, inviolable
unities has also been challenged in theories of what we may, in
abbreviated fashion, call textuality. As Pérez Firmat points out, even
if we rescue poetics by redefining it as the general theory of discourse (as Todorov suggests) there is "no reason to suppose, and
every reason to doubt, that a typology of discourse would organize
itself by reference to works."[12] The theoretical grounds of the project of literary classification, undermined from many directions,
seem to be crumbling under our feet. From this perspective genre
criticism looks very much like a dangerous dead end.

Given these difficulties, it is not surprising that critics tend to
retreat to more empirical and historical approaches to genre. Many
studies that fail to specify their theoretical assumptions simply
rely on impressionistic description of similarities between works,
prompting one to ask if all similarities are necessarily significant.
As Pérez Firmat points out, rigorously speaking one cannot define a
genre without identifying features "common to all the members of
the class and only to them."[13] These empirical analyses are also
particularly vulnerable to the accusation that they have explained
nothing about works but merely reported what is immediately observable about them.[14] However, they frequently go beyond noting
similarities to discuss a genre as an entity, as a creature that waxes
and wanes, grows or mutates and declines, in any case somehow
manifesting a substantial and transhistorical existence. Analyses
and taxonomies that appear purely descriptive implicitly appeal,
with some regularity, to a priori if rather unsystematic typologies.

Gustavo Pérez Firmat himself, as we might expect, argues a more
resolutely historicist position. The final, irreducible credentials of
genre criticism are constituted by the evidence that writers and
readers do in actual practice make use of generic categories. There
is certainly a place for a criticism that codifies the knowledge of
contemporary writers and readers about the literary kinds of a given
period. From this perspective genre is not immanent in literature or
in literary works but itself constitutes a kind of text; it is, as Pérez
Firmat puts it, "a verbal message that is durable, delimitable and
coherent," although not "always or easily retrievable," "in treatises
on poetics, interspersed in works of literature, scattered about in
prefaces, letters, anthologies, and other assorted documents."[15]
Genre is thus constructed in critical discourse rather than existing
independently in literature itself.

It is scarcely disputable that some such body of knowledge forms

8
Form
and
History
in
American
Literary
Naturalism

an indispensable part of the reader's equipment for encountering texts. Generic ascriptions and classificatory operations do much toward making texts intelligible (and thus, as contemporary critics have made us acutely aware, toward circumscribing and naturalizing them). As one critic puts it, "merely to say that a work is to be read ironically (i.e., as one reads works of an ironic kind) is to offer a new way of making sense of what might not otherwise seem sensible."[16] The comparisons between works that characterize genre criticism also enable a rich intertextuality that is an important context for interpretation. Recognition of this *activity* of the critic in generic operations is appealing and widespread. One can find it even in the work of that ardent typologizer Frye, who writes at one point in *Anatomy of Criticism* that the "purpose of criticism by genres is not so much to classify as to clarify such traditions and affinities, thereby bringing out a large number of literary relationships that would not be noticed as long as there were no context established for them."[17] But, of course, unless one believes that such relationships have an objective existence, that generic observations have validity of some sort, one will scarcely trouble to make them—so that the question of the source of genres has here been neatly sidestepped. In fact most genre criticism proceeds by some similarly elusive movement between implicit claims for "theoretical" genres and evidence for "historical" genres.

Genre is, certainly, a "text" in the sense that Pérez Firmat describes. But to confine oneself simply to collecting and summarizing contemporary views of genre, remaining agnostic about the validity of the similarities and differences that are described, is to consign such original articulations of generic affinities and systems to the theoretically naive and the daring (to, say, writers themselves, who cannot be expected to know any better and might not care if they did). Taken to its logical end, such an approach legislates itself out of existence, since it cannot defend the creation of the very generic formulations it takes as its object. And such a genre criticism seems a rather uninteresting and antiquarian enterprise—a project of collation rather than analysis. Indeed, strictly interpreted these principles would scarcely allow the construction of any generic descriptions, and Pérez Firmat must allow the critic sometimes to derive generic norms from observations not explicitly offered as such, thus making a place for the intervention of even the most severely historicist genre critic. We must wonder, with Pérez Firmat himself, "whether such lofty methodological aspirations can stand the wear and tear of painstaking research into individual genres."[18]

In any case we lose too much by so thoroughly yielding up the concept of genre to the case against classification. Without claiming to intuit a unique "literariness" in poetic language or a vast a priori system of theoretical possibilities, we can see that literature

9
The
Nature
of
Genre,
the
Genre
of
Nature

does exist as a social institution and that within it readers find genres distinguishable if not distinct. But the processes that constitute them are neither exclusively textual nor exclusively literary, so that a genre theory or generic description argued purely in *aesthetic* terms is fundamentally misconceived. Literary forms *exist*, not as embodied or disembodied essences, but as effects of historically specific practices of reading and writing; they have a weight, a material reality of their own, and offer a slow, stubborn resistance to the innovator. Nor of course are the needs answered by formal innovation or the constraints on imagination and articulation purely formal. Literary language interpenetrates with other discourses; the production, distribution, and consumption of tales takes place through particular social and economic structures; the experience out of which narration proceeds is always historically specific— and all these circumstances are not causes but limiting conditions for literary production. Genres and novels, like history, are made by human beings—but not just as they please. We must encounter literary texts that are internally discontinuous and diverse and a literary realm that is both inextricably implicated in society and endlessly inventive.[19] Studying the "generic text" is not enough, for works and forms are not cut from whole cloth spun in the imagination, but effortfully pieced together from available materials.

In a fully historical view the institutions of literature and genre themselves appear as mutable. Thus, as Fredric Jameson suggests, when literature in the modern period is increasingly cut loose from concrete situations of performance it becomes more and more difficult for texts to "enforce a given generic rule on their readers. No small part of the art of writing, indeed, is absorbed by this (impossible) attempt to devise a foolproof mechanism for the automatic exclusion of undesirable responses to a given literary utterance." And increasingly, as art itself becomes commodified, traditional genres come to be seen as "a brand-name system against which any authentic artistic expression must necessarily struggle."[20] From this perspective the present problematizing of genre in literary practice and literary theory is itself part of our object of study: it is characteristic of a period in which the codes that suggest appropriate strategies for reading also suggest strategies for merchandising, in which classification is intertwined with commodification. Not just the configuration of genres, not just the content of the generic text, but the very nature of generic operations is historically specific.

Literary history can be seen as the history of forms, as the study of the continual remaking of the possibilities of literary discourse in concrete historical circumstances rather than the traditional tale of a self-contained procession of great writers or literary movements. And in this analytic project generic concepts can mediate between the specific work and the conditions (both narrowly literary and

10
Form
and
History
in
American
Literary
Naturalism

more broadly social) of its production; as Jameson puts it, their value is to allow "the coordination of immanent formal analysis of the individual text with the twin diachronic perspective of the history of forms and the evolution of social life" (p. 105). Such coordination becomes possible when generic analysis is used to locate not the category to which a putatively unified work belongs in a relationship of simple identity but the crucial differences between works and the ways in which different generic strands coexist within a text. Genre becomes a concept uniquely capable of revealing the interrelations of ideological discourses, cultural practices, and social institutions. Generic concepts retain their explanatory power, indeed seem more urgent than ever, but cease to be prescriptive and constraining.

What then do I mean when I take as my object of study American literary naturalism? What claims do I make for naturalism as a genre? I do not, of course, claim that naturalism is a necessary element in a theoretical typology of literary kinds. On the other hand, "naturalism" certainly does refer to a "generic text"; writers and critics have designated works as belonging to that genre and offered closely related if not wholly consistent definitions of it. I will analyze that generic text, but I will also claim more: particular features do indeed mark the works ascribed to naturalism. Those texts do not "belong" to the genre in any simple way, and my purpose will not be to draw boundaries; they are traversed by many conventions, impulses toward form and aesthetic ideologies, some of them "naturalistic" and others not. But this group of texts, produced in America at a particular historical moment, assembles a characteristic set of conceptual oppositions, investments in characters, and organizational strategies; analyzing them through the concept of naturalism enables us to see how they constitute a significant and distinctive development in the ideology of form.

One cannot take for granted even that naturalism constitutes a genuinely distinct genre. Many critics have challenged its status, considering it merely a school within the realist movement or doubting its formal specificity. In fact, most scholars approach naturalism through its relation to realism, seeing naturalism either as a version of realism or as its negation. Certainly the history and self-conscious theoretical development of the two movements were closely intertwined, and their differences were rarely sharply formulated in the controversies surrounding them. The terms "real," "realism," "nature," "naturalism" (and their cognates in French) all have complex histories in the vernacular and in specialized discourses —Raymond Williams calls "nature" "perhaps the most complex word in the [English] language."[21] His discussion of the origins, metamorphoses, and current varied usage of these terms is extraordinarily informative, and I need not rehearse it here. Suffice it to say that "realism" was new in French in the early 1850s and that the term "naturalism," with its long history as a philosophical and scientific term and its relatively short history in art criticism, was adopted into literary criticism shortly afterward, almost certainly by Émile Zola in his 1867 preface to *Thérèse Raquin*.[22] Zola himself, founder of the naturalist school in France and original source of the "generic text" of naturalism, often used "realism" and "naturalism" interchangeably in writing about both art and literature.[23] Subsuming naturalism within realism would not, of course, solve any problems; we would merely be faced with the at least equally difficult task of describing realism and its varieties. But the constant association of the two categories demonstrates the need for us to come to terms with both.

11
The
Nature
of
Genre,
the
Genre
of
Nature

George Becker's essay "Modern Realism as a Literary Movement" is an exemplary statement of the view that naturalism is merely a variant of realism.[24] I choose this essay for analysis because although it was written twenty years ago it cogently states views that persist, less explicitly formulated, in many more recent works. His succinct statement of the aims and immediately visible traits of realism and naturalism introduces many of the categories critics have used in discussing naturalism, establishing the outline of the descriptions from which I begin. Becker treats realism as a phenomenon of the latter nineteenth century, considering it coincident with the development of a self-conscious realist program (although not equal to it, since he believes with William Dean Howells, the standard-bearer of American realism, that realism was not "invented" but "seems spontaneously to have come all at once and everywhere" [p. 8]). He implicitly rejects such persuasive discussions of formal realism as Ian Watt's *Rise of the Novel*, arguing that the "realistic elements" he admits were present in earlier works "rarely, if ever, dominated and controlled a whole work before the middle of the nineteenth century" (p. 4). Becker takes the meaning of "realistic elements" to be more or less self-evident, weaving into his discussion the very terms that are in need of definition: "Men seem always to have had a sneaking fondness for the *petit fait vrai*. . . . Heroes and villains, if they were to command belief, had to have some saving touch of nature; adventures had to touch at least on homely soil before they soared off" (p. 4). By assuming that the writer and reader spontaneously agree on the meaning of "realistic," "fact," and "nature," Becker places himself within the outlook of the movement he studies.

Naturalism and realism do indeed share the crucial mimetic convention that narrative can and does refer to a "real world" with a material existence somewhere outside the literary text. The names of both forms assert their privileged relationship to that assumed extratextual world, invoking an ability to embody "reality" or "na-

12
Form
and
History
in
American
Literary
Naturalism

ture" as constitutive of the genre itself. To understand why these terms and generic texts have such complex histories, we must recognize that a claim to represent reality accurately entails not only a descriptive but a prescriptive power, that an account of what *is* exerts considerable influence over what one thinks *can* be and *ought* to be done. We have only to think of the profoundly ideological uses of the concept of "human nature," or of the accusation that some view is "unrealistic," to see that influence at work. As Williams observes, " 'Let's be realistic' probably more often means 'let us accept the limits of this situation' (*limits* meaning *hard facts*, often of power or money in their existing and established forms) than 'let us look at the whole truth of this situation' (which can allow that an existing *reality* is changeable or is changing)."[25] This normative force is what is at issue in the continual reappropriation to new purposes of a term like "nature." In the most common contemporary vernacular use of the term, the naturalist studies plants and animals; he fixes them in a classifying, analytical gaze, and through his scientific credentials and his scientific project assumes a practical and symbolic power over his objects of study.[26] The literary naturalist too makes a powerful and polemical case for his tale merely by claiming the generic label—although to say so is scarcely to do full justice to the prestige of the concept of "nature," in both French and English, at the moment when Zola claimed it.

Becker offers lucid descriptions of the subject matter, technique, and philosophy of realism as three aspects that have been consistent since the beginning of the movement—descriptions that often, however, insensibly move us toward or implicitly locate us within the perspective of the realists themselves. First, readers are all assumed to inhabit the same "homely soil" when he writes that the realists insist that "the ordinary and near at hand are as suitable for literary treatment as the exotic and remote" (p. 23). Next Becker reports that the realists' technique aspires to objectivity and that their "method of authorial self-effacement necessitates reliance on documentation and observation" (p. 31); through this technique the realist strives for "truth":

> His ambition is the dispassionate approach of the scientist; his delusion, the one manifested by Zola, that he can actually manipulate data to a conclusion as coldly impersonal as that reached in the laboratory. At his best he serves no interest save that of truth; he has no preconceived view of how things should be; he observes and he states. Granting the impossibility of absolute objectivity, the essential thing is that such a principle eschews fancy and intuition, is reluctant to go beyond the facts, and is zealous in pursuit of all the facts.
> [p. 29]

(We can see here already the pejorative tone taken in so many descriptions of naturalism.) Finally, the philosophy of the realist, according to Becker, makes him skeptical of the idea that events can escape the "ineluctable laws of causality. It is this last term which is the key to the realist position: the universe is observably subject to physical causality; man as a part of the physical continuum is also subject to its laws, and any theory which asserts otherwise is wishful thinking" (p. 34).

13
The
Nature
of
Genre,
the
Genre
of
Nature

For Becker, naturalism is a variant of realism which places particular emphasis on this philosophical determinism; as he puts it, the "naturalists have been noisy about this position" (p. 35). In his work the terms realism and naturalism are

> deliberately used almost interchangeably. . . . There are those who equate the latter term with "stark realism," that is, any account which is unpleasant, sordid, and dubious about man's higher nature. It has been widely and loosely used to indicate any of the more forthright recent American realistic writers without regard for their precise philosophical position. Certainly usage may do what it will with a word, but in essence and in origin naturalism is no more than an emphatic and explicit philosophical position taken by some realists, showing man caught in a net from which there can be no escape and degenerating under those circumstances; that is, it is pessimistic materialistic determinism. [p. 35]

Becker's formulation here slips, as genre criticism so often does, from one assumption to another: usage may do what it will, but there exists nevertheless an "essence" of the genre—correlated somehow with its "origin"—to which the truly discerning, rejecting the misleading elements of the generic text that confuse "journeyman critics" (p. 35), will penetrate. But his association of naturalism and determinism is scarcely disputable, and the definition of naturalism in these strongly *conceptual* terms has been extremely influential; this is a perspective that will figure crucially in my analysis in Chapter 2.

Squalid scenes and pessimistic philosophy are two elements that are often used to distinguish naturalism from realism, whether they are considered distinct genres or not. In another classificatory strategy the cognitive claims of both forms become the basis for a distinction between them. A programmatic naturalist like Zola claims a special ability, through his "experimental" method, to convey knowledge of social life; critics hostile to naturalism, on the other hand, often accuse it of systematic distortion. Some even use "realism" and "naturalism" to distinguish, respectively, adequate and inadequate representations of reality, usually elaborating a definition of "naturalism" as a particular kind of literary falsehood. The

14
Form
and
History
in
American
Literary
Naturalism

arguments of this debate often trace a rather narrow and naive epistemological circle: both sides judge mimetic works by measuring them against another text called "reality" which is never *acknowledged* as a text but taken for granted as (to draw in the other operative term) natural. In order to clear the ground for my own analysis I will take the risk of appearing to some readers to belabor the obvious and thoroughly examine this question of the relation between naturalism and truth, between realism and reality.

The persistence of the notion of realism as the transparent vehicle of reality demonstrates above all the extraordinary power representation exercises over the minds of writers and readers, including critics. Becker's work symptomatizes the difficulty critics have had in distancing themselves (I should, perhaps, say ourselves) from the implicit and explicit claims of realism. Near the end of his essay, Becker suggests that "whatever reality is, it seems safe to say that it is not identical with a work of art and is anterior to it" (p. 36). The existence of such a realm may be disputable, but it is scarcely dubitable. My understanding of realism (and of all mimetic genres) like Becker's is based on the assumption that the real exists, but that no text embodies it. As soon as I speak of the real it has become a text, has been transformed into a shaped reality by the very language that made it accessible. We *can* attain knowledge, however; what I am suggesting is not at all Becker's platitude (quoted above) about the "impossibility of absolute objectivity." In fact, the idea that knowledge is always somehow flawed and contaminated by subjectivity is inextricably linked with the idea that except insofar as it is flawed its nature *is* to provide a transparent access to its object; in that formulation while some flavor of subjectivity is acknowledged to remain, the elements of objectivity and subjectivity are envisioned as essentially separable. Therefore Becker's careful distinction between reality and its representation is inevitably accompanied by lapses into critical judgments that are inconsistent with that distinction.

A statement that assumes the existence of an extratextual real and makes a descriptive statement about it might appear quite simple. Yet epistemology, the psychology of perception, and semiotics take the nature of such statements as a topic for rigorous investigation. Both the claim that naturalism records facts accurately and the accusation that it falsifies them imply that the mental processes involved in perception and cognition are more or less passive. But knowledge is not simply accepted, not simply impressed upon us by reality, but produced. And when a statement goes beyond description to abstraction or when it is part of a literary work, new layers of productive activity intervene. The notion of a passive and literal "photographic" realism has been thoroughly discredited, and, indeed, photography itself is rarely any longer seen as a literal transcription of reality. It has become almost a cliché to note that a photograph implies at the very least a photographer's choice and a camera's mediation, and we are all too familiar with the faked photograph and the falsified image—in John Berger's words, "we are surrounded by photographic images which constitute a global system of misinformation: the system known as publicity, proliferating consumerist lies."[27] Certainly the technology of the camera allows the creation of an image by light, which itself has no language, yet the image must always be taken up into a system of meanings in order to be meaningful. The documentary uses of photography— medical photographs, photographs made from airplanes or through electron microscopes, and so on—produce knowledge through particular procedures of investigation and interpretation, not as direct, self-evident impressions of "reality." As Berger puts it, "In itself the photograph cannot lie, but, by the same token, it cannot tell the truth" (p. 97). To claim that image or word *simply* records true facts, simply represents reality, effaces the productivity of knowledge and cultural practices, and uses the appearance of truth to guarantee an illusion.

E. H. Gombrich's *Art and Illusion* demonstrates at length and in very accessible terms that even the most basic perceptions are necessarily produced. For Gombrich all perception, whether of an object, a person, a landscape, or the representation of an object, a person, a landscape, entails a movement between "schema and correction." He writes: "All thinking is sorting, classifying. All perceiving relates to expectations and therefore to comparisons."[28] What we perceive is not all available sensory information, but a set of significant details always already selected according to previous experience. Thus the artistic image need not (and cannot) duplicate the real object, but it can represent significant elements of what it seems to duplicate. Gombrich's analysis of portraiture illustrates this process:

> All artistic discoveries are discoveries not of likenesses but of
> equivalences which enable us to see reality in terms of an image and an image in terms of reality. And this equivalence
> never rests on the likeness of elements so much as on the
> identity of responses to certain relationships. . . . What we experience as a good likeness in a caricature, or even in a portrait, is not necessarily a replica of anything seen. If it were,
> every snapshot would have a greater chance of impressing us
> as a satisfactory representation of a person we know. In fact
> only a few snapshots will so satisfy us. We dismiss the majority as odd, uncharacteristic, strange, not because the camera distorts, but because it caught a constellation of features
> from the melody of expression which, when arrested and frozen, fails to strike us in the same way the sitter does. [p. 345]

16

Form
and
History
in
American
Literary
Naturalism

Gombrich shows us *not* that the camera distorts, but that drawing a contrast between truthful image and distortion misconceives the nature of perceptive and representative processes, which *produce* rather than *transcribe* either faithfully or unfaithfully.

What is true of visual representations is certainly no less true of literature; the suggestion that language itself is a differential network of meaning scarcely comes as a surprise these days. Narratives like all texts work on already-structured material, and this recognition in itself would seem to prohibit a theory of literature as the reflection of reality. And in the literary text specifically aesthetic structures intervene to produce that material yet again. Generic categories themselves, of course, are part of this realm of perceptual and artistic codes opened up by Gombrich's work. In order to understand any text's relation to the real, whether that text is a literary work or not, one must consider the effects of these codes in opening and closing an always mediated access to what Gombrich calls the "veridical" (p. 327). The methodological controversies of social scientists and historians over how to achieve satisfactory knowledge and representations of social fact and historical event—and indeed whether those categories of fact and event are even legitimate—are devastating to the plausibility of novelists' and critics' "reality" and "realism." When Hayden White in *Metahistory* examines historical narratives through generic categories drawn from Frye's literary criticism, literary critics must think twice before expecting literary narrative to produce a knowledge of history.[29] Comparisons between texts and adequations between different sorts of texts can indeed lead us to conclusions about their accuracy—but these are not generic determinations; they are procedures that operate at a level and on grounds very different from any invoked by the realists, the naturalists, and their critics.

In fact although it is an article of faith for many readers that literature can and should reflect reality (as anyone who has taught a novel class for college students can attest), the authors who labor to produce texts are frequently more skeptical. Zola writes of "observed data," "the scrupulous study of nature," and the "impersonality" of the work: "That is reality: shudder or laugh at it, draw from it some lesson or other if you will, the sole task of the author has been to put true documents before your eyes."[30] But he also elsewhere acknowledges the necessary intervention of the artist's temperament and arrangement of materials and indignantly denies the accusation that the naturalists are literary photographers—Claude Bernard's experimental method appeals to him not only because it offers the guarantee of science but because it makes a place for the novelist's activity: "We begin certainly with true facts which are our indestructible base; but to show the mechanism of the facts, we have to produce and direct the phenomena; that is our part of invention and genius in the work."[31] The American naturalist Frank

Norris distinguishes between the "accuracy" of quotidian realism and the imaginative "truth" aimed at by romance, asserting that something that "has actually happened . . . is not necessarily true when told as fiction—not necessarily true even when told with the most scrupulous adherence to fact, even when narrated with the meticulous science of the phonograph or pictured with the incontestable precision of the photograph." In his view naturalism—which he treats sometimes as the highest form of romance, sometimes as here as "midway between the Realists and Romanticists, taking the best from each"—provides the most satisfactory reconciliation since it "strives hard for accuracy *and* truth."[32] At different moments naturalist authors manifest different degrees of self-consciousness about the fictions involved in turning the real into a text. They are consistently drawn to claims that they convey reality, even as they register an awareness of the contradictions of such a program.

A belief in the transparency of representation is a temptation for critics as well. In "Modern Realism as Literary Movement" Becker often fails to acknowledge the specificity of the operations of writing and reading literature, contradicting his own assertions elsewhere by treating realist narratives not only as true reports but as effectively identical with experience itself: "The realistic writer attempts to retrace the steps by which he arrived inductively and empirically at certain generalizations; in other words, he seeks to have his reader participate in the same act of discovery, the same 'experiment,' as he. The difficulty is that once he has arrived at these generalizations, he is tempted to use them functionally without reproducing the process of induction in later works which he writes" (p. 33). Becker echoes Zola's argument in *Le Roman expérimental* that the novel can be an objective scientific experiment in which characters are subjected to influences and observed so that the laws of their behavior can be deduced—only here the experiment is performed on the reader. The specifically literary procedures by which an equivalence between the processes of perceiving or learning operating on a concrete world outside the text and the extraction of meaning from a novel is attained are elided in favor of an evocative image of the reader participating in the writer's experience. Overtones of naive reflectionism creep into Becker's essay even more easily when he uses negative formulations: he assumes that we can all agree, at least, on what is *not* reality, writing for example that a "really faithful representation of life cannot be achieved within a dialectic based on teleological concepts" (p. 23) and that when "the facts presented are attached to some pre-existent body of doctrine or belief or myth, they cease to speak for themselves and speak only as directed" (p. 33). But of course the "facts" never "speak for themselves," any more than the impressions of light on film do: the contention and convention that they

18
Form
and
History
in
American
Literary
Naturalism

can forms part of the ideological baggage of the generic texts of realism and naturalism. These are not categories we can use to understand the form, but elements that enter into the production of naturalist narrative and into the production of critical discourse.

Becker suggests here and elsewhere that preconceptions distort perceptions, revealing his belief that it is both possible and desirable to be without preconceptions. I would argue that it is neither. As Gombrich observes, "This inductivist ideal of pure observation has proved a mirage in science no less than in art. The very idea that it should be possible to observe without expectation, that you can make your mind an innocent blank on which nature will record its secrets, has come in for strong criticism" (p. 321) (and that is surely putting it mildly). To efface the process of "schema and correction" is to overlook one's own schemata, exempting them from analysis because they are "natural" and inevitable. Roland Barthes among others has said that the essential task of modern myth is to rewrite the historical as the natural.[33] Thus the effect of Becker's strictures is to disparage the openly polemical and political and specifically to disparage Marxism (p. 33), while reinforcing common-sense assumptions that are themselves equally tendentious. He acknowledges, of course, that objectivity is impossible—but caught in an irresolvable dichotomy between objectivity and subjectivity, between truth and distortion, he forgets his qualifications and falls back on the insistence that after all we *do* seem to know what is out there in the world and when we have encountered a "really faithful representation." The word "really" marks Becker's iterated insistence on an unproblematized reality: a reality based on claims very much akin to those of the realists, a reality bound to the shared beliefs and values of reasonable people, a reality necessarily implying a severely circumscribed notion of who that (class-, race-, and gender-bound) reasonable audience is—a reality that is, to put it directly, profoundly ideological.

Becker falls prey to the same temptation of the inverted prescription and the obvious assumption when he complains that in naturalism "animal imagery easily becomes a system, a constant and pervasive referent which consistently downgrades every thought and act of the human protagonists. This is a violation of objectivity, since it does not permit the reader to see or judge the characters in any but one dimension" (p. 32). Stigmatizing such imagery as a "violation of objectivity" implies that the "self-effacing" realist technique of presenting characters without such imagery *is* objective; here Becker unequivocally occupies the ground of realism, going on to rule that one of Zola's animal images is "permissible," but that London and Norris reduce such metaphors to "absurdity."

But one can rewrite Becker's normative assertion, which contains a kernel of valuable observation, and transform it from a statement about the correspondence between realism and reality into a statement about the conventions of realism and their relation to perception. We might posit an equivalence between the sorts of information the narrator of a realist novel gives about characters and what one might learn about people by meeting them or hearing them described. According to the realist convention that the narrative refers to an objective world outside it, the character is treated as having sides the reader does not see, as continuing to exist off-stage, and thus is constructed as complex and "round." But neither I nor the writers and readers of Zola's, London's, and Norris's novels (nor, I expect, my own readers) in daily life systematically view other people in terms of animal imagery; such characterization emphasizes instead that the text is a literary construction and that the writer attributes significance to reported detail. Violating realism's claims to transparency, pervasive animal imagery suggests to the reader that the generic category of realism may not be appropriate for the work in question—or, depending on the reading practices being employed, that the work is a failure.

Yet the equivalence between what one ordinarily observes and the descriptions of realism cannot be simple, for such novels usually present a wealth of information about characters, and surely we do not ordinarily know the personal history, cannot ordinarily provide a detailed physical description of our acquaintances. (Where was your neighbor born? What color are his or her eyes?) The routine descriptions of settings in Balzac and Zola also include much more detail than most of us would note: the eye of the narrator has more in common with the camera eye than the human eye. This preoccupation with description, like the contention that the narrative embodies an unmediated reality and like the animal imagery Becker criticizes, is neither an accomplishment nor a flaw but an element of the texts we are striving to understand.

I have translated Becker's prescriptive statement into more satisfactory generic description, but my formulation still poses some problems. It fails to take into account how deeply metaphor is embedded in our language, so that I use a kind of animal imagery when I write that Becker "falls prey" to a temptation (one can argue, however, that such usages ordinarily do not constitute a system). It fails to question the notion that unified "characters" inhabit literary works. But most disturbingly, it transfers commonsensical assumptions about how one ordinarily perceives other people directly into literary convention, when such assumptions demand to be more closely bound to culture, class, gender, to have their content specified by reference to particular historical situations. In the past the image of the animal carried a quite different and much greater weight, and characterization through reference to the qualities of animals—in Homer, for example—had a rather different significance from the one Becker assumes.[34] The "we" in which I include my reader and the formulation "what one usually observes" both

20

Form
and
History
in
American
Literary
Naturalism

inscribe and conceal a concrete audience. Indeed, the detailed descriptions of realism seem in part to respond to the failure of shared assumptions, as they convey information to the fragmented publics that, as Jameson summarizes the phenomenon, follow upon "the atomization and monadization of contemporary society, and the increasing uncertainty as to whether your own local 'code' will be meaningful down the hall, let alone across the border."[35]

But let us take a very loose and impressionist sense of "what one ordinarily observes," accepting the uncertainty as to how far our code applies, and examine the functioning of these realist conventions. Such scrutiny necessarily undermines reflectionist claims to provide transparent access to reality. In *Structuralist Poetics* Jonathan Culler, although rejecting the more radical implications of this insight, usefully articulates the fundamental Saussurean recognition that language always entails a network of significations in an analysis of how code and convention make literary texts intelligible. He writes:

> what we speak of as conventions of a genre or an *écriture* are essentially possibilities of meaning, ways of naturalizing the text and giving it a place in the world which our culture defines. To assimilate or interpret something is to bring it within the modes of order which culture makes available, and this is usually done by talking about it in a mode of discourse which a culture takes as natural. This process goes by various names in structuralist writing: recuperation, naturalization, motivation, *vraisemblablisation*. [p. 137]

The first of the five levels of naturalization Culler defines is the one I have already described, the gesture toward "the socially given text, that which is taken as the 'real world'. . . . The most elementary paradigms of action are located at this level: if someone begins to laugh they will eventually stop laughing" (pp. 140–41). Characters are assumed to have two eyes that will be of certain colors—not orange, for example; if these assumptions are violated, the reader infers that the text belongs to a genre such as the fairy tale or science fiction which cannot be naturalized at this level. The second level "is a general cultural text: shared knowledge which would be recognized by participants as part of culture and hence subject to correction or modification but which none the less serves as a kind of 'nature'" (p. 140). As Culler acknowledges, this second level is not always easily separated from the first. Many of the 'natural' assumptions that the realist convention of the objective world expects the narrator and reader to share turn out to be cultural attitudes. Such cultural codes often function in the description of characters; for example, a phrase like "flashing dark eyes" summons up an image naturalized on the second level.

That phrase might also, in some novels, indicate a certain kind of heroine and be naturalized on the third level, "the texts or conventions of a genre, a specifically literary and artificial *vraisemblance*" (p. 140). The fourth and fifth levels of naturalization begin to refer back to the process of naturalization itself, when "the text explicitly cites and exposes *vraisemblance* of the third kind so as to reinforce its own authority" and when, as in parody, "one work takes another as its basis or point of departure" (p. 140). Except for the last we can identify each of these levels of naturalization functioning in naturalist novels. Realism and naturalism make particularly frequent use of the disruption of "literary" naturalization in order to assert their reference to reality although patently "artificial" conventions often stand side by side with that gesture of disruption. Thus when Becker writes that in the realist novel "artificialities of plot and characterization go out the window" (p. 29), what he recognizes is a change in generic convention, a shift of emphasis to the fourth level of naturalization, and not a return to reflection or a closer approach to the real. Certainly, however, we should also acknowledge that the impulses to merge literary and vernacular discourse and to accommodate heterogeneous raw materials— often previously unrepresented or historically new experience— within the novel are common to both realism and naturalism and are critical to an understanding of both genres. Chapter 5 will examine one important formal consequence of that impulse in what I call naturalism's documentary strategy.

The verbal resemblance between naturalization and naturalism is not mere coincidence; in both cases an appeal to nature constitutes a claim to legitimacy. Culler in one sense credits that claim when he takes for granted that texts almost inevitably evoke the proper naturalizing responses from the reader and that the construction of intelligibility proceeds without significant disruption, although he most definitely does not endorse novelistic claims to realistic representation. I would argue that the "competent reader" necessary to Culler's system is an unjustifiably abstract, ahistorical, and normative construct; texts are actually read in specific conditions by specific readers and not necessarily according to the codes and conventions recognized by their authors.[36] A similarly ideal reader seems to be assumed, for that matter, by quite different critics of the *Tel Quel* and *Screen* schools who have been severe on realism precisely for its acquiescence to convention, its "readability," and have tended to valorize avant-garde texts that resist or at least delay such recuperation; their cognitive, political, and, indeed, virtually spiritual claims for such texts are as ambitious and implausible as those of the realists and naturalists. We want, unquestionably, to make assertions about the effect and value of literary texts, but surely we want to make them in more concrete terms, for more limited contexts: we want, in other words, to historicize the question of value. Literary forms themselves carry what Jame-

21
The
Nature
of
Genre,
the
Genre
of
Nature

22
Form
and
History
in
American
Literary
Naturalism

son calls "socio-symbolic messages"—it is a vital part of my project to argue that form itself is an immanent ideology.[37] But it does not do justice to the full significance of genre to diagnose forms as progressive or reactionary, as truthful or mendacious.

One of the most penetrating accounts of naturalism, however, depends crucially on such judgments of value. Georg Lukács is one of the most important genre theorists of our period (he is, for example, one of the two critics to whom Hernadi in *Beyond Genre* devotes an entire chapter; the other is Frye). It is not only Marx and Engels on realism but Lukács's criticism to which Jameson refers when he asserts that genre criticism has "always entertained a privileged relationship with historical materialism," and Lukács's work is an important source of Jameson's and my own approach to the ideology of form.[38] Although I will not finally accept Lukács's generic system, his studies of realist and naturalist novels have great descriptive and explanatory power and deserve to be more widely read by critics of American literature.

Lukács's theory of novel forms is complex and difficult to summarize, particularly because it appears in a series of books and essays rather than in a single, connected exposition. He states the relevant characteristics of realism and naturalism, as he sees them, most succinctly in his essay "Narrate or Describe?":

> In Scott, Balzac or Tolstoy [that is, in realism] we experience events which are inherently significant because of the direct involvement of the characters in the events and because of the general social significance emerging in the unfolding of the characters' lives. We are the audience to events in which the characters take active part. We ourselves experience these events.
> In Flaubert and Zola [that is, in naturalism] the characters are merely spectators, more or less interested in the events. As a result, the events themselves become only a tableau for the reader, or, at best, a series of tableaux. We are merely observers.[39]

In Lukács's system genres are always defined in opposition to one another, and his theory of naturalism is as inseparable from his theory of realism as Becker's from his assumptions about reality. His preference for realism is constantly implicit in the distinctions he makes between realist narration and naturalist description: "Narration establishes proportion, description merely levels" (p. 127). "Description contemporizes everything. Narration recounts the past" (p. 130). Lukács claims, in effect, that realism is uniquely adequate to the representation of historical actuality and that naturalism systematically distorts it.

In another essay in the same volume Lukács suggests that realism is characterized by its ability, in contrast to both naturalism and modernism, to achieve the "typical" through a synthesis of the particular and the general, the concrete and the abstract: "Universal, typical phenomena should emerge out of the particular actions and passions of specific individuals" (p. 154). He writes of the reader's "experiencing" events through investment in characters, although he does not rely on a naive belief in the possibility of importing "facts" more or less directly into narrative but describes a formal procedure for achieving such an effect. Lukács's analysis of that process is at times reminiscent of Gombrich's description of equivalences between the relationship of elements in an image and a real object: "The detail in a work of art is an accurate reflection of life when it is a necessary aspect of the accurate reflection of the total process of objective reality, no matter whether it was observed by the artist in life or created through imagination out of direct or indirect experience" (p. 43). In *Marxism and Form* Jameson also invokes the ideas of totality and process in restating Lukács's argument for realism and defending it against the opposite charge of being excessively abstract:

23
The
Nature
of
Genre,
the
Genre
of
Nature

> a Balzac character is not typical of a certain kind of fixed social element, such as class, but rather of the historical moment itself; and within this, the purely schematic and allegorical overtones of the notion of typicality disappear completely. The typical is not at this point a one-to-one correlation between individual characters in the work (Nucingen, Hulot) and fixed, stable components of the external world itself (finance aristocracy, Napoleonic nobility), but rather an analogy between the entire plot, as a conflict of forces, and the total moment of history itself considered as process.[40]

Lukács never implies either that the realist novel directly transcribes the real, or that it simply dramatizes an idea; he sees realistic reflection as a complex transformative procedure that allows the literary text to represent and resemble the real.

This is certainly a more sophisticated and appealing view of realism than Becker's. But it is a very long step from a resemblance between person and portrait and an equivalence between "the total process of objective reality" and a narrative—and Lukács claims considerably more for the genre than a capacity to create recognizable representations. Realism does not merely transform expectations about "what one ordinarily observes" into generic conventions; convincing renderings of phenomenal experience are important only as they serve to reveal less accessible and more important aspects of reality. The great realists, Lukács writes, "all have in common that they penetrate deeply into the great universal problems of their time and inexorably depict the true essence of reality as they see it."[41] For Lukács the realist narrative necessarily

24
Form
and
History
in
American
Literary
Naturalism

conveys truth: thus realism is an epistemological as well as a generic category. And the transmission of such knowledge is what constitutes literary value, for "realism is not one style among others, it is the basis of literature."[42]

Although not direct reflection but dialectical procedures are invoked, the epistemological privilege accorded to realism does derive from a model of reality and representation in which the real can be conveyed into a literary text. In "Art and Objective Truth" Lukács writes that

> the task of art is the reconstitution of the concrete—in this Marxist sense—in a direct, perceptual self-evidence. To that end those factors must be discovered in the concrete and rendered perceptible whose unity makes the concrete concrete. Now in reality every phenomenon stands in a vast, infinite context with all other simultaneous and previous phenomena. A work of art, considered from the point of view of its content, provides only a greater or lesser extract of reality. Artistic form therefore has the responsibility of preventing this extract from giving the effect of an extract and thus requiring the addition of an environment of time and space; on the contrary, the extract must seem to be a self-contained whole and to require no external extension.[43]

Lukács does not suggest, as a naive realist might, that the text can be continuous with the world. It contains not a transparently rendered slice of reality but an extract from reality. What is extracted, however, remains real: it is an essence. Although realism does not reproduce reality, through artistic form it does "reconstitute" it.

Since realist narrative contains the essence of reality, for Lukács the experience of reading it actually provides not just knowledge of the literary text but knowledge and even experience of reality. The process that operates in reading is not the same as that performed on reality, as it is in Becker's suggestion that the reader retraces the writer's steps to arrive inductively at the same conclusions. In art correct knowledge is available in "direct, perceptual self-evidence," and in this sense the experience offered by realism is actually superior to that offered by reality. The essence is more real than the empirically real, the artistically true detail more true than the "purely accidental, arbitrary and subjective" photographic detail.[44] Lukács writes, for example, that through plot "the dialectic of human existence and consciousness [can] be expressed, . . . through a character's action . . . the contrast between what he is objectively and what he imagines himself to be, [can] be expressed in a process that the reader can experience."[45] Thus the reader of the realist narrative enjoys a privileged access to the dialectical causality of historical processes and gains insights into the true nature of society. He attains, if only for the length of time it takes to read a novel, what Lukács sees as the correct attitude toward reality.

25
The
Nature
of
Genre,
the
Genre
of
Nature

For Lukács realism is defined by its ability to reconstitute the concrete, naturalism and modernism by their failure to do so. In the latter forms, objects and events can "acquire significance only through direct association with some abstract concept which the author considers essential to his view of the world. But an object does not thereby achieve poetic significance; significance is assigned to it."[46] Each severs the unity of the particular and the general that realism achieves in the "typical," resting "on a solipsistic conception of man hopelessly isolated in an inhuman society. . . . Thus the individual living only in himself is abruptly cut off from the fatalistic universality within the literary composition. The individual is opposed directly to the abstract universal" (p. 169). For Lukács naturalism is an objectivist negation of realism, modernism a subjectivist negation of realism. They place the reader in a false position and distort the nature of reality. For Lukács both naturalism and modernism are, *as genres*, artistic and epistemological failures.

The categories of this generic system are logically continuous with the epistemological arguments Lukács makes in his *History and Class Consciousness*.[47] In that early work Lukács attempts to demonstrate that, because of the historical situation of the bourgeoisie, classical Western philosophy has been trapped in the antinomy between the subject and the object:

> man in capitalist society confronts a reality 'made' by himself (as a class) which appears to him to be a natural phenomenon alien to himself; he is wholly at the mercy of its 'laws', his activity is confined to the exploitation of the inexorable fulfilment of certain individual laws for his own (egoistic) interests. But even while 'acting' he remains, in the nature of the case, the object and not the subject of events. The field of his activity thus becomes wholly internalised: it consists on the one hand of the awareness of the laws which he uses and, on the other, of his awareness of his inner reactions to the course taken by events.[48]

The proletariat, however, because of its situation as the "identical subject-object of history" (p. 197), can create a dialectical synthesis of those categories. In Lukács's generic system, it is the realist novel that is capable of achieving a dialectical knowledge of the totality of the real. Naturalism and modernism, in contrast, remain trapped in the antinomy of subject and object. They can describe the external and abstract and the internal and individual, but are incapable of dialectically uniting them in "concrete" plot, characters, details. Lukács's generic system subsumes the specific, heterogeneous formal qualities of each genre in its essence, and defines its essence in terms of a role in this epistemological drama.

26

Form
and
History
in
American
Literary
Naturalism

Lukács links both the evolution of Western philosophy and the forms of the novel to particular stages in historical development. His examples of realism are usually drawn from the nineteenth-century novel, for he considers that realist novels were written by the bourgeoisie during the period when its ideology was still historically progressive. In France, for example, the June days of 1848 mark the point at which realism becomes impossible; afterward, Balzac declines into Zola.[49] Jameson offers a sympathetic reading of the causal connections Lukács implies between history and the literary work, writing that for Lukács "realism is dependent on the possibility of access to the forces of change in a given moment of history."[50] This formulation attributes to Lukács a position very much like Jameson's own persuasive argument that the historical moment should be understood to "block off or shut down a certain number of formal possibilities available before, and to open up determinate new ones, which may or may not ever be realized in artistic practice" and that genre criticism therefore properly "aims not at enumerating the 'causes' of a given text or form, but rather at mapping out its objective, a priori conditions of possibility."[51] I am not convinced that Lukács actually advocates so structural a view of the matter; often he seems rather to collapse history, philosophy, and literature into a single expressive system, as would be consistent with the language of reflection and essence we have already encountered in his characterization of realism. But we may accept Jameson's position on its own merits and pursue Lukács's suggestion of connections between the socioeconomic and the cultural, between form and history. We will find, too, that the qualities Lukács notes in naturalism—the tendency for the characters to become spectators and the reader an observer, the simultaneous presence of apparently insignificant concrete detail and abstract concepts—are indeed central to the genre.

My criticisms of Lukács are informed by the work of innovative Marxist philosopher Louis Althusser and those who have followed him over the past fifteen or twenty years. Like Lukács, Althusser has been both influential and implacably and convincingly criticized.[52] He initiated an immensely fruitful debate in Marxist theory, and his writings retain their astringent power as a critique of epistemological positions like Becker's and Lukács's. His perspective remains insufficiently familiar in the United States, particularly when compared with other versions of post-Saussurean thought. In contrast to Lukács Althusser insists on the irreducible complexity of social formations and historical causality; literary critics following his lead have pointed to the specificity and complexity of both literary institutions and the text itself. That text is seen no longer as a self-contained work that succeeds or fails to achieve organic unity, that can be recognized as essentially realistic or naturalistic, but as a necessarily heterogeneous production. Neither Althusserian

and post-Althusserian literary criticism nor Althusserian and post-Althusserian epistemology can accommodate the kind of realism envisioned by the critics cited so far. 27
The
Nature
of
Genre,
the
Genre
of
Nature

Althusser's epistemology entirely rejects the category of "essence." The naturalists' and implicitly Becker's naive realism and Lukács's reflectionism assume that some essential part of the real enters into abstractions about reality. Althusser stigmatizes all such views as empiricist, spelling out their implications for the concept of knowledge and the concept of the real:

> Knowledge is an abstraction, in the strict sense, i.e., an extraction of the essence from the real which contains it, a separation of the essence from the real which contains it and keeps it in hiding. . . . *The real*: it is structured as a dross of earth containing inside it a grain of pure gold, i.e., it is made of two real essences, the pure essence and the impure essence, the gold and the dross, or, if you like (Hegelian terms), the essential and the inessential.[53]

In the assertions of naive realism the process of extraction is scarcely examined and seems to be simple; in Lukács's theory it is envisioned as complex. But in both cases knowing reality entails reading through its surface to find an essence that is already there and can be transferred intact to the abstraction or the literary text. Thus both epistemologies depend upon a conception of the real object as already containing knowledge and on a purely instrumental conception of the operations of knowledge; as Althusser puts it, "the abstraction operation and all its scouring procedures are merely procedures to purge and eliminate *one part of the real in order to isolate the other*. As such, they leave no trace in the extracted part, every trace of their operation is eliminated along with the part of the real they were intended to eliminate" (p. 36). The text does, finally, hand the real thing over to the reader.

In order to escape this empiricism, according to Althusser, "we must completely reorganize the idea we have of knowledge, we must abandon the mirror myths of immediate vision and reading, and conceive knowledge as a production" (p. 24). The real certainly exists, but "thought about the real, the conception of the real, and all the operations of thought by which the real is thought and conceived, belong to the order of thought, the elements of thought, which must not be confused with the order of the real, the element of the real" (p. 87). The object we know is produced by the operations of knowledge; it is the object of knowledge, which is always distinct from the real object.

To say this is not to say that there is no adequate knowledge; there can be, in Jameson's phrase, a "scientific language . . . which designates the Real without claiming to coincide with it."[54] But such a science would perform its operations not on the "real" but

28
Form
and
History
in
American
Literary
Naturalism

on something that is already a human production: "however far back we ascend into the past of a branch of knowledge, we are never dealing with a 'pure' sensuous intuition or representation, but with an *ever-already* complex raw material, a structure of 'intuition' or 'representation' which combines together in a peculiar *'Verbindung'* sensuous, technical and ideological elements."[55] Althusser's original epistemological theory, caught in a fruitless opposition between science and ideology and fatally drawn, as the naturalists were, to the glamor of "science," has been thoroughly discredited; it may be that a satisfying epistemological theory is possible only on the basis of a reconstruction of the very language in which the discussion is conducted and a rejection of "science." Nevertheless, the refusal of solipsism and radical skepticism embodied in the term remains fundamental to a criticism based on historical materialism.

At any rate, literary texts like other texts are constructed not out of innocent "facts" but on the basis of already complex structures of representation. And the operations performed on this raw material in order to produce a novel are specifically literary operations; they are distinct from the operations that would be performed to produce, say, a monograph on genetics or economics or history, and it is inappropriate to expect a narrative to provide knowledge in the same sense. This does not mean that no narrative ever tells the truth. For example, Terry Eagleton, in a remark representative (in both content and style) of the early appropriation of Althusser in literary criticism, writes that

> Balzac was indeed able to achieve partial insight into the movement of real history, but it is mistaken to image such insight as a transcendence of ideology into history. No such displacement of realms occurs: it is rather that Balzac's insights are the effect of a specific conjuncture of his mode of authorial insertion into ideology, the relations of the ideological region he inhabited to real history, the character of that stage of capitalist development, and the "truth-effect" of the particular aesthetic form (realism) he worked.[56]

The insight acknowledged here, however, is inevitably partial, since the text is heterogeneous, and it is always specific to a "conjuncture" and not the automatic perquisite of a genre. Moreover, the critical acknowledgment of such insight must be made from a point situated outside the literary text. A narrative may claim or seem to offer a self-sufficient account of the real, but its offering must be examined in the light of a critical understanding that avails itself of other sources of knowledge, such as properly historical works.

We must always remember, of course, that our access to history is itself mediated through texts. And we may wonder whether Eagleton himself does not lapse into an uncritical and unjustifiable ges-

ture of legitimation with his appeal to "real history." The temptation 29
The
Nature
of
Genre,
the
Genre
of
Nature offered by "reality" is powerful, and at this point the very word "real" should alert our suspicions. In any case, such judgments of truth-value are only part of the task of criticism. We have also to compre-hend the work as a production in determinate historical circum-stances; as Eagleton puts it, to "show the text as it cannot know itself, to manifest those conditions of its making (inscribed in its very letter) about which it is necessarily silent" (p. 43). Naturalism does not provide a window into reality. Rather it reveals history indirectly in revealing *itself*—in the significant absences silhouet-ted by its narratives, in the ideology invoked by the very program that proclaims a transparent access to the real, in its transmutation of content into form and form into content. The search for the real must give way to a search for the historical.

Thus far I have discussed realism and naturalism in general terms, without distinguishing between French and English works and the American works I have taken as my topic. Unquestionably Zola is the source of the term "naturalism" as a recurrent point of reference for authors and critics defining an aesthetic program and a form called naturalism. Lars Åhnebrink has detailed Zola's influ-ence on the early American naturalists.[57] In the critical writings of Frank Norris, for example, one can find a "generic text" that pre-serves his reactions to Zola and defines naturalism—albeit in terms we have not yet encountered, for Norris considers it a version of romanticism rather than realism.[58] Yet when we come to a writer like Dreiser, we can find no such clear influence or generic text; those who consider Dreiser a naturalist do so on the basis of per-ceived affinities between his work and pronouncements about lit-erature and a model of naturalism. Indeed, the problem of the novel form in America—whether viewed through the realist move-ment, Becker's account of that movement, Lukács, the romance-novel question, or contemporary criticism—is in part a problem of translation. The generic text given to American writers has pre-scribed the terms of realism, romance, naturalism. Yet, as Eric Sundquist points out, "American realism virtually has no school; its most dominating and influential advocate, William Dean Howells, often seems to ride along in a strange vacuum, nearly unheeded in his continual insistence on the proprieties of the everyday, stable characterization, and moral certainty, while almost every other im-portant author of the period simply refused, in these terms, to be-come a realist."[59] And realism and naturalism are even less easily separated in American literature than in European literature. The claim for an American naturalism most often rests, like the claims of so much genre criticism, on a barely perceptible slippage be-tween theoretical and historical generic claims.

My assumption will be that the critics who have categorized

30
Form
and
History
in
American
Literary
Naturalism

American novels as naturalist *have* recognized meaningful affinities. Zola's program and example offered formal possibilities that certain American writers found enabling; even where the influence is not directly apparent, we may presume that there are identifiable similarities. Yet this does not tell us why the name taken by a clearly defined, relatively short-lived literary movement in France should become in America a broad term used by some writers and many critics to characterize a diverse group of works, works constituting a major body of American literature, over a long period of time.[60] That is a question which this study will not answer definitively; to do so would require not only what is to follow—a historical reading of American naturalism—but an equivalent reading of French naturalism.

Within the frame of one national literature and one national history, however, I use the concept of naturalism and the vocabulary critics have developed to describe it to coordinate the close analysis of individual texts with the history of literary forms and with social and economic history. Since I do not approach genre criticism as a classificatory project, my task is simpler than it might otherwise be: I need not show that a given work wholly "belongs" to the genre whose distinctive features I will demonstrate, and indeed to the contrary I will show that other forms also traverse the texts defined as naturalist. Although there are enough continuities to provide a basis for suggesting a "model" of the genre, that is not my intention. One must for the sake of economy of expression speak of "naturalism," and thus I may sometimes seem to suggest that an evolving entity exists somewhere, but my intent is rather to evoke a sense of naturalism as a mediating concept that enables us to perceive significant similarities *and* differences among texts. My contention will be that in a group of works written by American novelists during the late nineteenth and early twentieth centuries, we can see concepts, types of characterization, and strategies for sequencing narrative and producing closure articulated in a distinctive configuration that bears the marks of that particular historical moment.

In studying that moment, one begins with and repeatedly returns to the rapidity and completeness with which American life was transformed between the Civil War and the First World War.[61] The expanding and improving networks of transportation and communication were a tangible aspect of the market economy that was knitting the country more and more tightly together; the growing cities, concentrating both unparalleled wealth and the tremendous influx of immigrants, provided an even more impressive demonstration of the radical changes accompanying the expansion of the industrial capitalist system. The recurrent economic depressions, the struggle between capital and labor, organized agrarian protest, the renegotiation of social and political authority, the impact of commodified culture and the incipient culture of the commodity we call consumer society, the strains experienced by the dislocated (immigrant and native, geographically and psychically): all these combined to make this system seem, to many of those living in it, a uniquely precarious one.

31
The
Nature
of
Genre,
the
Genre
of
Nature

Production statistics can begin to suggest the scope of the transformation implied by the rapid industrialization of the period. Sustained economic growth did not of course abruptly commence in 1865; rather, it developed gradually during the first half of the century, probably emerging in the 1820s and 1830s and progressing more swiftly in the 1840s and 1850s.[62] The Civil War stopped that progress temporarily, but in the fifty years following its conclusion the pace of growth was unprecedented. At the most general level we can see that expansion reflected in the statistics of the Gross National Product. Real GNP per capita tripled over the period. Since the population was also growing rapidly—from 36 million in 1865 to 101 million in 1915—the statistics for total output are still more striking: there was an eightfold increase in production.[63] This growth did not proceed smoothly and evenly, but irregularly, interrupted by fluctuations in business and in particular by the depressions of the mid-1870s and mid-1890s. But, as economic historian Robert Higgs writes, "never before had such rapid growth continued for so long."[64]

These figures reflect not only an increase in total production but a remarkable rise in productivity. Agricultural output increased because more land was brought under cultivation and also because farms were mechanized. Before the Civil War 61 hours of labor were required to produce an acre of wheat; in 1900 only 3 hours, 19 minutes, were required.[65] Technological advances transformed manufacturing just as profoundly, making possible extraordinary growth like that of the steel industry: steel production increased roughly tenfold between 1870 and 1880 and tenfold again between 1880 and 1900—a hundredfold increase in thirty years.[66] Manufacturing as a whole expanded more rapidly than agriculture with the effect that the composition of production shifted. In 1869 53 percent of commodities were produced in the agricultural sector, 33 percent in the manufacturing sector; in 1899 those figures were precisely reversed. (The remaining production was in mining, which accounted for 2 percent of total output in 1869 and 5 percent in 1899; and in construction, 12 percent in 1869 and 9 percent in 1899.) By the end of the nineteenth century America's predominantly agrarian economy had become a predominantly industrial economy.[67]

Changes in the organization of business and commerce reciprocally made possible and resulted from these increases and shifts in production. Firms tended to become larger, and incorporation became far more common. Specialization both within and among firms increased.[68] Given the expanded markets that both manufac-

32
Form
and
History
in
American
Literary
Naturalism

turing concerns and agricultural producers served, information had to be exchanged and goods moved over increasing distances. One of the better-known statistics of expansion is that the miles of railroad track in the United States grew from 46,800 in 1869 to 190,000 in 1899.[69] (This construction itself represented a huge capital investment and a considerable stimulus to industrial production.) Communications too were expanded and transformed: between 1870 and 1900 the miles of telegraph wire increased ninefold, and the volume of messages increased sevenfold; the sale of postage stamps multiplied eightfold; the 3,000 telephones of 1876 had become 1.3 million by 1900.[70]

There are no similarly condensed ways in which to write about the tremendous social changes that were inseparable from these transformations of production, transportation, and communication. Both the structure of society and the texture of everyday life were profoundly affected. The statistic about postage stamps perhaps suggests, in its unassuming way, not only expanding trade but changing habits among ordinary people. A few striking examples may help to drive the point home, for twentieth-century Americans tend to take for granted many practices that were established only in this relatively recent period. The wide use of factory-made shoes, for example, is such a practice. It was only in the middle of the nineteenth century that ready-made "crooked shoes"—that is, shoes cut to fit the left or right foot rather than "straights" which made no distinction—became available. The working class began buying ready-made shoes in large numbers after the Civil War, and by the end of the century their rising quality had made them acceptable to the middle class and the affluent as well.[71] Examples of the transfer of production from households and local artisans to factories during this period could be multiplied virtually without limit.

The way in which business was transacted was also changing. The cash register, a machine we now consider indispensable to the operation of stores, was patented in 1879. As its use spread, it not only provided a defense against pilfering from the till but, particularly with later improvements, an increasingly detailed record of transactions. Daniel Boorstin writes that this information "made possible a revolution in business accounting. More and more [businessmen,] workers and employees began to think quantitatively about their activities, their products, and their income."[72] The new institution of time zones also reflected and fostered new ways of thinking. Times had always been set locally by the sun and announced by steeple clocks and the ringing of church bells. As Alan Trachtenberg describes it, "overlappings of regional times set by the larger cities and local times in the hinterlands formed a crazy-quilt pattern across the nation."[73] This lack of uniformity obviously presented a problem for the railroads, as their trains moved through the countryside and through varying local times. Rather than attempt constant adjustment each line set its own time, and finally, in 1883, all the lines agreed to divide the nation into four standard time zones. They, not the government, established the national time we take for granted today. In the process they dramatized the increasing degree to which local communities were caught up in, and conceived themselves in relation to, a web of national connections.

33
The
Nature
of
Genre,
the
Genre
of
Nature

The urbanization that accompanied industrialization was of course one of the changes of the period that required new forms of social authority and made an enormous, immediate difference in people's lives; even those who did not live in the cities were affected by their increasing economic and cultural power. In 1870, 26 percent of Americans lived in urban areas, and there were fourteen cities with populations greater than 100,000; in 1900, 40 percent lived in urban areas, and thirty-eight cities had populations greater than 100,000.[74] Part of this growth resulted from migration from the country to the city as, throughout the period, the percentage of the labor force engaged in agricultural work declined. Part of it resulted from the greatest volume of immigration ever recorded.[75] In 1880, 80 percent of the population of New York was foreign-born or born of immigrants; in Chicago the figure was 87 percent; in Detroit, 84 percent; in St. Louis and San Francisco, 78 percent.[76] It was of course the immigrants themselves who had to adjust to the most radical changes in their lives, but their presence had an impact on others as well. Those voicing warnings about rising social tensions and the state of the nation not infrequently emphasized the threat of uncontrolled immigration and uncontrolled immigrants, as we will see in more detail later.

The nation's growing wealth did not mean uniform prosperity. Even for those who were profiting most, there was uncertainty— markets shifted rapidly and the prospect of failure could never be utterly dismissed. Others faced relative or absolute deprivation. For farmers, after the Civil War "hard times" seemed to have come to stay. A contracting currency, the crop lien system, the unpredictability of prices for supplies, freight, and crops all worked to their disadvantage, and farmers complained loudly that they were denied their share of the new wealth.[77] Workers in the manufacturing sector were also at the mercy of the market—the availability of work, wages, the cost of the necessities of life all fluctuated widely. Conditions varied between and within industries, but in general, historian Melvyn Dubofsky writes, "for what were at best low wages and a marginal existence, workers labored long hours in unsafe environments."[78] References to the widespread sense of crisis at the end of the century more commonly indicate the alarm felt by the prosperous as they contemplated the discontent of the deprived; but workers would surely have been justified in feeling a need for urgent remedies when, every year in the period from 1880 to 1900, 35,000 of them were killed on the job and another 536,000 injured.

34

Form
and
History
in
American
Literary
Naturalism

Some work was particularly dangerous: in 1901, one of every 399 railroad men was killed, one of every 26 injured; among operating trainmen, one of 137 was killed, one of 11 injured.[79] The efforts of farmers and workers to organize and improve their circumstances, and the response of the comfortable and powerful to those efforts, will play an important role in my account of the period when, in Chapter 3, I consider how those living through them responded to the changes in American life in the late nineteenth and early twentieth centuries. Here I have, of course, only begun to sketch those changes.

Herbert Gutman attempts to contain these complex transformations in a structural description of the economic changes of the second half of the century: "Preindustrial American society was not premodern in the same way that European peasant societies were, but it was, nevertheless, premodern. In the half-century after 1843 industrial development radically transformed the earlier American social structure. . . . After 1893 the United States ranked as a mature industrial society."[80] To periodize so unequivocally is always perilous, of course, since if one looks closely at the different series of economics, politics, and literature, for example, one sees clearly that each develops according to its own temporality, which is only unevenly correlated with that of other causal series.[81] It is unquestionably oversimplifying to encapsulate such a decentered, divergent real in a homogenizing description. But the changes I identify here, without establishing punctual transitions, act as limiting conditions on a wide range of activities. One may characterize the period from 1870 to 1910 when the first generation of American naturalists was born, came to consciousness, and began to publish as a period in which the consequences of these transformations became virtually inescapable. We may decide that we cannot know precisely when America became a "mature industrial society," but by the 1890s it was clear that a profound change *had already* taken place. In this sense, the authors studied here are native-born citizens of modern America—a nation to which a writer like Henry Adams, one might ironically claim, brings the sensibilities of the immigrant. In another sense, of course, the penetration of all areas of life by a global market including not only commodity production and exchange but a commodified mass culture, is still proceeding today, simultaneously creating the possibility of nightmarish, totalitarian uniformity and the possibility of utopian collectivity.

The authors who will centrally concern me are Frank Norris, born 1870; Theodore Dreiser, and, to a lesser extent, Stephen Crane, both born 1871; Jack London, born 1876, and, again to a lesser extent, Upton Sinclair, born 1878. With a few exceptions the works I examine were published between 1893 and 1909; within that group of novels those most crucial to my analysis were published during an even briefer span of years at the turn of the century. Certainly one can trace elements of this characteristic form in earlier works (in the protonaturalist novels of Harold Frederic, for example) and in later works that avail themselves of the formal possibilities opened up by naturalism. Indeed, once the generic concept and its sometimes separable techniques exist, they enter into the systematizing discourse of writers and critics and it becomes possible to detach naturalism from its historical location and find "naturalistic" qualities in an enormous range of writers, from Rabelais to Faulkner, and beyond. But it is at its formative moment in the late nineteenth and early twentieth centuries that we can see most clearly the distinctive character of the phenomenon we call American literary naturalism.

2 Forces, The
       Freedom, Antinomies
       and   of American
       Fears: Naturalism

The thread that comes most readily to the hand of the critic seeking to unravel the definitions of naturalism and weave them into a new theory is the association of the genre with abstract concepts of reality and causality—specifically, with philosophical determinism. The observation most frequently made about naturalism must surely be that it is, in George Becker's words, "pessimistic materialistic determinism."[1] Lars Åhnebrink's definition provides a more extended illustration of this commonplace: "the author portrays *life as it is in accordance with the philosophical theory of determinism.* . . . a naturalist believes that man is fundamentally an animal without free will. To a naturalist man can be explained in terms of the forces, usually heredity and environment, which operate upon him."[2] Ideas of determinism were widely available and influential before and during the period of American naturalism. Ronald Martin writes that the determinist view of causality he calls the "universe of force" had an extraordinary impact in America: "Principally in its Spencerian formulation—indissoluably tied to the theory of evolution—not only did it become a factor to be reckoned with in American science, philosophy, and religion, but it penetrated to levels of the American population never before reached by any formal philosophy save Christianity."[3] Martin thoroughly examines both the philosophical systems based on this notion and their impact on American literature. Other critics too have considered naturalism's relation to the intellectual history of its period.[4] We will take these essential but more traditional and limited versions of literary history as given, but to understand American naturalism as a genre and not simply as the reflex of a philosophical position we must consider other elements of the novels.

After all, the next most frequently made observation about naturalism must surely be that it is *not* pessimistic determinism. Critics consistently assert that novels in one way or another fall lamentably short of—or from another perspective fortunately escape—the rigorous application of determinist principles. For example, V. L. Parrington writes that the naturalist is subject to certain "temptations," one of which is that from

concern over a devastating *milieu* he may end in desiring to
change that *milieu* to the end that men may achieve happiness. Hence he tends to lose his objectivity and scientific detachment, and becomes a partisan to a cause. Such was the
fate of Zola. The philosopher of naturalism, in practice he
abandoned his principles and became a reformer, attacking
the church, the capitalist order, etc. . . . . This was the failure of
the first group of American naturalists—Frank Norris, Robert
Herrick, Jack London.[5]

He also warns that by studying the "inner drives of low-grade characters the naturalist is in danger of creating grotesques," and by
emphasizing "animal impulses" he may "turn man into an animal"
(p. 325). Donald Pizer comments that naturalism seems always to
be either "damned for degrading man beyond recognition by de-
picting him as a creature at the mercy of 'forces' . . . or attacked for
inconsistency because of the presence of characteristics which fail
to debase him."[6] To evaluate a work according to its relationship
with a narrow generic standard is (as we saw in the previous chapter and as the best critics of naturalism have recognized) a theoretically questionable enterprise. Pizer argues that the

> traditional approach to naturalism through realism and
> through philosophical determinism is historically justifiable
> and has served a useful purpose, but it has also handicapped
> thinking both about the movement as a whole and about indi-
> vidual works within the movement. It has resulted in much
> condescension toward those writers who are supposed to be
> naturalists yet whose fictional sensationalism . . . and moral
> ambiguity . . . appear to make their work flawed specimens of
> the mode.[7]

And indeed, the inconsistencies cited by Parrington and Pizer are
so common in naturalist novels that one begins to wonder just
where one finds the novels that define the norm; reformism and
sensationalism are more the rule than the exception in American
naturalism and are elements of the novels which will concern me
throughout but particularly in Chapters 4 and 5 of this study.

Lilian Furst also observes that literary naturalism combines two
incompatible attitudes, but she considers this dualism intrinsic to
the form. Naturalism, she writes, was "torn between its theory and
its practice, between materialism and idealism, between pessimism
and optimism. . . . [The naturalists tried] to combine high-minded
idealism with the sobriety of detached observers. Looking at the
world and at man, they despaired and hoped at one and the same
time. This underlying dualism helps to account for some of the
apparent inconsistencies within naturalism."[8] Charles Child Walcutt

38
Form
and
History
in
American
Literary
Naturalism

insightfully places this apparent inconsistency at the very heart of his definition of naturalism. He proposes to reconcile the three dominant critical views of naturalism—that it expresses "an optimistic social purpose," that it reveals a "pessimistic determinism," a "philosophy of gloom and despair," and that it is incomprehensibly, hopelessly contradictory—by distinguishing between the literary work and the ideas that inform it. The "key to this puzzle," he suggests, is that the novelist, committed to both science and reform,

> has to establish the validity of two assumptions: that the state of man needs to be improved, and that human conditions are determined by the operation of material causes which can be traced, recorded, understood, and, finally, controlled. The . . . best possible way to illustrate and validate these two assumptions is to write a "naturalistic" tragedy in which a human being is crushed and destroyed by the operation of forces which he has no power to resist or even understand. The more helpless the individual and the more clearly the links in an inexorable chain of causation are defined, the more effectively documented are the two assumptions which underlie the scientists' program of reform, for the destruction of an individual demonstrates the power of heredity and environment over human destinies. And if the victim's lot is sordid, the need for reform is "proved." The more helpless the character, the stronger the proof of determinism; and once such a thesis is established the scientist hopes and believes that men will set about trying to control the forces which now control men.[9]

Notwithstanding its philosophical pessimism, what this "scientist-reformer" produces—a work of art—is itself, Walcutt argues, a victory that holds out the possibility of improving the human condition.

I would add that the validation of the role of the scientist-reformer, who is also the novelist, is no insignificant part of the victory Walcutt identifies. This important configuration of hopeful observer of events and helpless character in their midst is something to which I will return. At the moment, however, what concerns me is the way Walcutt cuts the knot other critics are worrying at by accepting both determinism and reformism as constitutive of the genre and defining the form through a dynamic opposition rather than a single concept. Although he has encapsulated both terms in a seemingly unified and logical narrative about the naturalist project, he has not, as he acknowledges in concluding his description of the generic model, disposed of the tension: "all 'naturalistic' novels exist in a tension between determinism and its antithesis. The reader is aware of the opposition between what the artist says about man's fate and what his saying it affirms about man's hope. Both of these polar terms are a part of the 'meaning' of a naturalistic novel" (p. 29). The antinomy between fate and hope, between determinism and human will, is not only implicit in the program of naturalism but is repeatedly dramatized in the action of novels; in Chapter 4 I will examine that tension through characters, such as Presley in Frank Norris's *Octopus*, who strive to effect reforms within their novelistic worlds.

But we encounter a tension between hope and fate more pervasively in characters' struggles to fulfill their own desires. In a later article Walcutt, distinguishing between naturalism and realism in almost Lukácsian terms, takes account of the opposition between will and determinism at this level as well: "No matter how complex and full are the surrounding forces in a realistic novel, . . . the interest is in the freedom of the characters. In the naturalistic novel the interest is unavoidably divided between the controlling forces, which are the novelist's avowed and intended subject, and the frail wills of the people who struggle against them."[10] Sydney Krause, in his introduction to *Essays on Determinism in American Literature*, attributes the inconsistency that he, like so many other critics, observes in naturalism to the characters' struggles on their own behalf:

> the characteristic mood of deterministic naturalism is mixed and paradoxical. Its key paradox centers on the brute refusal of the human to be sucked down into the vortex of natural law. It is because of their cheerless prospects that we are cheered by the moral drive of individual characters who suffer much, but who like Jean Macquart, Esther Waters, or Rose Dutcher still manage to hold themselves intact as human beings despite the animal ruthlessness of others and the natural and social causalities that confine them.[11]

In *Jennie Gerhardt* Dreiser gives Lester Kane a speech that succinctly expresses the plight of the naturalist character: " 'The best we can do is to hold our personality intact.' "[12] Our interest in the opposition of forces and freedom is, as Walcutt indicates, focused through characters and groups of characters; helplessness and volition become attached, as they are in Krause's description, to particular proper names as attributes of particular characters. For the purposes of thematic analysis in this chapter we may consider characters as the vehicles of recurrent ideas. Despite the investments we make in them, characters are, after all, only assemblages of meanings given proper names that provide them an illusion of unity (as we recognize with ease in an intellectual climate in which identity itself is increasingly seen as a construct). Thus the same opposition between will and determinism can function at several levels

40
Form
and
History
in
American
Literary
Naturalism

in a work: in the description of characters, in the narration of their actions, in the narrator's commentary, in the informing project of the novelist as scientist and reformer.

The themes of naturalism include, then, a characteristic opposition between human will and hereditary and environmental determinisms that both shape human beings and frustrate their desires. That opposition is also implicit, as Walcutt shows, in naturalism's aesthetic and philosophical premises. Although this formulation is considerably more adequate than the idea that because of those premises naturalism is or should be strictly deterministic, it is still too simple. To go beyond it requires that we examine the novels themselves and that we move from the themes of naturalism to what we might call its thematic: the fundamental conceptual oppositions that inform and structure those themes. It is not the sheer content of a novel but the organization of its semantic field that establishes its possibilities for meaning. The idea of "fate," for example, is operative both in Greek tragedy and in American naturalism, but it takes on a distinctive significance in each because it operates in different conceptual structures, because it is opposed to different terms. To put it another way: we will distinguish naturalism as a genre not by the answers texts give to questions, not even by the questions they ask, but by the terms in which they ask those questions and the very kinds of questions that they can formulate. We must begin, of course, with determinism—yet we must also take serious account of the reformism, sensationalism, and persistent assertion of human will that are so often noted as elements of naturalist novels.

At a very fundamental level this approach derives from Saussure's radical insight that in language there is only difference, without positive terms. A device that usefully embodies this insight for semantic analysis is A. J. Greimas's "elementary structure of signification," which represents an opposition between two "contraries" together with their simple negations or "contradictories":

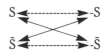

Greimas suggests that all meaning operates within certain semiotic constraints and must necessarily be built up from layers of such oppositions.[13] But we may use his semantic rectangle as an analytical tool without necessarily crediting its claim to "elementary" status. It scarcely seems possible, at least when dealing with literary works, to establish the pure logical possibilities of meaning—we are too familiar with the inevitably and profoundly constructed nature of such cultural objects as "themes."

I use Greimas's structure of signification, therefore, as a heuristic device, to rewrite themes in terms of oppositions rather than positive contentions, and thus to construct the thematic terrain of naturalism as an object of study.[14] Once constructed, that thematic can be used as part of a more wide-ranging analysis. I would agree with Fredric Jameson that the "operational validity of semiotic analysis, and in particular of the Greimassian semiotic rectangle, derives . . . not from its adequacy to nature or being, nor even from its capacity to map all forms of thinking or language, but rather from its vocation specifically to model ideological closure and to articulate the workings of binary oppositions."[15] In this spirit I will show that by revealing the conceptualizations beyond which a text cannot go—in Jameson's phrase, the antinomies "between which it is condemned to oscillate" (p. 47)—the characteristic oppositions of naturalism point the way toward an understanding of the historical situation to which the form responds. In this chapter I am concerned with deriving a thematic structure from close textual analysis and will defer reading naturalist novels in relation to their cultural and historical matrix until Chapter 3. But ultimately we will want to see the antinomies of naturalism not just as abstract oppositions but in terms of concrete social contradictions.

Let us begin with Theodore Dreiser's *Sister Carrie* (1900), which will serve throughout this investigation as an exemplary case.[16] Dreiser's naturalist thematic is operative in the very first chapter of the novel, which opens with Carrie Meeber aboard a train that will take her from her native village to Chicago. Carrie is simultaneously hopeful and fearful. She vaguely expects new pleasures, yet is almost overwhelmed at finding herself suddenly adrift in this immense "sea of life and endeavor"; the mysterious city both allures with "the gleam of a thousand lights" and threatens "the grimness of shift and toil."[17] This equivocal panorama, with the figure of the desirous and vulnerable Carrie set against it, is already the terrain of Dreiser's concepts as well as his story. It is constructed according to the metaphysical attitude that, as Ronald Martin summarizes it, informs all Dreiser's philosophizing: "his thinking both began and ended in a sense of awe at what he perceived as the harshness and beauty of a universe made up of determining forces indifferent to man and inscrutable" (p. 219).

Human desire is, we will see, one of those inscrutable forces—but it is also a.response to beauty, a form of the passionate awe and longing that Dreiser depicts as the sensitive individual's response to this universe. In a sense Carrie is the victim of her desires, as she is drawn after first one object, then another. Yet her peculiarly passive and dedicated pursuit of her dreams is also an exercise of will that draws her from one level of understanding to another and thus draws her closer to the realm of freedom. Carrie's desiring disposition is the dominant attribute of her character, and it is constantly conveyed to the reader in descriptions of Carrie and in reports of

42

Form
and
History
in
American
Literary
Naturalism

her thoughts and actions. As she travels toward Chicago in the opening scene, she is "dreaming wild dreams of some vague, far-off supremacy" (chap. 1, p. 2); as the novel progresses she does "not grow in knowledge so much as she awakened in the matter of desire. . . . She longed and longed and longed" (chap. 12, pp. 86–87). Carrie's passionate yearning makes her emotionally sensitive and responsive, and Dreiser portrays these qualities as the source of her power over other characters; in particular, it is her "sympathetic, impressionable nature" that makes her a successful actress (chap. 16, p. 117). Carrie signifies desire, for others and for the reader; the character Ames tells Carrie that her face has something "'the world likes to see, because it's a natural expression of its longing. . . . Sometimes nature . . . makes the face representative of all desire. That's what has happened in your case'" (chap. 46, p. 356). The nature of this central character places desire, ambiguously represented both as involuntary attraction and as an effort toward freedom, at the heart of the novel's themes.

A less generalized and spiritual longing affects Carrie when she enters a department store for the first time:

> Each separate counter was a show place of dazzling interest and attraction. She could not help feeling the claim of each trinket and valuable upon her personally, and yet she did not stop. There was nothing there which she could not have used —nothing which she did not long to own. The dainty slippers and stockings, the delicately frilled skirts and petticoats, the laces, ribbons, hair-combs, purses, all touched her with individual desire, and she felt keenly the fact that not any of these things were in the range of her purchase. [chap. 3, p. 17]

As in the first chapter—titled "The Magnet Attracting: A Waif Amid Forces"—Carrie here is passive; the trinkets and valuables assert claims on her, rather than she on them. She drifts into a relationship with Drouet largely because of his ability to purchase such things for her, and when she thinks of leaving him their arguments against it are too powerful to resist: "Fine clothes were to her a vast persuasion; they spoke tenderly and Jesuitically for themselves. When she came within earshot of their pleading, desire in her bent a willing ear. . . . 'My dear,' said the lace collar she secured from Partridge's, 'I fit you beautifully; don't give me up'" (chap. 11, p. 75). Objects and circumstances act upon Carrie, and even her desire is something "in her," separate from her self and enforcing itself upon her. But what is within and what is without are not easily separable, nor is an authentic self easily located. Surely one could ask for no more vivid description of commodity fetishism, of the life of objects that consumes the life of the human beings who produce and consume them. Alan Trachtenberg writes that in the just-invented department stores of the Gilded Age "the citizen met a new world of goods: not goods alone, but a *world* of goods, constructed and shaped by the store into objects of desire. . . . In department stores, buyers of goods learned new roles for themselves, apprehended themselves as *consumers*, something different from mere users of goods."[18] Carrie is an apt student of this world of images.[19] She constantly looks into mirrors and is constantly captured by possible images of the self: "She looked into her glass and saw a prettier Carrie than she had seen before; she looked into her mind, a mirror prepared of her own and the world's opinions, and saw a worse" (chap. 10, p. 70). *Sister Carrie* seems to offer itself as an immanent analysis of not only the commodity but the specular self in consumer society.[20] Carrie learns to desire more expensive possessions, mansions rather than trinkets, and her trying-on of attitudes and roles is magnified into a career as an actress, but throughout the novel she remains passive, her self provisional, unstable, endangered.

Carrie's desire is never satisfied by what she has. Glamor slides metonymically from one object to the next: "She wanted pleasure, she wanted position, and yet she was confused as to what these things might be. Every hour the kaleidoscope of human affairs threw a new lustre upon something, and therewith it became for her the desired—the all. Another shift of the box, and some other had become the beautiful, the perfect" (chap. 15, p. 107). Although Carrie's proliferating desires and perpetually deferred satisfaction mark her participation in the alienating signifying system of the commodity, they might also be said to mark the infinite, even utopian character of her desire. Carrie wants, first, the clothing and other things one can buy with money, but she wants more than that—she always wants something *better* than what she has. At the end of the novel, when Carrie has succeeded in attaining all the desires to which she can put a name, she is as desirous as ever. As Dreiser writes in his sentimental and widely deplored conclusion, for her "it was forever to be the pursuit of that radiance of delight which tints the distant hilltops of the world" (chap. 47, p. 369). Her desire—both in its practical and in its more metaphysical manifestations—motivates Carrie to struggle for what she wants and to develop a more complex emotional and (to some degree) intellectual life. The eagerness with which she embraces the role of consumer is inseparable from the impulse that leads her toward wider horizons, toward heightened awareness and the exercise of will.

Carrie is drawn to what she desires, but she is also a magnet herself—to a number of men in the course of the novel, but most importantly to Drouet and Hurstwood. Drouet, less imaginative than Carrie and unable really to understand her, finds in her for a moment that retreating radiance of delight and must pursue it; he "had his future fixed for him beyond a peradventure. He could not help what he was going to do. He could not see clearly enough to wish

44
Form
and
History
in
American
Literary
Naturalism

to do differently. . . . He would need to delight himself with Carrie as surely as he would need to eat his heavy breakfast" (chap. 8, p. 58). In all his novels Dreiser's male characters are more susceptible to the overwhelming "chemic" force of sexual desire and sometimes experience their own passion as something virtually uncontrollable and alien to them.[21] But this passion is certainly not simply lust—a diverse array of genetic, physiological, psychological, and social forces are invoked to explain behavior. Hurstwood is captured by a role he invents for himself; in writing to Carrie he begins "to feel those subtleties which he could find words to express. With every expression came increased conception" (chap. 15, p. 107). In naturalist novels characters face both external and internal forces. They are thwarted by nature and, particularly in Dreiser, by the man-made "second nature" of social forces. And they find themselves struggling with their *own* natures, with the forces of instinct and heredity that embody nature within the very boundaries of the self. The social too invades the self, as we have seen—indeed we may suspect in reading *Sister Carrie* that the self is more properly a self-image and is the creature of the social. The characters' freedom is assaulted by both nature and society, by both internal and external determining forces. But since the integrity of the self is so often precisely what is at stake, we will find that these categories are not finally separable.

The series of events that precipitates Hurstwood's flight from Chicago with Carrie is one of Dreiser's most famous dissections of the forces acting in what we call "choice." His irresistible impulse to pursue Carrie has put him in an intolerable situation with his wife when, by chance, he finds his employers' safe open and an unusually large sum inside. He does not *decide* to steal the money; rather, he is pushed and pulled by fear and desire: "He was drawn by such a keen desire for Carrie, driven by such a state of turmoil in his own affairs that he thought constantly it would be best, and yet he wavered. He did not know what evil might result from it to him—how soon he might come to grief" (chap. 27, p. 193). Hurstwood vacillates, takes the money, decides to put it back, returns it to the wrong boxes, takes it out again to correct his mistake—and "accidentally" closes the safe and seals his fate. As Donald Pizer comments, it is a remarkable "dramatization of the ways in which chance and subconscious desire blend into event."[22] In a sense Hurstwood chooses, but in classically determinist fashion the internal and external forces that shape his actions make nonsense of the notion of free will.

Once Hurstwood has taken this step his decline is inevitable. We see these determining agencies within the individual at their most extreme and mechanical in Dreiser's description of what happens to Hurstwood after he abandons his job, his property, and his

family: "it has been shown experimentally that a constantly sub-
dued frame of mind produces certain poisons in the blood, called
katastates, just as virtuous feelings of pleasure and delight produce
helpful chemicals called anastates. The poisons generated by remorse inveigh against the system, and eventually produce marked
physical deterioration. To these Hurstwood was subject" (chap. 33,
p. 240). Dreiser derives this specious theory from the "offbeat" psy-
chologist Elmer Gates (the adjective is Ronald Martin's [p. 223]),
and many readers have found it risible. We might ask, however, if it
is really qualitatively different from the widely held attitudes that
Susan Sontag analyzes in *Illness as Metaphor*, such as the deeply
rooted contemporary conviction that cancer can somehow be attributed to unhappiness. As she points out, "every illness can be
considered psychologically. Illness is interpreted as, basically, a
psychological event, and people are encouraged to believe that
they get sick because they (unconsciously) want to, and that they
can cure themselves by the mobilization of will; that they can
choose not to die of the disease."[23] The attitude is, surely, more
familiar than Gates's theory yet not utterly dissimilar. We will find
that the thematic of naturalism, if not its vocabulary, is not so alien
as contemporary critics who dismiss its ideas out of hand would
lead us to believe.

Carrie is not drawn by sexual desire so strongly as Hurstwood
and Drouet; in her relations with men she seeks rather affection,
admiration, security, seeks the new selves they can offer her. But
like them she is as much acted upon as acting, constantly vacillating in the grip of conflicting forces. In one critical early episode she
is drawn into a dependency on Drouet that results in her becoming,
in the figure of her sister's dream, a fallen woman. Dreiser glosses
this incident with a well-known meditation on the dilemma of the
desiring self wavering between reasoned choice and the internal
pressures of passion:

> Among the forces which sweep and play throughout the uni-
> verse, untutored man is but a wisp in the wind. Our civilisa-
> tion is still in a middle stage, scarcely beast, in that it is no
> longer wholly guided by instinct; scarcely human, in that it is
> not yet wholly guided by reason. . . . We see man far removed
> from the lairs of the jungles, his innate instincts dulled by too
> near an approach to free-will, his free-will not sufficiently de-
> veloped to replace his instincts and afford him perfect guid-
> ance. . . . He is even as a wisp in the wind, moved by every
> breath of passion, acting now by his will and now by his in-
> stincts, erring with one, only to retrieve by the other, falling by
> one, only to rise by the other. . . . When this jangle of free-will
> and instinct shall have been adjusted, when perfect under-

46
Form
and
History
in
American
Literary
Naturalism

standing has given the former the power to replace the latter entirely, man will no longer vary. The needle of understanding will yet point steadfast and unwavering to the distant pole of truth. [chap. 8, pp. 56–57]

Like many of Dreiser's philosophical musings, this is portentous but amorphous. One of its effects, certainly, is to suggest what Ronald Martin calls *Sister Carrie*'s "systematic deletion of conventional conceptions of volition and consequently of any sense of moral responsibility" (p. 251), thus in some part shielding Carrie from blame for her actions. But if moralism is revealed as an entirely inadequate response to events, is volition also discredited? What is at stake here is the possibility that human struggle has meaning, that human will exists as a distinct entity rather than as a mere manifestation of the impersonal forces that sweep through the self as well as the external universe—what is at stake is, in short, the chance that the personality can hold itself intact. And Dreiser's meditation, reflecting an optimistic notion of evolutionary teleology more often found in Norris's than in Dreiser's novels, asserts that free will is sometimes effective and should eventually prevail.[24]

Let us call on the semantic rectangle to open an analysis of the various categories Dreiser uses here. The passage clearly establishes basic oppositions between beast and human and between free will and instinct (these are of course commonplace in or out of literature). It also seems to imply that there is a difference between instinct, which is consistently identified with beasts and the bestial element of humanity, and passion. If instinct is the opposite or contrary of free will, given the preceding discussion of the ambiguities of desire, we may take passion as its simple negation or contradictory. Passion is not consciously willed, its object not chosen by reason—but it does not necessarily lead one astray. The term that offers a basis for volition is suggested in the last two sentences: the fourth term, the contrary of the contradictory, is understanding. The resulting semantic rectangle takes this form:

As I have suggested, Carrie's pursuit of the beautiful does lead her in the direction of understanding, culminating in her being drawn to a third man, Ames, late in the novel. Ames is relatively untouched by the forces that move the other characters; his enthusiasms are intellectual and altruistic, and he articulates a view of life informed, like the narrator's, by reason. He hopes not to gain his own ends but to improve the world; "interested in forwarding all good causes" (chap. 46, p. 357), he even tries to educate Carrie and draw her closer to understanding. Indeed Ames is scarcely an ex-

ample of "untutored man," for he is by far the most educated character portrayed in *Sister Carrie*; both his class and his consciousness mark him as belonging to a realm of freedom rather than
forces.

Ames's understanding is exceeded only by the narrator's. Mankind as a whole is expected to reach such understanding through
generations of evolution, but as he loftily pronounces on the progress of human civilization the narrator seems to speak from a place
where it has already been achieved. He looks down at the struggles of the characters and writes smugly, "blessed are the children
of endeavour in this, that they try and are hopeful. And blessed
also are they who, knowing, smile and approve" (chap. 17, p. 127).
The diagnosis of human development, like the psychologizing of
disease that Sontag describes, "seems to provide control over the
experiences and events (like grave illnesses)"—or like the overwhelming experience of urban life in the twentieth century and the
apprehension of the massive movements of history—"over which
people have in fact little or no control."[25] Chapter 4 examines such
gestures of control by the omniscient narrators of naturalist novels
and by self-aware characters like Ames and asks what kind of power
such narrators and characters are actually able to exert in these
fictional universes of force.

Omniscience, after all, is not necessarily omnipotence; holding
the personality intact does not insure control over external as
well as internal forces. The inscrutable, overwhelming forces that
"sweep through the universe" are manifested in physical and social
obstacles that in *Sister Carrie* and other naturalist novels we encounter above all as the city. In her first days in Chicago, for example, Carrie must confront a scene massively indifferent to the desirous self:

> She walked bravely forward, led by an honest desire to find
> employment and delayed at every step by the interest of the
> unfolding scene, and a sense of helplessness amid so much
> evidence of power and force which she did not understand.
> These vast buildings, what were they? These strange energies
> and huge interests, for what purposes were they there? She
> could have understood the meaning of a little stone-cutter's
> yard at Columbia City, carving little pieces of marble for indi-
> vidual use, but when the yards of some huge stone corpora-
> tion came into view, filled with spur tracks and flat cars,
> transpierced by docks from the river and traversed overhead
> by immense trundling cranes of wood and steel, it lost all sig-
> nificance in her little world. [chap. 2, pp. 12–13]

Dreiser here explicitly attributes the loss of human significance that
Lukács finds in naturalism to the historical circumstances in which
he writes, to the increasingly national and impersonal economy

48
Form
and
History
in
American
Literary
Naturalism

that is encountered most directly in the growing cities. Failing to find work, Carrie sees the city in an even grimmer light as the day wanes: "On every hand, to her fatigued senses, the great business portion grew larger, harder, more stolid in its indifference. It seemed as if it was all closed to her, that the struggle was too fierce for her to hope to do anything at all. Men and women hurried by in long, shifting lines. She felt the flow of the tide of effort and interest—felt her own helplessness without quite realising the wisp on the tide that she was" (chap. 3, p. 20). Dreiser's narration constantly assimilates this enormous, indifferent city and economic order to the more abstract and philosophical—and even more enormous and indifferent—terrain of the universe of force.

These passages from *Sister Carrie*, as well as the vocabulary of naturalist themes provided by my account of critical discussions of the genre, offer many terms that might be the basis for a semantic rectangle that accommodates these themes. We can specify some initial oppositions between human effort and determining forces outside the self using virtually the first words one encounters on opening the novel: the title of the first chapter, "The Magnet Attracting: A Waif Amid Forces."[26]

Waif◄-------------►Forces

Or, from the passage quoted immediately above:

Wisp◄-------------►Tide

The desiring, endeavoring self confronts an indifferent, impersonal field of force that seems to have nothing to do with, to utterly negate—to be the contrary of—individual hopes and efforts.

But the forces that determine events are not actively hostile to the waif; they simply disregard her. Immediately after she experiences Chicago at its most oppressive, Carrie gets a job: "She walked out into the busy street and discovered a new atmosphere. Behold, the throng was moving with a lightsome step. She noticed that men and women were smiling. . . . This was a great, pleasing metropolis after all" (chap. 3, p. 21). Carrie not only succeeds in finding work—she succeeds, eventually, in rising far beyond her first job and becoming a successful actress. The causal chain here is not quite clear. Carrie owes something to "her youth and her beauty" (chap. 38, p. 279), something to her imaginative nature and her ability to project desire. Chance certainly seems to play a role, too; the quoted newspaper account of her first important success ends, with apparent irrelevance, with the statement that " 'the vagaries of fortune are indeed curious' " (chap. 43, p. 327). We have seen that Carrie is relatively passive, that she is drawn to Drouet, Hurstwood, Ames rather than actively choosing them. Yet her sensitivity equips Carrie with a kind of compass powered by the magnet of desire, gives her a direction to follow if not the means to move. Carrie "had little power of initiative; but nevertheless, she seemed ever capable of getting herself into the tide of change where she would be easily borne along" (chap. 31, p. 225).

Here "tide" as a metaphor for the play of causal forces implies not that forces are irresistible but that they are unpredictable. The forces of chance—not really laws of causality, but rather the interstices between those laws—open the possibility for her success, and her developing sense of direction allows her to take advantage of it. She is "an apt student of fortune's ways" (chap. 11, p. 75). To anticipate a more rigorous argument in Chapter 4, we may think of Carrie's luck in terms of historian Robert Wiebe's comment that some social theorists of the period "pictured a society of ceaselessly interacting members and concentrated upon adjustments within it. Although they included rules and principles of human behavior, these necessarily had an indeterminate quality because perpetual interaction was itself indeterminate. . . . Thus the rules, resembling orientations much more than laws, stressed techniques of constant watchfulness and mechanisms of continuous management."[27] It is this indeterminacy, the incalculable complexity of the determining forces that are figured in Dreiser's narrative, that permits the watchful, desirous Carrie to prosper.

Dreiser describes Carrie (and humankind in general) as "a waif amid forces," a "wisp in the wind," a "wisp on the tide." The equation of forces, wind, and tide suggests that we are faced by powerful and mysterious forces. We do not know where we may be swept by winds or tides—they are, it seems, quite arbitrary. His metaphors seem to suggest that causality is too complex to be manipulated or even fully understood. Yet there are prevailing winds as well as inexplicable tempests and fitful breezes, and a tide, although it may contain eddies, is a powerful force moving in a particular direction. No human effort can reverse the direction of winds and tides. Dreiser's metaphors can imply not only that events are unpredictable, but that they are inevitable. In *Sister Carrie* Hurstwood, for example, is caught in what we may call an ebb tide. After he has stolen his employers' money and fled Chicago, his decline is predictable and inexorable. Once he is on it the "road downward has but few landings and level places" (chap. 33, p. 244), and Hurstwood meets a miserable end as a bum and eventually a suicide.

Here we may avail ourselves of the critical vocabulary about naturalism and term this a malevolent *fate* pursuing Hurstwood as it does characters in other naturalist novels. The special status of fate and fatalism in these novels is evident in the definition of naturalism as *pessimistic* determinism. It sometimes seems that the naturalists' "world" is constructed not according to indifferent laws but as a trap or even a torture chamber. The forces arrayed against Hurstwood conspire to deprive him not only of his prosperity but of his dignity and self-control, to subject him to internal pressures that

50
Form
and
History
in
American
Literary
Naturalism

reduce him to a less-than-fully-human condition; Hurstwood's brutalization will play an important role in the analysis of Chapter 3. Not all characters are exposed to the full cruelties of such sadistic forces—but for those who are, in Hurstwood's last words, " 'What's the use?' " (chap. 47, p. 367). The contrary of Carrie's good fortune is fate, a conception of the forces of nature and society as inevitably and malevolently crushing the character. Our completed rectangle, then, looks like this:

Effort◄------------►Forces
(the endeavoring waif)   (indifferent determinism)

Fortune◄------------►Fate
(the unpredictable eddy)   (the road downward)

This schema certainly does not *contain* the complex themes of *Sister Carrie*, but it does organize the novel's ideas in a revealing fashion—revealing both because it accurately describes the novel's very consistent use of these concepts, and because, as will become increasingly apparent, it makes sense of that use in relation to a wide range of other observations about American naturalism and its historical moment.

Jack London's early fiction constructs a terrain that looks very different from Dreiser's city but embodies surprisingly similar conceptual oppositions. The Northland of London's Alaskan stories is as inscrutable as Dreiser's Chicago and New York, and on its ground equally vulnerable characters hope and strive. Dreiser's city has transformed and dominated the natural landscape—as Carrie's train pulls in, Drouet points out the Chicago River, which proves to be "a little muddy creek, crowded with the huge masted wanderers from far-off waters" (chap. 1, p. 7). London's rivers are more formidable, for the forces that concern London are overtly more natural than social. Although his materials are often those of the adventure story (in Chapter 5 I will discuss the generic discontinuities that mark London's fiction so strongly), from the perspective of our thematic analysis of naturalism the Northland tales generate a remarkably coherent chain of conceptual oppositions.

The antinomy between nature and culture is perhaps the most fundamental of these oppositions, and the most characteristic and distinctive figure of London's effort to grasp and to resolve that difference is his complex image of the wolf.[28] From his first collection of stories, *The Son of the Wolf* (1900), London works with this image, even transposing it to the quite different setting of a sealing ship in *The Sea-Wolf*. Dreiser evokes beasts primarily as metaphors for tendencies in human beings, but London uses them as characters, and their role in constituting the semantic field of his fiction is correspondingly more complex. His most enduringly popular work,

The Call of the Wild (1903), is the story of a dog that becomes a
wolf. *White Fang* (1906), which embodies London's thematic most
effectively for my purposes, reverses the story of *The Call of the
Wild*: a wolf becomes a dog. Yet these summaries are too simple; it
would be more accurate to say that each story develops a network
of oppositions that makes it possible for the animal protagonist to
cross the boundary between nature and culture and thus makes it
possible to envision their reconciliation.

The first five paragraphs of *White Fang* generate an elaborate set
of antinomies between a wild terrain and the life represented by a
dogsled moving through it. Virtually every phrase contributes to the
development of this opposition. The first paragraph describes the
landscape:

> Dark spruce forest frowned on either side the frozen waterway.
> The trees had been stripped by a recent wind of their white
> covering of frost, and they seemed to lean toward each other,
> black and ominous, in the fading light. A vast silence reigned
> over the land. The land itself was a desolation, lifeless, with-
> out movement, so lone and cold that the spirit of it was not
> even that of sadness. There was a hint in it of laughter, but of
> a laughter more terrible than any sadness—a laughter that
> was mirthless as the smile of the Sphinx, a laughter cold as
> the frost and partaking of the grimness of infallibility. It was
> the masterful and incommunicable wisdom of eternity laugh-
> ing at the futility of life and the effort of life. It was the Wild,
> the savage, frozen-hearted Northland Wild.[29]

This silence—dark, but otherwise akin to what London calls, in the
eloquent title of the first story in *The Son of the Wolf*, the White
Silence—is not unchallenged: "there *was* life, abroad in the land
and defiant. Down the frozen waterway toiled a string of wolfish
dogs. Their bristly fur was rimed with frost. Their breath froze in the
air as it left their mouths, spouting forth in spumes of vapor that
settled upon the hair of their bodies and formed into crystals of
frost" (pp. 3–4). Two "unawed and indomitable" men accompany
the dogs; they are "not yet dead" (p. 5), but the sled also carries
another man:

> a man whom the Wild had conquered and beaten down until
> he would never move nor struggle again. It is not the way of
> the Wild to like movement. Life is an offence to it, for life is
> movement; and the Wild aims always to destroy movement. It
> freezes the water to prevent it running to the sea; it drives the
> sap out of the trees till they are frozen to their mighty hearts;
> and most ferociously and terribly of all does the Wild harry
> and crush into submission man—man, who is the most rest-

52
Form
and
History
in
American
Literary
Naturalism

less of life, ever in revolt against the dictum that all movement must in the end come to the cessation of movement.
[pp. 4–5]

The phrases most reminiscent of Dreiser's contrast between the
endeavoring, desiring self and indifferent forces come at the end
of this passage: the men "perceived themselves finite and small,
specks and motes, moving with weak cunning and little wisdom
amidst the play and interplay of the great blind elements and
forces" (pp. 5–6). And the pitiless fate that pursues Hurstwood
seems echoed in the active malevolence of the Wild as it aims at
the destruction of life.

This opening scene, then, establishes three of the terms of the
semantic rectangle proposed for *Sister Carrie*, and at the end of this
sequence the surviving man's fortuitous rescue from the hungry
wolf pack that besieges him certainly provides the fourth—good
luck. Yet the proliferation of meanings in this landscape and the
abstractions it evokes is not yet adequately recognized in that semantic rectangle; London constantly assimilates one opposition
to another, playfully correlating images and ideas so that it is difficult to identify stable contraries and contradictories. *White Fang*
stages a confrontation in constantly changing terms on a constantly
changing terrain.

The groupings that follow are to some extent arbitrary, since each
opposition is linked to the others; yet the terms do seem to com-
pose themselves into logical pairs. There are antinomies that are
entirely abstract:

Eternity◄------------►Effort
Infallibility◄------------►Futility

Other oppositions embody abstractions in somewhat more concrete images:

In the most concrete images, opposite terms are accommodated
in the same landscape and begin to seem less implacably incompatible:

In fact, terms representing life and movement can be stilled by the
Northland cold and transferred to the other side of the opposition:

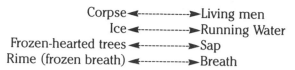

Corpse ◄------------► Living men
Ice ◄------------► Running Water
Frozen-hearted trees ◄------------► Sap
Rime (frozen breath) ◄------------► Breath

In such oppositions radical discontinuities such as stillness and movement, death and life, nature and culture become more accessible to mediation. The transformation of breath into rime, in fact, distantly suggests the function of mist as a mediator between earth and sky to which Lévi-Strauss alludes in "The Structural Study of Myth."[30] The substitution of categories enables mediation between polar terms. White Fang himself will constitute the most significant mediation between nature and culture, between the human and the inhuman.

There are few clearer illustrations of the arbitrary and structural nature of meaning than the functioning of such mediation. Placed in opposition to white, any color can signify black (as the many forms of racism attest). And the white fangs of hunger can turn any flesh into—food. In the early chapters of *White Fang*, humans are deprived of their traditional privilege by being cast as the hunted rather than the hunter:

> As he piled wood on the fire he discovered an appreciation of his own body which he had never felt before. He watched his moving muscles and was interested in the cunning mechanism of his fingers. By the light of the fire he crooked his fingers slowly and repeatedly, now one at a time, now all together, spreading them wide or making quick gripping movements. . . . It fascinated him, and he grew suddenly fond of this subtle flesh of his that worked so beautifully and smoothly and delicately. Then he would cast a glance of fear at the wolf-circle drawn expectantly about him, and like a blow the realization would strike him that this wonderful body of his, this living flesh, was no more than so much meat, a quest of ravenous animals, to be torn and slashed by their hungry fangs, to be sustenance to them as the moose and the rabbit had often been sustenance to him. [pp. 38–39]

The opposition between nature and culture—between the beast that crushes a man's hand in its teeth and devours him, and the domesticated animal that takes its food from his hand—is unsettlingly unstable in *White Fang*, particularly in this opening section. The she-wolf who will be White Fang's mother regards this man "with a great wistfulness" that the man knows to be born of great hunger, her longing for the meat she must have to survive a macabre echo of Carrie's yearnings (p. 39). Yet precisely what makes Kiche dangerous is that her longing is not simple, for she violates

54
Form
and
History
in
American
Literary
Naturalism

with ease that boundary between the savage and the domesticated that is established by the distinction between wolf and dog:

> "What'd it look like?" Henry asked.
> "Couldn't see. But it had four legs an' a mouth an' hair an' looked like any dog."
> "Must be a tame wolf, I reckon."
> "It's damned tame, whatever it is, comin' in here at feedin' time an' gettin' its whack of fish." [p. 16]

They conclude that " 'that animal's familyarity [*sic*] with campfires is suspicious an' immoral.' 'It knows for certain more'n a self-respectin' wolf ought to know. . . . That wolf's a dog, an' it's eaten fish many's the time from the hand of man.' " But Kiche—like her quarry—could cross the boundary between living flesh and food with equal ease: " 'if I get a chance at it, that wolf that's a dog'll be jes' meat' " (pp. 20–21).

The wolf's world is that of the Silence, the Cold, the savage Northland Wild, which is ruled by the harsh "law of meat":

> The aim of life was meat. Life itself was meat. Life lived on life. There were the eaters and the eaten. The law was: EAT OR BE EATEN. . . . Had the cub thought in man-fashion, he might have epitomized life as a voracious appetite, and the world as a place wherein ranged a multitude of appetites, pursuing and being pursued, hunting and being hunted, eating and being eaten, all in blindness and confusion, with violence and disorder, a chaos of gluttony and slaughter, ruled over by chance, merciless, planless, endless. [pp. 108–9]

The wolf is capable of surviving and conquering in this realm, unlike, for example, the "soft and helpless" (p. 197) Southland dogs White Fang kills with such ease at Fort Yukon, dogs who depend for their survival on the order imposed by the campfire and the law of man. The wolf's strength is desirable as well as threatening, and the effect of the progressive substitutions for the opposed terms of nature and culture is to make the potency of the Wild available to man.

White Fang constantly plays on and challenges the distinction between dog and wolf. Not only is Kiche a doglike wolf, but in these opening passages the huskies (who are, we might note, the first living beings to break the silence of the Wild in this narrative) are referred to as "wolfish dogs" (p. 3), "wolf-dogs" (p. 7). The development of the mediating term embodied in White Fang can be presented—very schematically—like this:

Movement ◄-----------► Silence
Life ◄-----------► Wild
Man ◄-----------► Beast

```
Dog (tame animal) ◄-------------►Wolf (wild animal)
    Wolflike dog ◄-------------►Doglike wolf
```

The protagonist's pedigree qualifies him to represent both nature and culture. He is "the son of the wolf," but he is not quite the wolf; his mother is half-wolf, half-dog, and his father is a wolf. He is born wild but returns with his mother to the Indian village where she was born. The cub is, as Kiche's Indian master says when he reclaims them, the "sign" (p. 118) of Kiche's life with the wolves—but at the same moment that he is so marked he is given "a name in the world" by the "mouth noises" (p. 118) of the Indians: White Fang, a name that carries a reminder of the law of meat into the second half of the book. But in London's explanatory system it is not these semiotic events but the interplay of heredity and environment that define White Fang's nature. Despite the fact that he is three-quarters wolf he becomes, the reader is informed, essentially a dog: "had White Fang never come in to the fires of man, the Wild would have molded him into a true wolf. But the gods had given him a different environment, and he was molded into a dog that was rather wolfish, but that was a dog and not a wolf" (p. 177).

Within the cultural system, however, he remains the sign as well as the son of the wolf, and other dogs torment him because he represents the Wild:

> Like him, they were domesticated wolves. But they had been
> domesticated for generations. Much of the Wild had been lost,
> so that to them the Wild was the unknown, the terrible, the
> ever menacing and ever warring. But to him, in appearance
> and action and impulse, still clung the Wild. He symbolized
> it, was its personification; so that when they showed their
> teeth to him they were defending themselves against the pow-
> ers of destruction that lurked in the shadows of the forest and
> in the dark beyond the camp-fire. [p. 190]

He is an outcast, and in civilization his nature, "savage by birth, . . . became more savage under this unending persecution" (p. 133). White Fang goes wild twice, and each time chooses to return to man—only to be sold, when his Indian master is corrupted by civilization and becomes a drunk, to a brutal white man. The Indians also serve as mediators, representing culture in relation to the Wild, nature in relation to the white man. In each case, in this unsettling fiction, culture proves crueler than nature. In the white man Beauty Smith's hands White Fang becomes the Wild incarnate, "a fiend," "the enemy of all things. . . . To such an extent was he tormented, that he hated blindly and without the faintest spark of reason" (p. 215). Smith enjoys cruelty for its own sake, but he also wants to turn a profit on White Fang's ferocity; he turns him into

56
Form
and
History
in
American
Literary
Naturalism

a professional fighting animal and exhibits him as "The Fighting Wolf": the sign of savagery created by civilization.

Weedon Scott rescues White Fang from this life and tames him again. For "The Fighting Wolf" to accept food from Scott's hand for the first time requires him to resist the determinism of both heredity and environment, both "the prod of his instinct and the warning of past experience." Enduring Scott's touch requires a tremendous effort of will: "White Fang was torn by conflicting feelings, impulses. It seemed he would fly to pieces, so terrible was the control he was exerting, holding together by an unwonted indecision the counterforces that struggled within him for mastery" (p. 253). White Fang is a beast, yet within him London depicts the same tension between instinct and free will that Dreiser describes in *Sister Carrie*. Only a conscious, effortful resistance to the forces of determinism permits the bond between Scott and White Fang to develop: "It required much thinking and endless patience on the part of Weedon Scott to accomplish this. And on the part of White Fang it required nothing less than a revolution. He had to ignore the urges and promptings of instinct and reason, defy experience, give the lie to life itself" (p. 256). White Fang's new circumstances open up the possibility of reshaping his character, and the very "plasticity" before environmental forces that has made him ferocious as an outcast is here represented as a laudable sensitivity and adaptability. As Carrie responds to the call of a better life, the wolf responds to Weedon Scott's love: "White Fang was in the process of finding himself. In spite of the maturity of his years and of the savage rigidity of the mould that had formed him, his nature was undergoing an expansion" (p. 260).

White Fang *is* capable of exerting his will and overcoming the pressures of instinct, as he must demonstrate again and again when Scott takes him to California to live. After he has killed some chickens, for example, Scott's father asserts that "'you can never cure a chicken-killer. . . . Once they've got the habit and the taste of blood . . .'" (p. 300). But White Fang is no mere beast, and when Scott has taught him that it violates human law to kill chickens, he never does again.

> Life was complex in the Santa Clara Valley after the simplicities of the Northland. And the chief thing demanded by these intricacies of civilization was control, restraint—a poise of self that was as delicate as the fluttering of gossamer wings and at the same time as rigid as steel. . . . Life flowed past him, deep and wide and varied, continually impinging upon his senses, demanding of him instant and endless adjustments and correspondences, and compelling him, almost always, to suppress his natural impulses. [p. 303]

White Fang's self-control entitles him to an honorable place in society—he is "becoming tame and qualifying himself for civilization"
(p. 304)—as it entitles the human beings who possess it to a place
in society. Although his parents ate human flesh, White Fang re-
spects even a chicken protected by the laws of civilization.

White Fang's ultimate accommodation to civilization is marked
by his acceptance by the sheepdog Collie, whose "instinctive fear of
the Wild, and especially of the wolf, was unusually keen. White
Fang was to her a wolf, the hereditary marauder who had preyed
upon her flocks from the time sheep were first herded and guarded
by some dim ancestor of hers" (pp. 285–86). She is safe from White
Fang because he will not attack a female. This implausible contention (implying retrospectively that all the dogs White Fang fought
were male) reveals the gender ideology that is assimilated into the
semantic field. Biological improbability notwithstanding, the Northland is an almost exclusively masculine world. Femininity and the
family, on the other hand, are the signs of civilization. Collie's puppies by White Fang—five-eighths dog, three-eighths wolf—mediate
between nature and culture not only by mingling the heredity of dog
and wolf, but also by creating a family that mimics the values of
human domesticity. Called "Blessed Wolf" by the women because
he has saved the household from a murderous attack by the criminal Jim Hall, weak from the injuries Hall inflicted and with Collie's
puppies clambering fearlessly over him, White Fang has been fully
domesticated. Yet his ferocity is assimilated, not abandoned. Scott's
return to California with White Fang brings back to the soft Southland both a wolf who can kill any dog within minutes and a man
who has won that wolf's devotion and who is strong enough to
survive in the world of the wolf. White Fang's devotion to his master
allies Scott with the principle of potency that the wolf evokes and
embodies.

Despite its initial focus *White Fang* in its constant correlation of
oppositions proves very much concerned with social as well as
natural forces. Weedon Scott's alliance with the Wild invigorates
and masculinizes the civilized values and society he represents.
White Fang's acceptance of the law fulfills what is best in his nature. But the confrontation of man and animal can also produce a
different mediating term; if White Fang can be a dog, a man can be
a beast. The first of the two men who represent this degraded category in *White Fang* is the ironically named Beauty Smith, who is
scarcely mentioned without evoking at least the adjective "bestial"
if not some more extended vilification. As Weedon Scott rescues
White Fang from Smith, he repeatedly exclaims, "'You beasts!'" to
Smith and the other men watching the dogfight (pp. 233–34), and at
one point he calls Smith "'Mr. Beast!'" (p. 238). When Smith complains, "'A man's got his rights,'" Scott answers, "'Correct. . . . But

58

Form
and
History
in
American
Literary
Naturalism

you're not a man. You're a beast.'" Someone in the crowd jokes, "'Look out! He'll bite!'" (p. 239). Unlike White Fang, Smith cannot control himself; helpless before determining forces, he is not morally responsible for his actions: "Beauty Smith had not created himself, and no blame was to be attached to him. He had come into the world with a twisted body and a brute intelligence. This had constituted the clay of him, and it had not been kindly moulded by the world" (p. 211). No fairer circumstance gives him the opportunity to find himself that Scott gives White Fang, nor does the narrator lament or even mention the lack. Because he has no volition he is exempted from blame; but, excluded from the realm of willed endeavor Weedon Scott and the narrator recognize as human, he is also denied any "rights."

The semantic rectangle suggested by this aspect of *White Fang* looks like this:

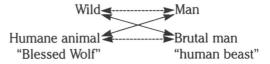

Jim Hall, the convict from whom White Fang saves Scott and his family at the conclusion of the narrative, is precisely the same sort of creature: "He had been ill-made in the making. He had not been born right, and he had not been helped any by the moulding he had received at the hands of society. The hands of society are harsh, and this man was a striking sample of its handiwork. He was a beast—a human beast, it is true, but nevertheless so terrible a beast that he can best be characterized as carnivorous" (p. 317). Brutalized by nature and culture alike, unjustly sentenced to prison, he is the human counterpart of the Fighting Wolf: he fights with his teeth and bare hands, he is kept in a cage. "When his food was shoved in to him, he growled like a wild animal. He hated all things. For days and nights he bellowed his rage at the universe. For weeks and months he never made a sound, in the black silence eating his very soul. He was a man and a monstrosity, as fearful a thing of fear as ever gibbered in the visions of a maddened brain" (p. 318). Beauty Smith and Jim Hall are human beasts who cannot escape determinism. They are at the mercy of the pitiless forces outside them and at the mercy of the blind brute inside them.

Weedon Scott, in contrast, possesses self-awareness and self-control. When Beauty Smith is enraged "the abysmal brute" in him rises up, "mastering the small bit of sanity he possessed" (p. 233). (The contemporary significance of the vocabulary of brutality omnipresent in descriptions of Smith and Hall will be discussed more fully in Chapter 3.) In this scene Scott is also in a rage, but his is "a sane rage" (p. 233). Scott not only exerts his will to control himself but in his way is a reformer. He chooses to "set himself the task of

redeeming White Fang—or rather, of redeeming mankind from the
wrong it had done White Fang. It was a matter of principle and conscience. He felt that the ill done White Fang was a debt incurred by man and that it must be paid" (p. 259).[31] Like Ames in *Sister Carrie*, Scott intervenes in events on the assumption that he is morally responsible and potentially effective.

These contrasts are already fully comprehensible in terms of the thematic we have established for naturalism. They suggest once again, however, that social class is inscribed, in some crucial way, in this semantic field, for Scott's freedom is clearly premised at least in part on his privilege. In the scene above, for example, the men he confronts refrain from reprisals because they recognize at once that he "'must be somebody.'" An inquirer learns that he is "'one of them crack-a-jack mining experts. He's in with all the big bugs. If you want to keep out of trouble, you'll steer clear of him, that's my talk. He's all hunky with the officials'" (pp. 239–40). What prohibits the law of meat from operating here is Scott's class privilege, endorsed by the equally harsh law of society, for otherwise even a hero could not single-handedly confront and insult a crowd with impunity. White Fang also appreciates class distinctions; although the dog-musher feeds him, he "divined that it was his master's food he ate and that it was his master who thus fed him vicariously" (p. 262) and will obey only Scott. An instinctive aristocrat, in California he "differentiate[s] between the family and the servants of the household. The latter were afraid of him, while he merely refrained from attacking them. This because he considered that they were likewise possessions of the master . . . appurtenances of the household" (p. 296). In this vein we may speculate that the escape of the dog-driver besieged by the wolf-pack, in the opening scenes of *White Fang*, may not be so utterly accidental after all. The men who rescue him have been drawn into the Wild in search of "Lord Alfred," we learn—the third man whose body is to be found hoisted out of reach of the wolves, "'roostin' in a tree at the last camp'" (p. 46). Perhaps it is fanciful, but if a wolf can be a snob, perhaps in the thematic logic of the tale Lord Alfred's privilege can, even after his defeat by the cold of the Wild, protect his faithful, fortunate dependents. He seems indeed to belong to a different species—neither flesh nor meat, neither wolf nor man, but bird.

In *Martin Eden* (1909), London deals more directly with issues of class. This book was written slightly later than the central group of novels I examine in this study, and to some degree it moves away from the concerns of that formative moment of naturalism. But it invokes a semantic field very much like the one I have been describing, at which we may briefly glance to see terms familiar from our analysis of *White Fang* transposed into a new context. The image of the beast is evoked at the very beginning of the book, when the sailor Martin Eden enters the bourgeois home of the

60

Form
and
History
in
American
Literary
Naturalism

Morses. He feels completely out of place: "He mopped his forehead dry and glanced about him with a controlled face, though in the eyes there was an expression such as wild animals betray when they fear the trap."[32] The Morses perceive Eden as a "wild man" (p. 570), a "man from outer darkness" (p. 574), just as the other dogs saw in White Fang "the powers of destruction that lurked . . . in the dark beyond the camp-fire" (p. 190). Ruth reacts to Martin as if to the Wild itself: "In similar ways she had experienced unusual feelings when she looked at wild animals in the menagerie, or when she witnessed a storm of wind, or shuddered at the bright-ribbed lightning. . . . He was untamed, wild, and in secret ways her vanity was touched by the fact that he came so mildly to her hand. Likewise she was stirred by the common impulse to tame the wild thing" (p. 617). London dramatizes in this reaction something of the projective, fantasy component of images of the Other, which I will discuss in Chapter 3, and with the name "Eden" also begins to suggest the inadequacy of those images; like White Fang, Martin Eden signifies the Wild, but wildness proves not at all what Ruth Morse thinks it is. Yet Martin Eden himself sometimes sees other working-class characters in bestial terms; when he returns from the Morses', his brother-in-law "affected him as so much vermin"; Higginbotham's eyes are "weasel-like and cruel," and contact with him makes Martin's "blood crawl" (pp. 581–82). Martin's image of Ruth, equally exaggerated and fantasy-imbued, provides the other half of the opposition: "He likened her to a pale gold flower upon a slender stem. No, she was a spirit, a divinity, a goddess; such sublimated beauty was not of the earth" (p. 560).

The "impassableness of the gulf" (p. 575) between the classes establishes a radical antinomy. But Martin, like Carrie, is drawn toward what he perceives as a higher plane of life: "All his childhood and youth had been troubled by a vague unrest; he had never known what he wanted, but he had wanted something that he had hunted vainly for until he met Ruth. And now his unrest had become sharp and painful, and he knew at last, clearly and definitely, that it was beauty, and intellect, and love that he must have" (pp. 615–16). The opposition Martin confronts can be mediated through a sexual relationship, as in different senses such oppositions are in both *Sister Carrie* and *White Fang*. Martin is a proletarian, but a man; as he talks to Ruth "all that was essentially masculine in his nature was shining in his eyes" (p. 564). Although the wild creature is the opposite of the spirit, the masculine is simply its contradictory. Ruth is a bourgeoise, but a woman, and as such she is not the contrary of the natural but its contradictory. As a woman she is drawn to Martin: "She was clean, and her cleanness revolted; but she was woman, and she was just beginning to learn the paradox of woman" (p. 564). The terms are familiar, and another semantic rectangle falls into place:

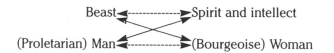

Beast ←------------→ Spirit and intellect

(Proletarian) Man ←------------→ (Bourgeoise) Woman

The mediation achieved here will fail, however, later in the novel when it becomes apparent that Ruth represents not beauty and intellect but narrow-minded respectability.

The masculine ideal embodied in Martin Eden and in London's other heroes combines the strength and vitality of the wild man with the self-discipline and sensitivity of the civilized man. The novel is in part a celebration of Martin Eden's ability to remain in contact with a primitive potency and yet develop his will, from the beginning where despite his fear his face is "controlled," to his suicide when at the end of the novel the sexual mediation collapses and he finds his values emptied of meaning and his sense of purpose failing. Here a play on the word "will" evokes the tension between instinct and conscious choice: "the moment he felt the water rising above his mouth the hands struck out sharply with a lifting movement. The will to live, was his thought, and the thought was accompanied by a sneer. Well, he had will,—ay, will strong enough that with one last exertion it could destroy itself and cease to be" (p. 930). Martin Eden's suicide is given a significance the reverse of Hurstwood's—but to go on to discuss the development of Martin Eden's self-consciousness and his growing disgust with life after his estrangement from Ruth and his success would take us far beyond our immediate concerns here.

Naturalism in this novel as elsewhere mingles with many other genres (*Martin Eden* is also a bildungsroman, for example), and many of the elements of naturalism are also self-consciously examined within *Martin Eden* itself. As I have suggested, the reader is shown from the beginning that Martin Eden's and the Morses' views of each other, which lay the groundwork of the semantic field that correlates Martin with the beast and Ruth with the spirit, are profoundly mistaken. By the end of the book Martin is exclaiming, "'The beasts! The beasts!'" (p. 851) of the educated men he once looked up to; the book's critique of bourgeois values is pervasive and bitter. But the equation of the working class with brutality is subjected to no such questioning except insofar as it is shown to be inaccurate in reference to Martin Eden himself; the images of his proletarian companions that occur to him—and are unquestioned by the narrator—are consistent throughout the novel. At its beginning Martin is revolted by the house he lives in and those with whom he shares it: "How could he, herding with such cattle, ever become worthy of her [Ruth]? He was appalled at the problem confronting him, weighted down by the incubus of his working-class station" (p. 593). The image of cattle, evoking as it does passivity in the face of determining forces, rather than viciousness

62
Form
and
History
in
American
Literary
Naturalism

or ferocity, as the salient element of brutality, recurs later when Martin tells himself, "You belong with the legions of toil, with all that is low, and vulgar, and unbeautiful. You belong with the oxen and the drudges, in dirty surroundings among smells and stenches" (p. 650). At the end of the novel, Martin still sees the working class—in this case, the sailors among whom he once lived—as made up of cattle and himself as another breed entirely: "He could find no kinship with these stolid-faced, ox-minded bestial creatures" (p. 927).

The domesticated ox, of course, has none of the masculine glamor of the wolf. The "toil-beast" (p. 698) London evokes occasionally in *Martin Eden* is a version of the brute that frightens not because of its ferocity but because it represents a surrender to the danger that Carrie also faces when she takes a factory job which reduces her to "one mass of dull, complaining muscles, fixed in an eternal position and performing a single mechanical movement which became more and more distasteful, until at last it was absolutely nauseating" (chap. 4, p. 29). In these novels the worst imaginable fate is to cease to resist such degradation. One can be swallowed up and devoured and destroyed not only by the carnivores of nature and society but by an anonymous, grim world of toil represented in both *Sister Carrie* and *Martin Eden* by the proximate, proletarian lives of a sister and brother-in-law.

From the Morses' point of view, however, the danger suggested by the beast—wild, not domesticated—that Eden evokes is more mysterious and more sinister. In her initial reaction to Martin Eden, Ruth Morse dramatizes the projection of bourgeois fantasies onto the working class; she is both attracted and repelled, able to resist his force only because she sees "horror in her mother's eyes— fascinated horror, it was true, but none the less horror. This man from outer darkness was evil" (p. 574). Martin evokes for them the sexual and violent realm outside the pale that the novels critics call naturalistic have persistently explored, from Zola's *Thérèse Raquin* (1867) to Selby's *Last Exit to Brooklyn* (1964). Donald Pizer describes this aspect of the genre when he asserts the difference between quotidian realism and naturalism:

> The naturalist populates his novel primarily from the lower
> middle class or the lower class. His characters are the poor,
> the uneducated, the unsophisticated. . . . the naturalist dis-
> covers in this world those qualities of man usually associated
> with the heroic or adventurous, such as acts of violence and
> passion which involve sexual adventure or bodily strength
> and which culminate in desperate moments and violent
> death. A naturalistic novel is thus an extension of realism only
> in the sense that both modes often deal with the local and

contemporary. The naturalist, however, discovers in this material the extraordinary and excessive in human nature.[33]

Critics who define naturalism as a variant of realism that adheres to a philosophy of pessimistic determinism find melodramatic action or systematic animal imagery "unrealistic," improbable, inappropriate. Pizer recognizes such elements as integral to the form, as I do; like the reformism that is also often labeled an anomalous element, the naturalist fascination with the brute is inscribed in the characteristic conceptual oppositions of the genre.

The discovery of the extraordinary and excessive within the local and contemporary finds its most extreme development in Frank Norris's work and particularly in his first completed novel, *Vandover and the Brute* (written 1894–95, published posthumously 1914). *Vandover and the Brute* combines now familiar terms into an opposition, insisted on explicitly and repeatedly throughout the novel and implicit in its title, between the self-aware, self-controlled human being and the subhuman brute. The narrative of Vandover's decline is the story of a degenerating will. The original defect in Vandover's character is that "he could be contented in almost any environment, the weakness, the certain pliability of his character easily fitting itself into new grooves, reshaping itself to suit new circumstances."[34] Gradually he loses the ability to exert himself either to attain a goal or to hold his personality intact. His habitual indolence and indeed all relaxations of self-discipline are treated by the narrator as significant failures; one of the first steps Vandover takes on his road downward is to take an afternoon off from work (pp. 26–29). His sensual enjoyment of sleeping late, eating delicacies and chocolates, sitting over the stove, and taking "enervating" (p. 88) hot baths is marked as a sign of deterioration, although his somewhat less openly recounted sexual indulgences are "animal pleasures" (p. 160) even more clearly dangerous to his character.

The brute that is part of Vandover is closely associated with his sexuality. When his boyish innocence begins to give way before the stirrings of "a blind unreasoned instinct," the adolescent Vandover finds himself deriving "vague and strange ideas" from what he reads in the Bible; he notices in the church service the prayer for women in the perils of childbirth and puzzles over it, "smelling out a mystery beneath the words, feeling the presence of something hidden, with the instinct of a young brute" (p. 7). The most pathogenic experience of the period is his discovery of an illustrated encyclopedia article on obstetrics:

He read it from beginning to end.
It was the end of all his childish ideals, the destruction of

64
Form
and
History
in
American
Literary
Naturalism

all his first illusions. The whole of his rude little standard of morality was lowered immediately. Even his mother, whom he had always believed to be some kind of an angel, fell at once in his estimation. . . .

It was very cruel, the whole thing was a grief to him, a blow, a great shock; he hated to think of it. Then little by little the first taint crept in, the innate vice stirred in him, the brute began to make itself felt, and a multitude of perverse and vicious ideas commenced to buzz about him like a swarm of nasty flies. [p. 8]

The brute is Vandover's secret self and becomes his personal nemesis—yet it is worth noting that it is first awakened by those lawgivers of respectable society, the Bible and *Brittanica*.

The blind but ardent pursuit of "vice" embodied in this powerfully charged image of the brute is, certainly, the contrary of the self-aware, self-controlled human being. The contrary of Vandover's slothful sensuality, on the other hand, is the self-discipline required by his art. Vandover's painting mediates between virtue and vice because it draws him toward exertion and humanity rather than the brutal, but also gives a sublimated sexual satisfaction (he becomes interested in drawing by copying pictures of women). Vandover is always lazy, however: "it bored him to work very hard, and when he did not enjoy his work he stopped it at once" (p. 54). Indolence drops into place as the contradictory of the human, art as the contradictory of the brute:

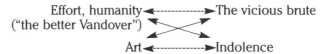

Effort, humanity ◄------------► The vicious brute
("the better Vandover")

Art ◄------------► Indolence

This rectangle models a semantic field structurally quite similar to what we have seen in the preceding analyses.

Vandover quickly loses his desire, then his ability to work at his painting as the brute grows in him. The overwhelming image of the brute dominates the novel too thoroughly for any other term to be developed. The central, virtually obsessive interest of the narrative lies not in Vandover's attempt to rouse his will and reform but in his degeneration. The brute gains strength when Vandover seeks sexual experience: "He commenced to chafe under his innate respect and deference for women, to resent and despise it. As the desire of vice, the blind, reckless desire of the male, grew upon him, he set himself to destroy this barrier. . . . the animal in him, the perverse evil brute, awoke and stirred" (p. 24). There is in *Vandover and the Brute* no scientific, amoral, "naturalist" approach to sexuality. Rather we find what one critic has labeled Norris's "Victorian interpretation of sex as evil."[35] As the brute grows, it devours Vandover—it is a carnivore, indeed a cannibal, within him: "The brute had grown larger in him, but he knew that he had the creature in hand. He was its master, and only on rare occasions did he permit himself to gratify its demands, feeding its abominable hunger from that part of him which he knew to be the purest, the cleanest, and the best" (p. 25). The fascinated horror with which Norris demonstrates the necessity of repression and sublimation and, for Vandover at least, its impossibility invites us to read the novel in terms of Norris's own sexual fantasies and feelings of guilt, and certainly the author's personal history is one of the conditions of *Vandover's* production. But these fantasies, particularly uncensored as they are in this (posthumously published) novel, are collective as well as individual. Norris's obsession with the brute is—as we will see still more clearly in Chapter 3—understandable in generic terms.

London's and Dreiser's images of animals and of sexuality are neither so unequivocally negative nor so emotionally charged as Norris's. Yet the realm of the brute is not unknown to them. Surely it is the evil outer darkness by which Ruth and her mother are fascinated and repelled—although it proves in *Vandover* to be an *inner* darkness, embodied by a member of the Morses' own class. And certainly it is the realm of Beauty Smith and Jim Hall. Dreiser alludes to Hurstwood's familiarity with "that under-world where grovel the beast-men of society" (chap. 13, p. 91); here again it is the "man of the world" who indulges in vice. But it is only in this single allusion to a sinister underworld that Dreiser evokes the intensely charged semantic field of the bestial and the human to describe sexual desire; for all his interest in uncontrollable chemisms, for Dreiser sexuality is a human phenomenon, passionate and unreasonable but not vicious and perverse as it is for Norris. London and Dreiser represent the circumstances of sexual life as different in different social classes. A certain fastidiousness (not necesarily morality) about interactions with the opposite sex seems to qualify the upwardly mobile characters for their rise, for that matter. Martin Eden loses interest in girls of his own class after he meets Ruth, Carrie is distressed by the flirtations of the other factory workers: "As Carrie listened to . . . familiar badinage among the men and girls, she instinctively withdrew into herself. She was not used to this type, and felt that there was something hard and low about it all" (chap. 4, p. 30). But in neither author do we see Norris's constant correlation of the realm of toil and the realm of the sexual.

In *Vandover and the Brute* the reader encounters the sexualized underworld most directly in the person of one of its denizens, the prostitute Flossie. Everything about her suggests sexuality—not only in Vandover's eyes, but in the narrator's: "her slightest action suggested her profession; as soon as she removed her veil and gloves it was as though she were partially undressed, and her uncovered face and hands seemed to be only portions of her nudity" (p. 44). Not only her open sexuality but her class identify Flossie

66
Form
and
History
in
American
Literary
Naturalism

as dangerous, for she "betrayed herself as soon as she spoke, the effect of her appearance was spoiled. Her voice was hoarse, a low-pitched rasp, husky, throaty, and full of brutal, vulgar modulations" (p. 45). The potential consequences of any contact with such a woman are absurdly illustrated by what happens to Vandover's friend Dolliver Haight. "Dolly" is a virginal paragon of morality, but his life is ruined because he submits to a kiss from Flossie while he has a cut on his lip and contracts an incurable venereal disease. This image of the wicked woman has its counterpart in the elevated image of the nice girl, which London bitterly attacks in his portrait of Ruth Morse but which Norris uncritically accepts. Naturalism and extreme sentimentality stand side by side on the shelf of Norris's works in *McTeague* and *Blix*, and they stand side by side in *Vandover* as well. Although Flossie appeals "to the animal and the beast in him, the evil, hideous brute that made instant answer" (p. 44), the pure Turner Ravis, the girl from a bourgeois home where the "'old fashioned virtues'" (p. 85) are maintained, is an uplifting influence on Vandover, "calling out in him all that was cleanest, finest, and most delicate" (p. 44). The lack of this uplifting feminine influence is cited as part of the environmental determination of Vandover's degeneracy. When he is about fifteen "there was a crying need for the influence of his mother. Any feminine influence would have been well for him at this time: that of an older sister, even that of a hired governess. The housekeeper looked after him a little, mended his clothes, saw that he took his bath Saturday nights, and that he did not dig tunnels under the garden walks. But her influence was entirely negative and prohibitory and the two were constantly at war" (p. 5). A governess, but not a housekeeper, can provide the proper influence—ultimately because she is and the housekeeper is not of the proper, asexual class.

Vandover's life as a young man about town and the "career of dissipation" (p. 181) that leads to his decline into brutality are traced with relish and detail. Again and again it is his willingness to cross the boundaries of his class and venture into the outer darkness beyond—we might say, his willingness to go slumming in the perilous realms of determining forces and brutality—that exposes Vandover to danger, whether when he associates with common women or when he takes passage on a second-class instead of a first-class boat in order to have time for one more coveted pleasure before a journey. The latter self-indulgence has disproportionately serious consequences. It is not only uncomfortable—"he had never been upon a second-class boat before and had never imagined that anything could be so horribly uncomfortable or disagreeable. The *Mazatlan* was overcrowded, improperly ballasted, and rolled continually. The table was bad, the accommodations inadequate, the passengers hopelessly uncongenial" (pp. 107–8). It leads to his being shipwrecked and indirectly to his father's death and the end of Vandover's brief reform. But the sordid scenes and sensations to which this episode exposes him are merely a hint of the depths to which Vandover plunges at the end of the novel.

Eventually the brute grows much stronger than Vandover's human self. An overwrought passage like the following suggests the emotional charge of the image:

> He had been lured into a mood where he was himself at his very best, where the other Vandover, the better Vandover, drew apart with eyes turned askance, looking inward and downward into the depths of his own character, shuddering, terrified. Far down there in the darkest, lowest places he had seen the brute, squat, deformed, hideous; he had seen it crawling to and fro dimly, through a dark shadow he had heard it growling, chafing at the least restraint, restless to be free. For now at last it was huge, strong, insatiable, swollen and distorted out of all size, grown to be a monster, glutted yet still ravenous, some fearful bestial satyr, grovelling, perverse, horrible beyond words. [p. 188]

Vandover is subject to an internal force more extraordinary and excessive even than Dreiser's katastates and becomes a human beast more literally and loathesomely than Beauty Smith or Jim Hall: he is the victim, the reader is informed, of "*Lycanthropy-Mathesis*" (p. 243) and is intermittently transformed into a wolf. "His intellectual parts dropped away one by one, leaving only the instincts, the blind, unreasoning impulses of the animal. . . . he swung his head from side to side with the motion of his shuffling gait, his eyes dull and fixed. At long intervals he uttered a sound, half word, half cry, 'Wolf—wolf!' but it was muffled, indistinct, raucous, coming more from his throat than from his lips. It might easily have been the growl of an animal. A long time passed. Naked, four-footed, Vandover ran back and forth the length of the room" (p. 272). It will hardly surprise the reader to learn that George Becker considers *Vandover and the Brute* naturalism's most egregious example of unrealistic animal imagery.[36] Yet however improbable its sequence of events may seem, the novel remains committed to philosophical determinism. Vandover is emphatically not a werewolf, and the causes invoked to explain his transformation are natural and not supernatural. It is not only that a moral and a medical system of explanation coexist in *Vandover and the Brute*— the moral is inscribed *as* the medical, the energies and events of melodrama are rewritten through the conventions of causality.

By the end of the novel Vandover's lucid moments offer no relief from the horror of his malady. He has spent his capital and must struggle to hold a menial job and earn enough to be able to eat. His moral degradation is also a social degradation; as with Hurstwood the deterioration of his clothing registers his loss of status and self-

68
Form
and
History
in
American
Literary
Naturalism

respect, and finally he has "even lost regard for decency and clean-liness" (p. 277). Norris quite openly equates Vandover's brutaliza-tion with his downward mobility; when he lodges in a house for "transients" ("sailors lounging about shore between two voyages, Swedes and Danes, farmhands, grape-pickers, and cow-punchers from distant parts of the state, a few lost women, and Japanese cooks and second-boys"), he

> sank to the grade of these people at once with that fatal adapt-ability to environment which he had permitted himself to fos-ter throughout his entire life, and which had led him to be contented in almost any circumstances. It was as if the brute in him were forever seeking a lower level, wallowing itself lower and lower into the filth and into the mire, content to be foul, content to be prone, to be inert and supine. [p. 278]

His will utterly degenerated, his money gone, nothing now sepa-rates Vandover from the brute—both as wolf and as social being he has "literally *become the brute*" (p. 278). Vandover sinks into the slums, and he can no longer return from the outer darkness.

In the novel's closing scenes humiliation upon humiliation is heaped on Vandover; the depth of his degradation is such that he is not even capable of perceiving it. To be bullied and ordered about, to say nothing of pitied and tipped, by a factory worker and his family is clearly marked in the text as the nadir of brutality. Norris charges his description of the work to which Vandover has sunk with an intense disgust. When ordered to—" 'You'll have to crawl way in to get at it—go way in!' "—Vandover crawls under the sink in a house he is cleaning; he acquiesces, just as he did when he immersed himself in vice:

> The sink pipes were so close above him that he was obliged to crouch lower and lower; at length he lay flat upon his stom-ach. Prone in the filth under the sink, in the sour water, the grease, the refuse, he groped about with his hand searching for the something grey that the burnisher's wife had seen. He found it and drew it out. It was an old hambone covered with a greenish fuzz. . . . [He brought out] a rusty pan half full of some kind of congealed gravy that exhaled a choking, acrid odor, next it was an old stocking, and then an ink bottle, a broken rat-trap, a battered teapot lacking a nozzle, a piece of rubber hose, an old comb choked with a great handful of hair, a torn overshoe, newspapers. [pp. 308–9]

Norris is profoundly revolted by and yet obsessed with dirt, as he is with sex. And in both cases he attempts to exclude the horror from the familiar precincts of middle-class life, attributing it to the brutal Other. Yet we have seen that the genesis of the brute was within the circle drawn by that gesture of exclusion; and as elements of the semantic rectangle, of course, the antinomies represented by Vandover's better self and his brutal self are inseparable.

This filthy cupboard and those "darkest, lowest places" where the brute crawls back and forth are the ultimate, claustrophobic space of *Vandover and the Brute*. Yet the semantic field that organizes that space of meaning has more in common with London's Northland and Dreiser's city than one might think at first glance. The characteristic conceptual opposition of all three novels—of the novels of this moment of naturalism—is an antinomy between human effort and determining forces, or, to put it another way, between the human and the brutal. The forces that press on them and the nature of their submission or resistance take different forms, but the choices characters make and the chances that befall them assume meaning in these terms; the meaning and relations of these concepts are negotiated in terms of the stories it proves possible to tell about the paths characters like Carrie, Hurstwood, White Fang, and Vandover trace in naturalist novels.

This formulation of the thematic of naturalism is not inconsistent with the tensions previous critics have noted in the genre: with Walcutt's interplay of optimism and pessimism, Pizer's portrayal of the extraordinary and excessive in human nature, Krause's description of attempts by characters to "hold themselves together as human beings," Parrington's "temptations" for the naturalist to become a reformer or from "much study of inner drives of low-grade characters" create grotesques and "turn man into an animal." Yet it enables us to see this collection of observations as elements of a coherent pattern of oppositions. The naturalist characters of the brute and the spectator follow from this characteristic conceptual register and provide us with categories for further exploration—moving past, but not abandoning, the notion of naturalism as pessimistic determinism.

3 Casting Out the Outcast: Naturalism and the Brute

The thematic register outlined in Chapter 2 belongs to a particular historical period: the characteristic oppositions of naturalism are constrained not only by the abstract, logical possibilities of meaning but also by the meaningful materials available in concrete circumstances. To realize the significance of American literary naturalism in its historical moment, we must appreciate those circumstances. I cannot of course undertake a comprehensive history of late nineteenth- and early twentieth-century America. To do so would require an accumulation of detail and an engagement with controversies in historical interpretation that would make this a rather different, and much longer, book. But let us go beyond the statistical and descriptive traces of change sketched in Chapter 1 to examine how those living through it responded to the transformation of American life in this period.

I have already rejected the notion that naturalism "reflects" its historical period; my task is not to set literary texts against a "history" or "reality" whose own textuality is for that purpose repressed, but rather to trace how naturalism is shaped by and imaginatively reshapes a historical experience that, although it exists outside representation and narrative, we necessarily approach through texts. A number of different theories attempt to account for literary texts as productions, using different vocabularies in which an indispensable term like "ideology" takes on an intricately variable meaning. But fundamental to any perspective that rejects reflection is a decisive break with the view of ideology as illusion, "false consciousness," or a pack of lies of any sort—although the ideological *includes* both truth and falsehood. Althusser in his now-classic formulation of what Fredric Jameson calls "the first new and as yet insufficiently developed conception of the nature of ideology since Marx and Nietzsche"[1] defines ideology as "not the relation between . . . [men] and their conditions of existence, but *the way* they live the relation between them and their conditions of existence: this presupposes both a real relation and an '*imaginary*,' '*lived*' relation." This imaginary relation inevitably "*expresses a will* (conservative, conformist, reformist or revolutionary), a hope or a nostalgia, rather than describing a reality," but it is never purely instrumental or mystificatory.[2] According to Althusser, a system of representations for imagining our own place in a world that pre-exists us is both an *active* force, reinforcing or modifying the relation between human beings and their conditions of existence, and a necessary part of *any* society (including a classless society). This lived relation is not merely or even primarily a matter of consciousness; ideology may indeed be inscribed in an *un*consciousness (we fail to ask what it means that a book is a commodity), a material practice (we buy books), a social institution (books are published, copyrighted, reviewed, sold).

Ideology then is "not a simple relation but a relation between relations, a second degree relation" (Althusser, p. 233). And to encounter ideology embodied in a concrete artifact such as a literary text adds yet another order of complexity to an already complex problem. As Julia Kristeva writes (in work indebted both to a climate of discussion that succeeded Althusser's redefinition of ideology and to the work of Mikhail Bakhtin in a much earlier and rather different discussion), a text is "a permutation of texts, an intertextuality: in the space of a given text, several utterances, taken from other texts, intersect and neutralize one another." The elements of the thematic register of naturalism examined in Chapter 2 are not unconditioned inventions, new-minted in these novels, but necessarily derive from ideological discourses outside the particular text and in part outside literature. As Kristeva puts it, these "functions defined according to the extra-novelistic textual set . . . take on value within the novelistic textual set."[3] When an element of an extranovelistic discourse is embedded in a text, it must be accommodated with other such discourses, must be processed according to the aesthetic ideology informing the novelistic project. Indeed, it is scarcely proper even to speak of embodying or embedding, since the novel does not reproduce but re-produces such elements. Naturalism contains such ideologies only in the same sense that naturalist novels are contained by the genre—that is to say, both generic and ideological discourses function in the narrative dynamic. The text is itself, in Kristeva's term, "a productivity."[4]

Naturalist novels are traversed by many ideological discourses. It will be my task in this chapter to trace the filiations between elements in American naturalism and such discourses; I will draw examples from other contemporary texts to manifest the intertextuality that is inscribed within naturalist narratives. My contention is that the naturalist novels I examine in this study process ideological material that characteristically invents a lived relation to two increasingly inescapable aspects of the conditions of existence in late nineteenth-century America: the decisive dominance in economic and social life of market relations in a national and even global economy; and the presence of class struggle in a nation with a constantly increasing, largely immigrant urban proletariat that

72
Form
and
History
in
American
Literary
Naturalism

was both very vulnerable to the recurrent economic depressions and relatively visible to other classes.

In the 1880s and 1890s it appeared obvious to many Americans that the huge, impersonal system of industrial society was indifferent to human needs. Controlling the economy seemed to present an enormous and perhaps insuperable problem, although as we will see, throughout the period individuals and groups claimed to have found the answer and, with varying success, garnered political support on the strength of that claim. The unpleasant and uncompromising "facts" of industrial capitalism were brought home in particularly painful fashion during the latter nineteenth century by the depression that followed the financial panic of 1873 and the even more severe depression that followed the panic of 1893. In the quarter century after 1873 all sectors of the economy were troubled by business failures, heightening competition, chronic overproduction and declining prices, tightening credit, wage cuts, and widespread unemployment which meant hardship, sometimes starvation, for industrial workers. Alan Trachtenberg writes that "recurrent cycles of boom and collapse seemed as inexorable as the quickening pace of technological innovation. Thus, even in the shadow of glorious new machines . . . , the public sense of crisis deepened."[5] Even in the intervals between the hard times, according to historian Robert Wiebe, the impact of the impersonal processes of a complex, widely extended interdependent economy on the lives of individuals and communities was increasingly apparent: "urban centers were collecting more and more power over regional finance, over the marketing of farm products and the distribution of finished goods, and over the dispensing of news and opinion. Although few city dwellers held any of that power, still fewer recognized that they had it, and fewer yet knew what to do with it, country people cared only that someone in a distant center was pulling the strings that moved their affairs."[6] And in the fast-growing cities the cash nexus (the receipt or payment of wages, the purchase of commodities) rather than traditional obligations between people defined the individual's place in society. The title of *Sister Carrie* marks Carrie Meeber's familial and traditional point of departure; we may read her subsequent course in the light of Wiebe's remark that "the growing numbers of clerks and salesmen and secretaries of the city [did not] share more than a common sense of drift as they fell into jobs that attached them to nothing in particular beyond a salary, a set of clean clothes, and a hope that somehow they would rise in the world" (p. 14). The elites were less vulnerable and vulnerable in different ways from those who struggled to make ends meet on a farm or worked for a wage, but not invulnerable to the unsettlingly mutable values and economic dislocations of the period.

Wiebe's account includes descriptions of both economic changes and the ways in which people lived those changes. The

objective conditions described in his account are indeed precisely
those that Marx identifies as the transformations wrought by capitalism: the substitution of the cash nexus for traditional relations, the creation of a global economy, the subjection of the country to the city, the periodic recurrence of crises of overproduction. To evoke the discomfort of the effort to apprehend this transition, of inventing a lived relation to these conditions of existence, Wiebe appeals to the naturalists: "When writers first adapted naturalism to America . . . they turned automatically to the huge and the vast. . . . Crane, Norris and Dreiser were merely giving singular form to the perplexity of a nation. As the network of relations affecting men's lives each year became more tangled and more distended, Americans in a basic sense no longer knew who or where they were. The setting had altered beyond their power to understand it, and within an alien context they had lost themselves" (pp. 42–43). I dissent, of course, from Wiebe's "automatically" and his "merely," seeking rather to understand the interaction of images of immensity and intricacy with the many other elements of naturalist narratives. Yet his suggestion provides a useful way to begin thinking about the function of causal theories in these novels.

One of the important ideological discourses that attempts to come to terms with this huge and vast system and the perplexity it engenders is the political debate over the inadequacies of the social structure and the possible ways to improve it. For example, the continuing "hard times" faced by farmers led them to form economic self-help organizations that laid the foundation for the populist movement. The cooperatives proved to be, Lawrence Goodwyn writes, "a powerful mechanism of mass recruitment," and the "subsequent experiences of millions of farmers within their cooperatives proceeded to 'educate' them about the prevailing forms of economic power and privilege in America."[7] When the opposition of bankers, wholesalers, and manufacturers frustrated their efforts within existing institutions to improve their circumstances, the farmers turned to political insurgency to try to change those institutions and created the People's party.[8] They were eventually defeated, as much by the party's loss of autonomy in nominating Bryan, the Democratic candidate, as by his subsequent loss of the 1896 presidential election; but they had created a mass democratic movement for which subsequent American history provides no parallels.[9]

The populists directed much of their energy against the "corporations, national banks, rings, trusts" that were increasingly identified as manifestations and beneficiaries of the impersonal economic order.[10] Not only farmers but many, perhaps most, other Americans believed that something ought to be done about the economy, and the problem was not infrequently defined as that of devising a way to control corporations and monopolies. In his descriptive survey of

74
Form
and
History
in
American
Literary
Naturalism

American magazine literature from 1900 to 1914 Maxwell Bloom-field summarizes such discussion, providing an example from an article in a popular family magazine:

What chiefly impressed John Q. Citizen about any corporation was its massive impersonality. He was accustomed to operating in a world of men, a world in which right and wrong standards of behavior were defined in terms of individual responsibility. . . . Was there not something frightening about these sprawling industrial empires that were at once so real and yet so impalpable? One felt their influence everywhere, but if he tried to lay hands on them they dissolved into sinister shadows. A popular columnist described the general effect in these terms:

"A corporation, as every lawyer knows, is an artificial person, begotten by the Law, a vast being composed of many individuals, with powers both greater and less than the sum of all its parts; invisible, and without the imbecilities of the body.

"It is not tempted by wine, woman, or song, like the rest of us, but its whole life is ruled and directed by one desire and passion which is never quenched nor satisfied. It is created for profit; it gets its life-breath, its muscles and thews, its intellect, and its size by profit. It has a vast acquisitive mind, but no heart of pity nor bowels of compassion.

"This uncanny race of incorporeal but corporate persons has begun to multiply among us of late, and to grow to unearthly size, towering among us mortals as the skyscraper towers among the plain old homes of our cities. It is doing our work for us with giant hands, and doing it well; but it demands to be fed with profit, and its hunger is insatiable. At times a cold horror creeps over us as we see its fingers feeling where our children play."[11]

Sometimes, too, corporeal persons are imagined behind the corporations: a number of naturalist novels (Dreiser's trilogy, *The Financier*, *The Titan*, and *The Stoic*, and Norris's *Pit*, for example) in complex and diverse ways take up the fascination of John Q. Citizen, or what is commonly called the "middle class," with the titans of business. They may be treated as themselves formidable forces, imposing their will on others and satisfying their hungers at the expense of the weak; or the captain of industry himself may be shown as vulnerable to forces, his ultimate impotence demonstrating the futility of even the most energetic human endeavor. In any case, this political discussion opens a place for the reformer who wants to control the corporation and thus overcome the laws of force and achieve a rational and regulated society. The project, as we might expect, assumes a privileged status among the themes of naturalism, and we will encounter it again in Chapter 4.

Any study of late nineteenth-century and early twentieth-century America encounters not just a vague discomfort but the sense, widely articulated by contemporaries and uniformly reflected by historians, that there is an immediate threat to social order, a sense that the very foundations of American life are endangered. Not only uncontrolled economic forces but populism itself could appear as a threat. Particularly in a period already perturbed by industrial conflict, gentlemen-reformers who themselves deplored the depredations of the large corporations saw radical farmers who allied themselves, as the populists did, with labor as "a concrete embodiment of the anarchy they dreaded," as Wiebe puts it. "In the past they had freely disdained both the uncouth masses and the new industrial kings. Now, in response to an immediate danger, they felt they had to choose, and without hesitation the large majority embraced the monopolist for the duration of the crisis. Save civilization first; otherwise there would be nothing to purify" (p. 89).

It is this apparently pervasive anxiety that gives Wiebe's book its title—*The Search for Order, 1877–1920*. But the assumption of a preceding and succeeding order implied here is unproven and, I would argue, unjustified: Wiebe's approach is informed by an ideology of stability, by the assumption that order is the natural condition of society. A different eye might find class conflict inscribed continuously although variably in different historical periods. The perspective from which one constructs this historical moment as a search for order is that of public discourses, of articulate men who dominate the media in which such matters are discussed. Often when Wiebe writes of widespread feelings "of danger and defeat" (p. 51), he writes—in this case explicitly—from the point of view of the established authorities, who "considered the true and simple America in jeopardy from foes of extraordinary, raw strength —huge, devouring monopolies, swarms of sexually potent immigrants, and the like. . . . Accustomed to a steady ripple of attacks, these men of breeding now saw a tidal wave that might sweep away all of legitimate society" (p. 52). This is not to say that only members of the elites found the period disorderly—we have already seen that the populists did, and impoverished workers certainly did—but rather that the descriptions of disorder we most commonly encounter are formulated from the perspective of the hegemonic groups.

The magazines and books of the late nineteenth and early twentieth centuries make it clear that their reading public was intensely interested in comprehending—let us say, in inventing a lived relationship to—a group that seemed even more menacing than insurgent agriculturalists, the increasingly visible and largely immigrant industrial proletariat living in the cities. Wiebe cites 1877, the year of the first national strike, as a time when the working class—and especially the inhabitants of the slums—forced itself upon the at-

76
Form
and
History
in
American
Literary
Naturalism

tention of other Americans; he chooses that year to punctuate the beginning of his period and the "search for order." There had of course been strikes before—many of them, some large, long, or bitter; but this great strike against the railroads, spreading between the lines and across the country, riveted the nation's attention as never before. It seemed to threaten another civil war. The events of 1877 in America might be compared to the June days of 1848 in France, which for Lukács divide the progressive from the conservative period of the bourgeoisie and thus divide Balzac from Zola. In 1848 in France, in 1877 in the United States, a new phase of class struggle was initiated—or rather, more accurately, we find a point at which it is clear to contemporaries and to historians that a new phase has already begun.

Philip Foner comments on the impact of the events of 1877: "Although the Great Strike was spontaneous and unorganized—it had nothing in the nature of central leadership and direction—this first nationwide rebellion of labor frightened the authorities and the upper classes as nothing before in our history. On July 24, John Hay, soon to become assistant secretary of state, wrote in alarm to his wealthy father-in-law: 'Any hour the mob chooses it can destroy any city in the country—that is the simple truth.'"[12] The tone of an account by a contemporary journalist, Joseph Dacus, titled *Annals of the Great Strikes in the United States: A Reliable History and Graphic Description of the Causes and Thrilling Events of the Labor Strikes and Riots of 1877*, is extreme but indicative:

> An epoch in the history of the nation is here marked, and from it will be dated the beginning of political discussions, and social movements which are destined to enlist the profound attention of thinking minds throughout the civilized world. These events are phenomenal. The world is witness to a spectacle, the like of which has never before been presented. . . . Hundreds and thousands of men belonging to the laboring classes, alleging that they were wronged and oppressed, ceased to work, seized railroads, closed factories, founderies, shops and mills, laid a complete embargo on all internal commerce, interrupted travel, and bid defiance to the ordinary instruments of legal authority. Commencing at Camden Station, Baltimore, and at Martinsburg, West Virginia, in three days the movement had extended to Pittsburgh, Newark, Ohio, Hornellsville, Fort Wayne and a hundred other points. State militia forces were encountered and repelled. The whole country seemed stricken by a profound dread of impending ruin. In the large cities the cause of the strikers was espoused by a nondescript class of the idle, the vicious, the visionary and the whole rabble of the Pariahs of society. No standing

army was available, and these classes absolutely controlled the country.

During these few days of the reign of the strikes, it seemed as if the whole social and political structure was on the very brink of ruin. From the Atlantic to the Pacific the laws were momentarily subverted.[13]

I quote this passage not to claim that everyone or anyone accepted hyperbole like Dacus's uncritically, but to demonstrate that the fear of class warfare that is part of the material worked by naturalism must be recognized as a powerful element of the ideology of the period. The employing classes might not *believe* that revolution and chaos were imminent—but they feared it.

This fear remained powerful long after 1877. Bloomfield writes that in the magazine literature of 1900 to 1914 "social critics . . . found unfailing satisfaction in exploring the broader dangers posed by organized labor. To them the very idea of class divisions suggested appalling vistas of bloodshed and destruction. Prophets of doom, preaching an imminent social catastrophe of some sort, flourished throughout the period" (p. 90). Labor unrest and industrial violence continued throughout the late nineteenth and early twentieth centuries; to name only a few of the most memorable, from the Great Strike of 1877 through the Haymarket affair of 1886 and the Homestead Strike of 1892 to the violence in the Colorado coal fields (of which the Ludlow Massacre was only one episode) in 1913 and 1914—the list could go on. We may see such struggle historically, almost coldly, as one of the conditions of existence in this moment of industrial capitalism; although Dacus writes that "sudden as a thunder-burst from a clear sky, the crisis came upon the country" (p. iv), Foner informs us that in 1876 "an economic depression was entering its fourth year; millions of Americans were unemployed, and for those who were still working, wages—already at starvation levels—were being cut in half" (p. 7). But class conflict was often imagined, by those whose privileges were threatened, as a "thunder-burst," a suddenly revealed conspiracy against civilization, an impending bloodbath.

Wiebe writes that "men in power . . . with incredible exaggeration . . . interpreted the Knights of Labor as disciplined mass sedition and the brief epidemic of local labor parties in 1886 and 1887 as a preface to political revolution. References to an American Reign of Terror and a domestic version of the Paris Commune were now heard everywhere, and the most discussed wonder of modern science was the dynamite bomb, symbol of mob terror" (pp. 77–78). Both the development of repressive political measures for the protection of property and the preservation of "law and order," and the elaboration of such ideological discourses about the mob, manifest

78
Form
and
History
in
American
Literary
Naturalism

the bourgeois response to changed conditions of existence; and in each case the new developments necessarily began from already existing political and legal or ideological materials. Specifically, the pejorative term "mob" used here by Wiebe and above by John Hay has a long history in political discourse dating from at least the seventeenth century. The image of the mob enters into naturalism in passages from *The Octopus*, which will be examined in Chapter 4, for example. We must recognize, however, that the image does not mean precisely the same thing at different historical moments; it is culturally available, persisting across a range of periods and offering possibilities for meaning that are intermittently revived and remade.

Similarly, the image of the brute that is characteristic of American naturalist novels can be seen as a transformation of the powerful ideological material that has long surrounded the idea of the savage. In his contribution to the debates over what was wrong with America, Henry George, for example, invokes the image of the savage quite explicitly: "I am no sentimental admirer of the savage state. I do not get my ideas of the untutored children of nature from Rousseau, or Chateaubriand, or Cooper. I am conscious of its material and mental poverty, and its low and narrow range. . . . But, nevertheless, I think no one who will open his eyes to the facts can resist the conclusion that there are in the heart of our civilization large classes with whom the veriest savage could not afford to exchange."[14] George evokes not only the noble savage but a tradition whose powerful influence in America is traced by Roy Harvey Pearce in *Savagism and Civilization*. Beginning with the earliest records of voyages to America, Pearce writes, "American Indians were everywhere found to be, simply enough, men who were not men, who were religiously and politically incomplete. If it was a brave new world, Caliban was its natural creature, Ferdinand one of its discoverers and planters. America had to be planted so that sub-humans could be made human. . . . Meantime, the Indian, in his savage nature, stood everywhere as a challenge to order and reason and civilization."[15] Although George is arguing for economic equality, he imagines the impoverished as effectively sub-human and potentially dangerous to society; as Richard Hofstadter describes George's view, "in its [the existing order's] squalid cities were already breeding the barbarian hordes which might overwhelm it. Civilization must either prepare itself for a new forward leap or plunge downward into a new barbarism."[16] (Those barbarian hordes, I suspect, invoke yet another set of images which given enough space and time might also be fruitfully pursued.) George continues to imagine America's political problems in terms that divide humanity between men and not-men along the lines of class and race; even in lamenting Caliban's wrongs, he remains a reforming Ferdinand.

Herbert Gutman's description of the images of the working class
mobilized in hegemonic discourse puts George's vocabulary in
context:

> Immigrant groups and the working population had changed in
> composition over time, but the rhetoric of influential nine-
> teenth- and early twentieth-century elite observers remained
> constant. Disorders among the Jersey City Irish seeking wages
> due them from the Erie Railroad in 1859 led the Jersey City
> *American Standard* to call them "imported *beggars*" and "*ani-
> mals*," "a mongrel mass of ignorance and crime and supersti-
> tion, as utterly unfit for its duties, as they are for the common
> courtesies and decencies of civilized life." . . . In 1869 *Scienti-
> fic American* welcomed the "ruder" laborers of Europe but
> urged them to "assimilate" quickly or face "a quiet but sure
> extermination." Those who retained their alien ways, it in-
> sisted, "will share the fate of the native Indian."[17]

The continuity briefly adumbrated here suggests the accuracy of the
generalization that Gutman quotes from Gramsci, who wrote under
quite different circumstances "that 'for a social elite the features of
subordinate groups always display something barbaric and patho-
logical'" (p. 72). The stereotypes of workers offered to naturalism
by extranovelistic ideological discourse seem already to depend on
the mechanism called in psychoanalysis projection; indeed, perhaps the image of the savage has mobilized the psychic energies of
repression throughout its existence. In writing of conservative gentlemen's fear of "sexually potent immigrants," Wiebe implicitly attributes at least some bourgeois anxiety to such sources. Historian
Melvyn Dubofsky comments directly on this point:

> When American-born elites thought of industrial workers in
> the late nineteenth century, especially of recent immigrants,
> they often projected onto workers images of untamed brutish-
> ness and potential violence. Lacking the well developed
> superego of the good *bourgeois* citizen, the immigrant worker,
> it was thought, easily succumbed to alcohol, sex, crime, and
> violence. In short, the middle class perhaps projected its own
> anxieties about sex, drink, and violence onto the working
> class at the same time that it sometimes perceived lower-class
> life as more human, natural, and perhaps, happier.[18]

The libidinal investment of the image of the proletarian as brute
increases its ideological power immensely—indeed, it might be
proper to say that this *is* its ideological power, for it is through such
imaginary relations that the collective fantasy we call ideology takes
shape.

We might refer the images of the savage and the brute to the more
general category of the wild man—evoked in that very phrase by

80
Form
and
History
in
American
Literary
Naturalism

London in *Martin Eden*—which has a long-documented history in Western thought. Hayden White writes that

> the notion of "wildness" (or in its Latinate form, "savagery") belongs to a set of culturally self-authenticating devices which includes, among many others, the ideas of "madness" and "heresy" as well. These terms are used not merely to designate a specific condition or state of being but also to confirm the value of their dialectical antitheses: "civilization," "sanity," and "orthodoxy" respectively. Thus, they do not so much refer to a specific thing, place, or condition as dictate a particular attitude governing a relationship between a lived reality and some area of problematical existence that cannot be accommodated easily to conventional conceptions of the normal or familiar.[19]

White describes the functioning of this image in cultures ranging from those of the ancient Hebrews and Greeks to our own; in different cultural matrices the many versions of the wild man remain in some sense consistent as possibilities for meaning, but they carry different meanings in systems structured differently. I devote much of this chapter to specifying the particular historical content of naturalism's reinvention of the wild man and savage as the brute. In naturalism the creature who defines humanity by negation and represents a problematical area of existence is imagined as living not outside the bounds of human society, not in the wilderness (where images of the American Indian as savage placed it), but within the very walls of the civilized city.

Jean-Paul Sartre takes a still wider view in developing his theory of the outcast as an image powered by projection. He writes:

> And whom does one strike in the person of the "dirty, greedy, sensual, negating" Jew? One's self, one's own greed, one's own lechery. Whom does one lynch in the American South for raping a white woman? A Negro? No. Again one's self. Evil is a projection. I would go so far as to say that it is both the basis and aim of all projective activity. As for the evildoer, we all have our own: he is a man whose situation makes it possible for him to present to us in broad daylight and in objective form the obscure temptations of our freedom. If you want to know a decent man, look for the vices he hates most in others. You will have the lines of force of his fears and terrors, you will breathe the odor that befouls his beauteous soul.[20]

Thus, as Sartre asserts, "the evildoer is the Other"—in this case, the sexual, the violent, the unaware, the uncontrolled and uncontrollable, the proletarian, the criminal, and above all—the brute.

This polarization of self and Other in terms of good and evil of course runs directly counter to the objective, analytic attitude proposed by the aesthetic ideology of realism and even more emphatically by naturalism. Causality, not morality, is to concern the novelist. Indeed, if forces rather than free will determine action, how can we speak of evil? But such determinism effectively dehumanizes the character and thus makes him available to projection. Beauty Smith and Jim Hall in *White Fang*, for example, although they did not make themselves and are not responsible for their own depravity, constantly threaten to slip into the category of evildoer. The Other, Sartre writes, is always "on the side of the objects named, not of those who name them. I am aware that honest people are also objects to each other. I am given names: I am this fair-haired man who wears glasses, this Frenchman, this teacher. But if I am named, I name in turn. Thus, naming and named, I live in a state of reciprocity. Words are thrown at me, I catch them and throw them at others" (pp. 40–41). Within the system that constructs him (or her, or perhaps more properly it) the Other is not only unspeakable but silent; in naturalism's ideology of brutality the Other is imagined as necessarily inarticulate, *incapable* of reciprocal naming since he is unable to achieve self-awareness or self-expressive speech.

One model implied in the category "brute" is the dumb beast, the animal who does not use language and is named but never names. The pervasive animal imagery critics note in naturalism belongs to the same ideology. John Berger has argued that this attitude toward the animal is itself historically specific; where once animals looked back at man, similar yet different, their lives parallel to man's yet distinct, in capitalism animals are physically and culturally marginalized and "that look between animal and man, which may have played a crucial role in the development of human society, and with which, in any case, all men had always lived until less than a century ago, has been extinguished."[21] The reduction of genuine alterity to Otherness is extended to human beings as well, in naturalism and in the culture of capitalism—Berger cites work by Frederick Winslow Taylor, which we will examine in Chapter 4. He argues eloquently against such reductionism, writing elsewhere, for example, that one must resist the temptation of "the false view that what people cannot express is always simple because they are simple. We like to retain such a view because it confirms our own bogus sense of articulate individuality, and because it saves us from thinking about the extraordinarily complex convergence of philosophical traditions, feelings, half-realized ideas, atavistic instincts, imaginative intimations, which lie behind the simplest hope or disappointment of the simplest person."[22] And, we may add, of the most complex and articulate, for it will prove to be precisely such influences and atavisms, such interpenetration of forces and self, that must be excluded with the Other.

Much contemporary critical thought is fascinated by versions of Otherness (although not necessarily by Sartre's version), taking up

82
Form
and
History
in
American
Literary
Naturalism

categories like madness and the feminine in theories that can be useful but can also end by once again abolishing the Other's difference. There are similarities in the way outsiders are defined from the perspective of the "center," but the groups and realm of experience so indicated also have an irreducible specificity; Berger's work embodies an exemplary attention to their concrete individuality. In the pages that follow I take for granted that the actual historical experience of the nonhegemonic groups described in naturalist novels can only be even approximately reconstructed by going outside these texts, a task I do not attempt here. Yet the ideological discourses of the period are not simply those of the bourgeoisie, for although my concern in this study is to draw out the way in which the working class is, again and again, represented as mute, those discourses are also a terrain of struggle over meanings.

To these qualifications I must also add the insistence that an account of naturalism is not a comprehensive consideration of the ideology of the period. There are many stereotypes of the working class that I have not discussed—the notion that proletarian life is natural and happy to which Dubofsky alludes above, for example. Bloomfield writes that in magazine fiction the American worker had "traditionally . . . been served up to the public with a condescending flourish, and this attitude persisted, to some degree, throughout the period. . . . All workers were visualized as essentially child types, who needed the guidance of the managerial classes" (p. 76). This too is an image of class relations that has a very long history and that remains effective in this period and, at times, in naturalist novels.

However, Bloomfield goes on to observe that "the mere existence of labor unions, capable of waging protracted strikes and boycotts, suggested a certain lack of harmony in the industrial family" (p. 77). Such dissension could be explained by positing a pernicious influence from Outside—an influence that, it is also sometimes admitted, might take advantage of dangerous elements already existing in the working class. (The same strategy was at work in the 1960s when campus unrest was attributed to "outside agitators.") Dacus writes, for example, that the strikes of 1877 were "aggravated . . . by the early appearance on the scene, of a vast number of theorists, and dangerous characters, who sought their opportunity, during the reign of general tumult to subvert the very fundamental principles of the social order" (p. iv). The subversives had their natural allies, however, in the "vicious" and "visionary" urban pariahs who created a constant problem of social control as well as participating in intermittent rebellions. William Dean Howells caricatures this way of thinking in *A Traveller from Altruria* when the naive literary man who is Howells's narrator expounds the theory he has drawn from the newspapers that the traveling labor organizer or "walking-delegate" is the cause of the working man's discontent. He is

> an irresponsible tyrant, who emerges from the mystery that habitually hides him and from time to time orders a strike in mere rancor of spirit and plenitude of power, and then leaves the workingmen and their families to suffer the consequences, while he goes off somewhere and rolls in the lap of luxury, careless of the misery he has created. Between his debauches of vicious idleness and his accesses of baleful activity he is employed in poisoning the mind of the workingman against his real interests and real friends.[23]

Even the milder version of this idea is tenable, of course, only on the assumption that the working man and woman have neither genuine grievances nor genuine self- or class-consciousness that might be the source of political demands and, in Sartre's sense, a claim to reciprocity. Dullness and incomprehension, as well as bestiality and depravity, are essential to the image of the brute; Martin Eden may be a "wild man," but his fellows are cattle.

This ideological configuration is expressed with remarkable directness in *The Breadwinners* by John Hay, the politician and diplomat quoted earlier on the disorders of 1877. This popular novel, published anonymously and never publicly acknowledged by its author during his life, was, according to Hay's son, written as a direct response to those strikes and the threat they posed to property and order. In *The Breadwinners* the "agitator" Andy (also known as Ananias) Offitt is fully as exaggerated as the clichéd villain Howells sketches. His face's "whole expression was oleaginous," his forehead "low and shining . . . covered by reeking black hair"; his countenance "could change in a moment from a dog-like fawning to a snaky venomousness," and his eyes "were too sly and furtive to belong to an honest man."[24] Even the chairs in Offitt's room are of "doubtful integrity" (p. 82). The workmen who attend the meetings of his "Brotherhood" are of course "the laziest and most incapable workmen in the town—men whose weekly wages were habitually docked for drunkenness, late hours, and botchy work. As the room gradually filled, it seemed like a roll-call of shirks" (p. 82). The subversive's natural allies are identified by their unfitness. This "greasy" fellow Offitt (p. 75) lays his hand on the arm of an honest workman, Sam Sleeny, and proceeds to flatter and try to corrupt him: " 'My dear boy, I've wanted to talk to you a long time,—to talk serious. You're not one of the common kind of cattle that think of nothin' but their fodder and stall—are you?' " The narrator comments: "Now, Sam was precisely of the breed described by his friend" (p. 77). In the context of the ideology we have been

84
Form
and
History
in
American
Literary
Naturalism

examining, this characterization and counter-characterization take on their full meaning.

The strike that forms the central public action of *The Breadwinners* does not amount to much, yet the hero Arthur Farnham (a gentleman and a millionaire) is nevertheless exposed to severe danger from the greasy socialist described above. The danger derives not from Offitt's political but from his criminal activities. While Farnham is alone in his library, peacefully totting up the rent money piled before him, Offitt enters the house surreptitiously, steals up behind Farnham, and—maliciously intending to murder as well as rob him—strikes him on the head with a hammer. The honest worker Sam Sleeny is also implicated in this crime: Offitt was able to reconnoiter the house only with Sam's reluctant connivance, and he uses Sam's hammer for the job. Still more significantly, we have already seen this tableau of the unsuspecting, unoffending gentleman enjoying the fruits of prosperity but menaced by the dispossessed, discontented proletarian. In this case the desired object is cash; in the other, earlier scene it is Maud, the pretty, social-climbing girl Sam loves. As Farnham talks to Maud—given the sentimental conventions of the novel he has, of course, no intention of taking advantage of her obvious admiration—behind him stands the working man, hammer poised to strike, but with a jealous Sam in Offitt's place. Later Sam describes the scene to Maud in this "brutal speech": "'I had my hammer in my hand. I looked through the pear trees to see if he kissed you. If he had'a' done it, I would have killed him as sure as death'" (p. 70). This obsessively repeated tableau images quite precisely Hay's view of the contemporary political situation: "the rich and intelligent kept on making money, building fine houses, and bringing up their children to hate politics as they did" (p. 246), taking no measures to protect themselves and civilization against the bloodbath of class war that approaches. The curious doubling of this image and its link to *The Breadwinners'* explicit political imperative marks the fear that it is not merely a few outsiders but the class as a whole—including honest workingmen—that poses a threat to the privileged and marks the difficult and disturbing connections between aggression, sexual desire, and class conflict that strike dissonant notes in this apparently conventional and complacent novel.

The names Hay gives his characters suggest the widespread identification of political radicalism and immigrant workers that tended to confirm the alien status of each. John Higham writes in his study of American nativism that "revolutionary doctrines and organizers, although pathetically weak, came almost entirely from Europe. . . . Class conflict could appear an un-American product of foreign agitators."[25] (The radical left still struggles with this "un-American" image.) Higham writes out of rather than simply about this stereotype when he neglects radical movements of the native-

born such as populism, but he usefully reflects the ideological
discourses that traverse naturalism, concerned as it is more with urban than with rural scenes and tensions. The immigrant population, divided by language and culture from the native-born population, seemed to the latter visibly a foreign body—an Other—within the city and within the nation. Nativism constitutes a complicated system of representations within the general ideology of this period and has its own complex responsiveness to historical experience; to explore it fully would take me beyond my concerns here.[26] We would need to discuss, for example, the topic that Herbert Gutman's work explores: the imperative to reshape the work habits of preindustrial laboring classes to suit the demands of the factory, a process that was complicated on this continent by the continued influx of immigrants from preindustrial societies. Gutman writes: "Just as in all modernizing countries, the United States faced the difficult task of industrializing whole cultures, but in this country the process was regularly repeated, each stage of American economic growth and development involving different first-generation factory workers" (p. 14). The shift in the mid-eighties from immigration from northern and western to immigration from southern and eastern Europe exacerbated the tensions of this process of proletarianization. As the passage quoted earlier from Gutman makes apparent, the full vocabulary of savagery was put to use in the hegemonic ideology that responded to the tensions of assimilation.

Nativism and its close cousin "scientific" racism recast discourses about humanity and degradation in a new and momentous form. Their solicitude for the integrity of the gene, although it is rarely any longer stated so frankly, is very much still with us today—for example, in laments over the supposed irresponsible fecundity of welfare mothers and equally irresponsible infertility of the educated. But during the period of naturalism such concern reaches an extraordinary pitch of fervency. Francis A. Walker, for example (not at all a risible fanatic, but a prominent economist who served at various times as a professor at Yale, president of the Massachusetts Institute of Technology, and superintendent of the census), saw immigration as a threat to the American way of life. He wrote:

> The entrance into our political, social, and industrial life of such vast masses of peasantry, degraded below our utmost conceptions, is a matter which no intelligent patriot can look upon without the gravest apprehension and alarm. These people have no history behind them which is of a nature to give encouragement. They have none of the inherited instincts and tendencies which made it comparatively easy to deal with the immigration of the olden times. They are beaten men from beaten races; representing the worst failures in the struggle for existence.[27]

86
Form
and
History
in
American
Literary
Naturalism

Walker feared that Anglo-Saxons would commit "race suicide," simply refusing to breed because they were "unwilling to live and work under the depressed conditions produced by immigration."[28] The idea that the native-born population would be not supplemented but supplanted by the foreign-born became after 1890 "a minor phobia in American thought."[29]

Jack London's *Valley of the Moon* (1913) casts this phobia quite directly into narrative form. Saxon Brown Roberts—her Christian name even more directly than her surname and her married name proclaiming that she is an "old American" from "the stock that crossed the plains," as we are reminded time and time again—actually miscarries in the midst of urban industrial violence. After a long journey through a landscape that constantly demonstrates the ways in which immigrants have triumphed economically over the native-born, Saxon and her equally Anglo-Saxon husband find a pastoral paradise; only then does she begin to bear children.[30] The contradiction between the accusation that the immigrants are "beaten men of beaten races" and the fear that they will overwhelm the worthier native-born stock is troubling if one considers this as logic; as an expression of inter- and intra-class conflict through the categories of ethnicity and race in a hereditarian ideology, on the other hand, it makes perfect sense—and was, as its widespread influence demonstrates, extremely persuasive.

Criminal anthropology articulated a powerful image of the Other by linking heredity and social problems. Anthony Platt writes that "a basic thrust of nineteenth-century criminological thought in the United States was an emphasis on the non-human qualities of criminals. Darwinist and Lombrosian rhetoric suggested that criminals were a 'dangerous' and discredited class who stood outside the boundaries of morally regulated and reciprocal relationships."[31] Indeed, the Italian Cesare Lombroso in his early work "suggested the existence of a criminal type distinguishable from non-criminals by observable physical anomalies of a degenerative or atavistic nature. He proposed that the criminal was a morally inferior human species, one characterized by physical traits reminiscent of apes, lower primates, and savage tribes" (pp. 20–21). Here the opposition between human and brute becomes a purportedly scientific argument that a criminal literally belongs to a subhuman species. Criminological discourse of the period manipulates and elaborates the image of the brute at great length, in a tone and rhetoric already becoming familiar to us.

Henry M. Boies, for example, one of the many Americans influenced by Lombroso, writes that "a professional criminal is a beast of prey constantly endangering society."[32] "The 'unfit,' the abnormals, the sharks, the devil-fish, and other monsters, ought not to be liberated to destroy, and multiply, but must be confined and secluded until they are exterminated" (p. 293). The vicious and the

helpless are tarred with the same brush, for the monsters Boies
wants to exterminate include "the incapable, by nature unable to
maintain themselves without assistance; the physically, mentally,
or morally defective; cripples, deformed, deaf, blind, imbecile,
weak-minded, diseased, insane, or criminal" as well as "beggars,
vagrants, tramps; the incorrigibly idle, dissolute, and criminal"
(p. 206). In fact, Boies considers the "idle" to be criminals who
should be sent to a penal institution "and either transformed into
honest self-supporters, or transferred into the State penitentiary, for
life. The attempt to procure an unearned living, the practice, or
habit of securing it, is in itself a theft from society. It is a crime
against social order and divine law" (pp. 209–10). We may set
against this assertion the historical information that low wages and
high unemployment—Foner reports that in 1876 one-fourth of the
workers in New York City were without jobs (p. 7)—kept most workers always on the verge of pauperism. Thus the proletarian's very
vulnerability in the labor market is ideologically represented as an
act of aggression.

In mass media and common sense ideology these conflicts are
still today imagined in moral terms, through an opposition between
honest and dishonest individuals. Although contemporary criminology has moved away from openly ethical theories of crime, the
battle over whether it is to be explained in terms of psycho- or
socio-pathology, or in completely different terms, is still being
fought. What is at stake is less the adequacy of theories of individual, social, or structural causality than the political program implied by each explanation. Are lawbreakers mentally ill? Does the
subculture of the slum or the Black family somehow turn people
into criminals through no fault of their own? Or are the theories of
criminology an example of the ideology we may call "blaming the
victim"? Their elaborated causal arguments may well draw us away
from a more structural analysis in which we would note the circumstances that define only certain kinds of lawbreaking as criminal
and define the activities of the young, the working class, and men
and women of color as concerns of the police and place members
of those groups with disproportionate frequency in situations of
potential and actual conflict with the police and courts.[33] The attitudes and practices of the ideology of criminality fundamentally
respond to class and racial conflict and the need to maintain social
order. In the late nineteenth century, as we have seen in *The Breadwinners*, individual disruptions of "law and order" are experienced
as profoundly threatening not only in themselves but because they
are metonymically linked with the threat of class warfare. The iniq-
uity of the criminal, the evildoer, represents as well the stigma
carried by the proletariat as a class imperfectly assimilated into the
civilized social order and potentially dangerous to it. Once again
the ideology of the late nineteenth and early twentieth centuries

88
Form
and
History
in
American
Literary
Naturalism

seems to me not so unrelated to our own period as we might at first expect.

The various incarnations of the Other I have explored in these general ideological discourses of the period of naturalism are fluidly but consistently coordinated. We will continue to see them in the analyses that follow, re-produced in narrative form and thus transformed, yet still carrying their ideological messages. Reading naturalism synoptically with this general ideology renders one more acutely aware of how strongly class-marked the oppositions that divide the characters of naturalist novels are. The determined and helpless yet menacing "naturalist" characters are drawn from or drawn into the working class and the underclass. The terrain they inhabit is imagined as squalid, dangerous, but exciting—even exotic, for it is alien territory to the middle-class perspective (sometimes that of a character or characters, generally that of the narrator) from which it is explored. Chapter 4 will examine that apparently safer, more orderly center of perception. Let us here merely sketch the brute and suggest the nature of the contrast, turning to Norris's early sketches for *The Wave*—a journal whose "small and homogeneous" audience clearly shared the perspective of that second category of characters—for the simplest, clearest examples.[34]

We may take a brief piece Frank Norris published in the San Francisco *Wave* in 1897 as a cameo portrait of the image of the laborer as brute—"Brute" is in fact its title—that enters naturalism from the general ideology of the period. I quote the sketch in its entirety:

> He had been working all day in a squalid neighborhood by the gas works and coal yards, surrounded by lifting cranes, pile drivers, dredging machines, engines of colossal, brutal strength, where all about him were immense blocks of granite, tons of pig iron; everything had been enormous, crude, had been huge in weight, tremendous in power, gigantic in size.
>
> By long association with such things he had become like them, huge, hard, brutal, strong with a crude, blind strength, stupid, unreasoning. He was on his way home now, his immense hands dangling half-open at his sides; his head empty of thought. He only desired to be fed and to sleep. At a street crossing he picked up a white violet, very fresh, not yet trampled into the mud. It was a beautiful thing, redolent with the scent of the woods, suggestive of everything pretty and delicate. It was almost like a smile-made flower. It lay very light in the hollow of his immense calloused palm. In some strange way it appealed to him, and blindly he tried to acknowledge his appreciation. He looked at it stupidly, perplexed, not

knowing what to do; then instinctively his hand carried it to
his mouth; he ground it between his huge teeth and slowly ate
it. It was the only way he knew.[35]

Here Norris passes in review a number of the most important elements to be found, in various combinations, in the images of the
brute: his strength, his incapacity for self-consciousness and self-
control, the coarse nature that is the result of the "squalid" environment of industrial labor and, probably, the heredity that bred those
instincts and huge teeth. Confronted by something that is beyond
him, he can feel only a glimmer of desire without understanding,
and therefore he destroys the object of his desire. The brute's blind
strength makes him dangerous even here, at his most stolid and
least vicious; the fear that a bloodbath and the destruction of civilization loom on the horizon remains potent.

In another group of sketches for *The Wave* Norris juxtaposes
courtship among the middle class and the working class. The first
of the group of pieces titled "Man Proposes" (1896) takes place in a
resort hotel. The innocent young couple whose quiet walk in the
moonlight is the subject of the little tale communicate their feelings
with subtlety and restraint; indeed, the exaggerated delicacy of their
sentiments is such that the light touch of his arm around her waist
becomes immensely significant. In the "proposal" at the end no
words are spoken:

> He partially closed the door with his heel, and as she
> straightened up he put his arm about her neck and drew her
> head toward him. She turned to him then very sweetly, yield-
> ing with an infinite charm, and he kissed her twice.
>
> Then he went out, softly closing the door behind him.
>
> This was how he proposed to her. Not a word of what was
> greatest in their minds passed between them. But for all that
> they were no less sure of each other.
>
> *She* rather preferred it that way.[36]

In this sketch Norris does not consider it necessary to write about
the physical appearance or background of the characters; everything is taken for granted, common ground—indeed, predictable
and clichéd. In the second sketch, in contrast, he gives detailed
descriptions:

> He was an enormous man, strong as a dray horse, big-boned,
> heavily muscled, slow in his movements. His feet and hands
> were huge and knotted and twisted, and misshapen by hard
> usage. Through the grime of the coal dust one could but in-
> distinctly make out his face. The eyes were small, the nose
> flat, and the lower jaw immense, protruding like the jaws of
> the carnivora, and thrusting the thick lower lip out beyond the

90
Form
and
History
in
American
Literary
Naturalism

upper. His father had been a coal heaver before him, and had worked at that trade until he had been killed in a strike. His mother had drunk herself into an asylum and had died long ago.[37]

This description, it is readily apparent, depends upon meanings generated in the ideological discourses already discussed.

The difference in the terms the two sketches use to represent femininity and sexuality is particularly marked. The object of the coal heaver's affections "was not very young, and she was rather fat; her lips were thick and very red, and her eyes were small, her neck was large and thick and very white, and on the nape the hair grew low and curling" (p. 60). Like the girl in the previous sketch she is engaged in womanly work, but she is doing the wash rather than kissing a child goodnight. As she works, the man takes a frank interest in her body that would be unthinkable in the sentimental idiom of the first piece: "The tips of her bare elbows were red, and he noted with interest how this little red flush came and went as her arms bent and straightened. . . . As her body rose and fell, he watched curiously the wrinkles and folds forming and reforming about her thick corsetless waist" (pp. 60–61). This unrestrained flesh contrasts with the control implied by the "firm, well-laced waist" (p. 56) of the middle-class girl.

The form of the proposal reveals both the man's emotions and his ability to express them as coarse: " 'Say,' he exclaimed at length, with the brutal abruptness of crude, simple natures, 'listen here. I like you better'n anyone else. What's the matter with us two gett'n' married, huh?' " (p. 61). Norris's association of sexuality and violence appears in the scene's conclusion:

> She, more and more frightened at his enormous hands, his huge square-cut head, and his enormous brute strength, cried out, "No, no!" shaking her head violently, holding out her hands and shrinking from him. . . .
>
> Suddenly he took her in his enormous arms, crushing down her struggle with his immense brute strength. Then she gave up all at once, glad to yield to him and to his superior force, willing to be conquered. She turned her head to him, and they kissed each other full on the mouth, brutally, grossly.
> [pp. 61–62]

The contrast between the two kisses could scarcely be more striking. This is indeed virtually a generic opposition—in the middle class love is a sentimental courtship vignette, in the working class it is a fragment of sordid "naturalism." Parts of this second sketch, in fact, also appear in the proposal scene in *McTeague* (1899). In these brief examples two classes and two worlds are defined by sheer opposition and contained within the frames of their separate

texts.[38] As we return to the naturalist novel proper, the task of defining their relation becomes more complex, since the opposition is
inscribed in a single narrative and is often complexly displaced or
mediated.

The ideology of brutality sometimes carries fairly elaborated systems of explanation for the existence of such degraded beings. We
have already seen how Norris links physical, moral, and social
degradation in *Vandover and the Brute*. The reference in "Man Proposes" to the coal heaver's parents suggests, in one of the most
powerful causal theories invoked by naturalism, that such brutality
is encoded in the genes. McTeague's lust for Trina, for example, is
(in a passage immediately preceding the proposal scene) directly
attributed to his tainted heredity:

> . . . the brute was there. Long dormant, it was now at last
> alive, awake. From now on he would feel its presence contin-
> ually; would feel it tugging at its chain, watching its opportu-
> nity. Ah, the pity of it! Why could he not always love her
> purely, cleanly? What was this perverse, vicious thing that
> lived within him, knitted to his flesh?
>
> Below the fine fabric of all that was good in him ran the
> foul stream of hereditary evil, like a sewer. The vices and sins
> of his father and of his father's father, to the third and fourth
> and five hundredth generation, tainted him. The evil of an en-
> tire race flowed in his veins. Why should it be? He did not de-
> sire it. Was he to blame?
>
> But McTeague could not understand this thing. It had faced
> him, as sooner or later it faces every child of man; but its sig-
> nificance was not for him. To reason with it was beyond him.
> He could only oppose to it an instinctive stubborn resistance,
> blind, inert.[39]

McTeague is doubly, triply condemned to brutality. Like every "child
of man" he is acted on by his heredity, but he also comes of a
defective line and lacks the distinctively human capacity that could
enable effective resistance: reason. The determining force of heredity can produce manly strength as well as bestial vice, however;
in Norris's story "Thoroughbred" (1895) the apparently effeminate
scion of a prominent, wealthy family shows his true mettle in a
crisis and proves that "good blood is what makes all the difference"
in men as in dogs.[40] But in naturalism bad blood always proves
more fascinating than good.

Norris's account of McTeague's bad blood relies upon the vocabulary of contemporary criminal anthropology. Two more early fictions
which draw quite directly on that source demonstrate that the brute
inscribed in the gene does not necessarily stay in the outer darkness of the slums. "A Reversion to Type" (1897) focuses on a commonplace, respectable department-store floorwalker. Schuster is

92

Form
and
History
in
American
Literary
Naturalism

described by the first-person narrator as "too damned cheeky" because he flirts with his lady customers and "entertained ideas on
culture and refinement"; thus, failing to accept his humble place in
society, he mildly endangers class boundaries and begins to reveal
himself as potentially disruptive to society. When he indulges in a
drinking bout he runs wild and eventually attempts highway rob-
bery—the very crime, we learn at the end of the story, for which his
grandfather was sent to San Quentin. It is this unsuspected criminal
ancestry that turns a respectable man into a "free-booter":

> Schuster, like all the rest of us, was not merely himself. He
> was his ancestors as well. In him, as in you and me, were gen-
> erations—countless generations—of forefathers. Schuster had
> in him the characteristics of his father, the Palace Hotel bar-
> ber, but also he had the unknown characteristics of his grand-
> father, of whom he had never heard, and his great-grandfather,
> likewise ignored. It is a rather serious matter to thrust yourself
> under the dominion of unknown, unknowable impulses and
> passions. That is what Schuster did that night. Getting drunk
> was an impulse belonging to himself; but who knows what
> "inherited tendencies," until then dormant, the alcohol un-
> leashed within him?[41]

Heredity can conceal a criminal self even within a respectable man.

In "A Reversion to Type" Schuster is able to return to his incon-
spicuous job and reveals his lapse only on his deathbed. In "A Case
for Lombroso" (1897) the consequences of hidden genetic defects
are more devastating, and there can be no return. The characters
have farther to fall: they are well-born, wealthy, educated. Norris
ostentatiously allies his narrator and male protagonist with a read-
ership supposedly belonging to a social elite; of Stayne's achievements in college, for example, he writes that "you others who have
been at Harvard will know just what all this means" (p. 35). But
Stayne abandons his self-control, yielding to the temptation represented by Cresencia Hromada. Cresencia has an extraordinary,
morbid sensitivity that is attributed to the fact that she "had come of
a family of unmixed blood, whose stock had never been replen-
ished or strengthened by an alien cross. Her race was almost exhausted, its vitality low. . . . To-day Cresencia might have been
called a degenerate" (p. 36). In Norris's version of the fashionable
notion of hereditary degeneracy not only interbreeding but any contact between certain people produces disaster for both—the reaction is virtually chemical. Cresencia's uncontrollable passion for
Stayne degrades her, and his response to it degrades him: "He
realized that she would take anything from him—that she would
not, or rather, that she could not, resent any insult, however gross.
And the knowledge made the man a brute" (p. 41). The sexual
excess and violence implied in their relationship constitute an in-

tolerable eruption of brutality within the elite, and social degradation follows: "Stayne's name has long since been erased from the
rolls of his club. Miss Hromada is thoroughly déclassé, and only
last month figured in the law courts as the principal figure in a
miserable and thoroughly disreputable scandal" (p. 42). If these
invasions of the brute into the realm of the human being are possible, civilization and stable identity seem at best provisional privileges, to be guarded at all costs against the most minute disruptions of social order and self-control.

Not only the themes but the very titles of these stories declare
their debt to Cesare Lombroso and the widely influential theories
of criminal anthropology. In *The Novels of Frank Norris* Donald
Pizer has provided an invaluable account of the impact of this and
other intellectual movements on Norris's work.[42] What concerns
me, however, is not so much questions of influence as the way in
which these concepts, incorporated into the novels, continue to
emit ideological signals and shape possibilities for meaning. For
Norris as for others of his period hereditary determinism offers a
satisfying way of understanding individual destiny in terms of biology, social problems in terms of the evolution of the species—in
short, the historical as the natural. But its consequences as worked
out in the narratives themselves often reinscribe the disturbing social contradictions that the abstract theories claim to resolve.

The idea of the atavism in particular seems to fascinate the
naturalists, offering a way of representing disruptive forces as the
primitive embedded within civilization and indeed within the individual.[43] London also makes frequent use of the atavism, although
he generally takes a more benevolent view of such reversion than
Norris does; we have already seen in *White Fang* that the primitive
can be vitalizing. Although Vandover and McTeague are consumed
and destroyed when the dormant brutes within them awaken, the
protagonists of *Before Adam* (1906) and "When the World Was
Young" (1910) manage, although not always comfortably, to live
double lives. The hero of "When the World Was Young" literally
shares his body with an atavistic personality, the two selves alter-
nating in a bizarre circadian rhythm. The narrator of *Before Adam*
also has a nocturnal double: through dreams he reexperiences the
life of an ancestor of the mid-Pleistocene. He writes that "this other-
personality is vestigial in all of us, in some of us it is almost obliter-
ated, while in others of us it is more pronounced. Some of us have
stronger and completer race memories than others. . . . My other-
personality is almost equal in power with my own personality. And
in this matter I am, as I said, a freak—a freak of heredity."[44]

In *Before Adam* as in *White Fang* the themes of naturalism are
transmogrified in a nonhuman world. Within that world we find
the atavism reinscribed; the narrator's other self also has atavistic
dreams that take him still farther back into man's past, "back to

94

Form
and
History
in
American
Literary
Naturalism

the winged reptiles and the clash and the onset of dragons, and beyond that to the scurrying, rodent-like life of the tiny mammals, and far remoter still, to the shore-slime of the primeval sea. I cannot, I dare not, say more. It is all too vague and complicated and awful" (p. 139). And to the denizens of the mid-Pleistocene the most terrifying being is still the "mighty monster, the abysmal brute" Red-Eye (p. 209), who has reverted to a still more primitive stage of evolution. This brute's uncontrollable strength menaces the fragile social order developing among the protohumans. The obsessive quality of the tale's concern with the atavism is captured—as well as it can be in an excerpt—in its last words, as the creature comes stalking in among the tribe from the outer darkness: "I can see him now, as I write this, scowling, his eyes inflamed, as he peers about him at the circle of the Tree People. And as he peers he crooks one monstrous leg and with his gnarly toes scratches himself on the stomach. He is Red-Eye, the atavism" (p. 242). London, exploring the Other within, meets him again as the Outsider.

The fascination of the atavism persists into our own period.[45] Themes related to those of *Before Adam* are reworked in the time-travel dreaming of Michael Bishop's *No Enemy But Time* and in the exploration of racial memory of Paddy Chayefsky's *Altered States*.[46] The significance of the atavism, the fears and even more strongly now the hopes it evokes, are different. Nature seems in these contemporary works a receding, elusive Other rather than a brute straining at its chain. *No Enemy But Time* retains the inarticulate vulnerability of the brute, *Altered States* the possibility that the Other is not merely a fierce potency but a ravening beast. *Altered States* has perhaps most in common thematically with naturalism: its scientistic fascination with the gene, its obsession with the predator, its emphatic suggestion that if the explorer-scientist ventures too far into the unknown he may not be able to return, and its ultimate redemption of the hero through the agency of the woman and the family. In Chapter 5 we will see how an appeal to domestic ideology is incorporated in a number of naturalist novels, just as in *Altered States* the scientist's astonishing reversions lead him, in a resounding anticlimax, to rediscover the family:

> "that ultimate moment of terror that is the beginning of life . . . is nothing, simple hideous nothing. . . . It's human life that is real! Truth is the illusion! . . . that moment of terror is . . . a real and living horror living and growing within me now, eating of my flesh, drinking of my blood. It's real because I have made it real. It's not just talk. It's alive. It's in me. It is me. And the only thing that keeps it from devouring me is you." "I think you're trying to tell me you love me," she said.[47]

This is an existential terror that one would want to trace to rather different sources than the naturalist nightmare of class struggle. Yet there is a significant continuity, for the vertiginous view down the evolutionary scale to primordial man and beyond that opens before the hero is astonishingly similar to what we see in *Before Adam*. And as so often in naturalism, the ultimate terror is the loss of stable personal identity, the collapse of self into Other.

We encounter the brute in its far-flung manifestations as a creature perpetually outcast, yet perpetually to be cast out as it inevitably reappears within self and within society. The terror of the brute includes, certainly, the fear of revolution and chaos, of the mob and the criminal, as invoked, for example, in *White Fang* by the prospect of being torn apart by the hungry wolf-pack or attacked by the murderous Jim Hall. It also includes the fear of becoming the outcast through the social degradation and psychological disintegration depicted in *Vandover and the Brute*; the brute can devour one from within, as it does Vandover: "At certain intervals his mania came upon him, the strange hallucination of something four-footed, the persistent fancy that the brute in him had now grown so large, so insatiable, that it had taken everything, even to his very self, his own identity—that he had literally *become the brute*."[48] These fears, powered at least in part by the mechanism of projection, are not ultimately separable. Naturalism's image of the brute is not simply a misrecognition of the actuality of the Other, an inaccurate, ignorant stereotype of the proletariat or lumpenproletariat (although certainly it is that), but a representation of the relation of a relatively privileged class to conditions of existence that produce this range of inconsistent fears. In this system of meanings, at this level, the social and the psychological can no longer usefully be distinguished.

We may call the "persistent fancy," the obsessive fear that haunts naturalism, by the scandalous name of *proletarianization*. It is an anxiety traditionally associated with although certainly not limited to the petty bourgeoisie who, possessing small capitals or professional skills, passionately defend their narrow footholds of economic security. In that structurally vulnerable position, trapped between the working class and the corporation, individuals may well experience themselves as "above" the interests of classes—as in Chapter 4 we will see the naturalist spectator and the progressive reformer proclaim themselves—and yet menaced by both. I call the term scandalous because American public discourse so often strives to efface class division in a rhetoric of equality; indeed, I sometimes suspect that one of the reasons naturalism has proven such an uncomfortable form for contemporary literary critics is its open interest in class. But I do not mean to imply that its representations of class are somehow the truth of the varied material naturalism processes. All the components that enter into the representation of the Other are genuine and irreducible; anxieties about social

96
Form
and
History
in
American
Literary
Naturalism

class have no predetermined priority over, for example, anxieties about masculinity, and each can serve as a way of carrying or managing the other. But the privileges of autonomy, awareness, control that characters and narrator struggle so desperately to establish and maintain are deeply marked as class privileges, and loss of those privileges is figured as the destruction of intellect, humanity, even civilization itself. We might wish for a term that alluded to the criminal and the tramp as well as the laborer—the relation between the categories of "lumpenproletariat" or underclass and "proletariat" is itself, of course, controversial. But proletarianization seems an appropriate rubric under which to explore naturalism's recurrent strategy of sequencing a narrative according to the progress of a character's deterioration.

In the work of Frank Norris, for example, this characteristic plotting can be seen in epitome in the declassing of Stayne and Cresencia Hromada in "A Case for Lombroso," dominates *Vandover and the Brute*, crucially informs *McTeague*, and enters into *The Octopus* (1901) as well. Although I have approached this point through the ideological discourses surrounding genetic determinism, this persistent fancy takes many forms—Dreiser's *Sister Carrie* and Crane's *Maggie* are both structured in part by progressive deteriorations, yet neither is particularly concerned with heredity. *The Octopus* incorporates the racial ideology that is a persistent element of Norris's and London's work as a peripheral concern, for example in the passing comment that at the jackrabbit drive the "Anglo-Saxon spectators roundabout drew back in disgust, but the hot, degenerated blood of Portuguese, Mexican, and mixed Spanish boiled up in excitement at this wholesale slaughter."[49] But the two characters in that novel who decline most precipitously have no such tainted blood. Magnus Derrick is an Anglo-Saxon, a "fine commanding figure, imposing an immediate respect, impressing one with a sense of gravity, of dignity, and a certain pride of race" (1:59). He is educated and articulate, wealthy and powerful: "In whatever circle he moved he was the chief figure. Instinctively other men looked to him as the leader. . . . He even carried the diction and manner of the rostrum into private life. It was said of him that his most colloquial conversation could be taken down in shorthand and read off as an admirable specimen of pure, well-chosen English. He loved to do things upon a grand scale, to preside, to dominate" (1:61). Yet as early as the third chapter, tempted by profit and power but also genuinely seeing no other solution to the wheat ranchers' problems, Derrick listens to arguments for a bribery scheme and allows his son to take part; thus he takes his first steps in corruption and his first steps on the road downward.[50]

Each subsequent step involves Derrick more deeply: "He began to see how perilously far he had gone in this business. He was drifting closer to it every hour. Already he was entangled, already

his foot was caught in the mesh that was being spun" (1:181). Soon
he is "hopelessly caught in the mesh. . . . He was blinded, dizzied, overwhelmed, caught in the current of events, and hurried along he knew not where. He resigned himself" (2:8). Derrick ceases to exert his will—and we already know the danger of such an abandonment of effort. His deterioration ends only when he has lost his money, his ranch, his sons, his honor, his eloquence, his authority, his belief in himself. He is destroyed as a human being; as the character Presley puts it, he is not only beggared but broken:

> "If it had only killed him, . . . but that is the worst of it. . . . It's broken him; oh, you should see him, you should see him. A shambling, stooping, trembling old man, in his dotage already. He sits all day in the dining room, turning over papers, sorting them, tying them up, opening them again, forgetting them—all fumbling and mumbling and confused. And at table sometimes he forgets to eat. And, listen, you know, from the house we can hear the trains whistling for the Long Trestle. As often as that happens the Governor seems to be—oh, I don't know, frightened. He will sink his head between his shoulders, as though he were dodging something, and he won't fetch a long breath again till the train is out of hearing. He seems to have conceived an abject, unreasoned terror of the Railroad." [2:272–73]

Finally, Derrick has sunk so low that he is willing to accept a menial position with the railroad that has destroyed him. He is brutalized and, quite literally, proletarianized.

Dyke begins as an employee of the railroad. Fired from his job, his hopes for a profitable farm destroyed by the railroad's freight charges, he too joins battle with the Pacific and Southwestern and is devoured. Like Derrick, he makes choices early in the novel that from the reader's perspective inevitably lead him to ruin, although their catastrophic consequences astonish him. Other characters, too, see where Dyke is heading; Annixter exclaims at one point, " 'Drinking at Caraher's. . . . I can see *his* finish.' . . . [They] contemplated the slow sinking, the inevitable collapse and submerging of one of their companions, the wreck of a career, the ruin of an individual; an honest man, strong, fearless, upright, struck down by a colossal power, perverted by an evil influence, go reeling to his ruin" (2:73). Dyke becomes a train robber, a murderer, a hunted man; his "finish" is a life sentence to the penitentiary:

> Jailed for life! No outlook. No hope for the future. Day after day, year after year, to tread the rounds of the same gloomy monotony. He saw the grey stone walls, the iron doors; the flagging of the "yard" bare of grass or trees—the cell, narrow, bald, cheerless; the prison garb, the prison fare, and round all

98
Form
and
History
in
American
Literary
Naturalism

the grim granite of insuperable barriers, shutting out the world, shutting in the man with outcasts, with the pariah dogs of society, thieves, murderers, men below the beasts, lost to all decency, drugged with opium, utter reprobates. To this, Dyke had been brought, Dyke than whom no man had been more honest, more courageous, more jovial. This was the end of him, a prison; this was his final estate, a criminal. [2:329]

Criminal Dyke and weak-minded Derrick have joined the ranks of the defective, a fate that appears in its full horror when set against contemporary treatments of the "unfit" like Henry Boies's. Dyke and Derrick have "become the brute."

The Octopus is a novel woven of many diverse elements, and I will analyze it more fully in Chapter 4. But the plot of decline provides one of the novel's important organizational structures, a strategy that generates narrative and enables closure. The sequence of a deterioration plays an even more important role in a novel like Stephen Crane's *Maggie: A Girl of the Streets* (1893), which is otherwise virtually without plot. *Maggie* seems Crane's most "naturalist" work, yet its relation to the form is still somewhat oblique.[51] Certainly, Crane evokes images of brutality; the slum world he creates is pervaded by an uncouth cruelty exemplified by the battling urchins of the first chapter, "the whirling mob of Devil's Row children [in whose yells] there were notes of joy like songs of triumphant savagery," and by the monstrous apparition of Maggie's mother: "Her face was inflamed and swollen from drinking. Her yellow brows shaded eye-lids that had grown blue. Her tangled hair tossed in waves over her forehead. Her mouth was set in the same lines of vindictive hatred that it had, perhaps, borne during the fight. Her bare, red arms were thrown out above her head in an attitude of exhaustion, something, mayhap, like that of a sated villain." At this moment in the novel the perspective from which this apparition is viewed is embodied in the little boy bending over her, "fearful lest she should open her eyes, and the dread within him . . . so strong, that he could not forbear to stare, but hung as if fascinated over the woman's grim face."[52] This dread and fascination are to a considerable degree shared by the narrator and reader; Crane's slum is part of the exotic terrain of the naturalist novel.

Yet the purposes to which the novelist turns these images are very different from those we have seen so far. I take the exposure of the artificiality and inadequacy of human representations and precepts to be central to Crane's project in *Maggie*; the novel is, as Alan Trachtenberg calls it, "a complicated piece of parody written with a serious regard for the task of rendering a false tale truly."[53] Crane's stylized prose can revitalize perceptions, can defamiliarize and transform the very process of reading in a fashion more familiar in the twentieth century than in the period of realism and naturalism.

The fictions reveal a skepticism about their own tourist's point of view on the slums in the works themselves, as in the frame story of the sketch "An Experiment in Misery." When the narrator's friend asks him if he has discovered the tramp's point of view by his experiment, he replies, "I don't know that I did . . . but at any rate I think mine own has undergone a considerable alteration."[54] This sophistication, however, has not prevented Crane from sometimes being read as unself-consciously representational nor his images of slum-dwellers from being taken as simple contributions to the ideology of brutality.

I think it is true that, as Walcutt contends in his reading of the novel, none of the characters in *Maggie* is "free." But I would argue that this is less because Crane is a determinist than because he is a fatalist. He is not concerned with tracing the sources of individual and social pathology with the implicit or explicit hope of eventually bringing them under control: Crane is in fact utterly uninterested in causality. We have little information about the specific determinants of Maggie's character and choices, no direct analysis of the causes of her despair, but rather a series of almost disconnected scenes unified by style, by defamiliarization, above all by the plot of fatality. Like the flower found and devoured by the "Brute" of Norris's sketch, Maggie appears from nowhere, uncaused; she makes no resistance and understands nothing about why she is destroyed. All that Maggie sees, and virtually all that the reader knows, is that she cannot survive in this brutal world. The very subtitle of the novel—*A Girl of the Streets*—preconcludes its outcome; the fact that Maggie grows up in the streets of New York is figured in the same words and is essentially *the same* as her doom as a girl of the streets, a prostitute.

Hurstwood's story in *Sister Carrie* is also organized according to the plot of fatality, as the thematic analysis of Chapter 2 suggests. Let us retrace the already familiar stages of his slow but gradually accelerating deterioration. In retrospect we may look back at choices Hurstwood makes in Chicago and see how they lead to his downfall, as he increasingly neglects his home for unlawful pleasures. The turning point, of course, comes when he steals his employers' money and flees Chicago. In New York Hurstwood is excluded from his former pleasures and sources of self-esteem, and although there is no apparent decline, the narrator writes that "psychologically there was a change, which was marked enough to suggest the future very distinctly indeed. This was in the mere matter of the halt his career had received when he departed Chicago. A man's fortune or material progress is very much the same as his bodily growth. Either he is growing stronger, healthier, wiser, as the youth approaching manhood, or he is growing weaker, older, less incisive mentally, as the man approaching old age." From this point he is irretrievably committed to "the road down-

100
Form
and
History
in
American
Literary
Naturalism

ward." Here Dreiser invokes an explicitly determinist, even bio-logical explanation for Hurstwood's decline—the passage on the pernicious influence of the katastates produced by remorse, for example, occurs in this chapter.[55]

Yet throughout *Sister Carrie* Dreiser also offers detailed accounts of more delicately balanced social forces that could also help to explain Hurstwood's decline. Hurstwood has become an outsider to the prosperous world he once inhabited; it is like "a city with a wall about it. Men were posted at the gates. You could not get in. Those inside did not care to come out to see who you were. They were so merry inside there that all those outside were forgotten, and he was on the outside" (chap. 33, p. 241). Like Dyke, he is walled away from the respectable world, the world of warmth, humanity, satis-fied desire. Dreiser constantly reports a complex interaction be-tween Hurstwood's self-image, others' reactions to him, and his reaction to their reactions. Carrie in particular, that "apt student of fortune's ways" (chap. 11, p. 75), is exquisitely responsive to his successive losses of status and self-esteem. *Sister Carrie* is above all, as we have seen, a novel of the image and the code of commodities, and Dreiser carefully describes the gradual deteriora-tion of Hurstwood's wardrobe and grooming. When a potential em-ployer takes him for a prosperous man Hurstwood cannot bear to undeceive him; when Mrs. Vance sees him shabby and unshaven he is deeply shaken. As carefully as any ethnomethodologist, Dreiser studies the intersubjective processes that construct identity, for oneself and for others; again, the psychological and the social are inseparable.

Hurstwood finds his new identity as a failure intolerable, and in-creasingly withdraws from interactive, intersubjective connections into a private world of fantasy and an impersonal, public world of journalistic spectacle: "He was getting in the frame of mind where he wanted principally to be alone and to be allowed to think. The disease of brooding was beginning to claim him as a victim. Only the newspapers and his own thoughts were worth while" (chap. 33, pp. 243–44). Both his capital and his capacity for self-exertion slip away, and as the process of proletarianization progresses Hurst-wood drifts into menial work and then into begging. He becomes a pitiable figure: "An old, thin coat was turned up about his red ears—his cracked derby hat was pulled down until it turned them out-ward. His hands were in his pockets. . . . People turned to look after him, so uncouth was his shambling figure" (chap. 47, pp. 361–62). Hurstwood's degradation is at once social, moral, and intellectual, for he has also become incapable of coherent thought: "Hopelessly he turned back into Broadway again and slopped onward and away, begging, crying, losing track of his thoughts, one after another, as a mind decayed and disjointed is wont to do" (chap. 47, p. 363).

Mindlessly, he seeks only food and warmth. Hurstwood has been utterly brutalized.

Hurstwood has lost not only his place in the world but himself. He is no longer capable of realizing how he appears to others or comprehending what is happening to him; the brute has no understanding, cannot regard himself or explain himself. It falls to Presley to observe and describe the fates of Derrick and Dyke, to the modern narrator of *Before Adam* to tell the story of his atavistic dream-self. The self is always human, the brute always Other; thus when Hurstwood is plunged into the world of determinism he cannot recognize himself in it. Working as a motorman during a streetcar strike, he holds himself apart from the other men: "he felt a little superior to these two—a little better off. To him these were ignorant and commonplace, poor sheep in a driver's hand. 'Poor devils,' he thought, speaking out of the thoughts and feelings of a bygone period of success" (chap. 41, p. 302). But that driven Other is—most explicitly in *Vandover and the Brute*—a nightmarish double of the self.

The narrative of proletarianization, demonstrating that one can tumble down as well as climb up the social ladder, implicitly proposes a frightening question to the reader: is anyone safe? Dreiser especially gives us an outcast with whom we must empathize, and as we follow Hurstwood down into his abyss the distinction between self and Other seems fearfully precarious. The gesture of exclusion reinforces the antinomy between human and brute without rendering the image of the brute any less potent, and the assertion of superiority always inscribes a doubt: "that isn't me (is it?)—that couldn't happen to me (could it?)." The sympathetic emotion provoked in the reader by Hurstwood's misfortunes itself contains this fear, as the naturalists' cynical contemporary Ambrose Bierce suggests when he defines "pity" as "a failing sense of exemption, inspired by contrast."[56]

But the trajectory of his fall tends to carry Hurstwood beyond the reach of empathy. We see him, still sympathetically, but more and more from outside as his point of view enables an exploration of "The Curious Shifts of the Poor"—the world of mission meals, flophouses, charity hospitals which is the same alien ground within the civilized city that Crane explores in "An Experiment in Misery." We can never quite see him, as other people do, simply as "a chronic type of bum and beggar" (chap. 47, p. 360), but he begins to merge into the mass of pitiable, helpless drifters who are portrayed in a version of the familiar imagery of the brute—they have "ox-like stares" (chap. 45, p. 346), wait patiently "like cattle" (chap. 47, p. 358). As Hurstwood waits to be admitted to a cheap lodging house, he is not only among but has become one of the unfit who bear on their bodies and in their minds the marks of degradation:

102
Form
and
History
in
American
Literary
Naturalism

There was a face in the thick of the collection which was as white as drained veal. There was another red as brick. Some came with thin, rounded shoulders, others with wooden legs, still others with frames so lean that clothes only flapped about them. There were great ears, swollen noses, thick lips, and, above all, red, blood-shot eyes. Not a normal, healthy face in the whole mass; not a straight figure; not a straightforward, steady glance. [chap. 47, p. 366]

These damaged men stand passively in the cold, looking at the door "as dumb brutes look, as dogs paw and whine and study the knob" (chap. 47, p. 367). It was to this, to the inevitable catastrophe of his brutalization and suicide that Hurstwood's road was, all along, leading him. Unlike the reader, who in the act of reading experiences himself as free, Hurstwood is and always was the doomed victim of forces beyond his comprehension and control. The disturbing question, "Could it happen to me?," can never be abolished. But the very *fatality* of the narrative of proletarianization works to contain its threat.

Dreiser's typical image of the brute is not Norris's vicious, violent beast but a weak, pitiable animal. Certainly, his brutal characters are dangerous and can harm others; yet even when, as in the play *The Hand of the Potter* or the early story "Nigger Jeff," Dreiser writes about a rapist, it is the criminal's vulnerability that concerns him. (The purple prose such a criminal evokes from Norris is recorded in passages from *The Octopus* discussed in Chapter 4). In *The Hand of the Potter* Isadore cries, expressing the sentiments implicit in the title, " 'I couldn't help it, could I? I didn't make myself, did I?,' " and the implication of the play as a whole bears out his appeal.[57] Jeff begs, " 'I didn't go to do it. I didn't mean to dis time. I was just drunk, boss.' " It is not lust or rage but his fear of the lynch mob that reduces him to complete brutality: "He was by now a groveling, foaming brute. The last gleam of intelligence was that which notified him of the set eyes of his pursuers."[58] Even when Dreiser deals with outright political violence during the streetcar strike, the anger he depicts is understandable human anger, not the rage of the brute. But imbecility and incomprehension can consume the self as surely as savagery. It is the helpless submission to the brutal world of toil that is the terrifying possibility in Dreiser's work, for if these characters are not unspeakable horrors neither are they fully human. Working with complex materials in the general ideology of the period, the naturalists invent an Other that is revealingly consistent but also significantly variable; thus, Dreiser's characteristic image of the brute is the ox, while Norris's is the wolfish monstrosity, and London's is the dangerous but potent and therefore glamorous wolf.[59]

The ritual act of casting out the obsessively recurrent apparition

of the brute is dramatized in naturalism in the narrative strategy I
have called the plot of decline. This plot provides a powerful ordering force in naturalist storytelling (we will encounter other such
narrative strategies in Chapter 5). It is enacted under the sign of
philosophical determinism, but carries its own conviction and carries naturalism well beyond that realistic program. The inexorable
process of Hurstwood's deterioration is assigned a cause, indeed
several causes, yet it belongs to the realm of fatality rather than that
of causality. Nor are the ends of Maggie and Vandover, for example,
ever really in doubt—from the beginning they are clearly no match
for the forces arrayed against them. In "A Case for Lombroso," too,
the reason cited for the protagonists' fatal effect on one another is
not remotely adequate to its result: "had they never met, Miss Hromada and young Stayne would yet have been as fine specimens of
womanhood and manhood as you could wish to know. Once having
met, they ruined each other" (pp. 41–42). Determinism and fatality
alike tend to reduce brutality to victimization, yet without rendering
it any less threatening. Whatever form it may take, whatever effort
may be made to capture and control it in webs of causality or plot,
the brutal Other signifies danger. It inescapably inscribes in the
represented social and psychological order and in the order of the
text an anxiety that ultimately has its source not in antinomies nor
in narratives but in the historical moment of naturalism.

4 Slumming in Determinism: Naturalism and the Spectator

If the brutal characters we have seen in the previous chapter are men "from outer darkness," if these degraded inhabitants of the naturalist terrain represent the "extraordinary and excessive in human nature," then surely an inner circle in the light and a normative human nature are implied as their opposite terms.[1] Critics of American literary naturalism have spent more time dissecting the characters victimized by determinism than they have discussing the perspective that complements them. Thus Warren French writes, quite accurately as far as he goes, that

> the striking distinction between the characters that Dreiser creates for *Sister Carrie* and that James creates for *Roderick Hudson* is that the former are not represented as being conscious of what they are doing or capable of any self-analysis of their motivations; whereas the latter are almost obsessively preoccupied with self-conscious analysis. . . . A useful distinction may thus be made between fictions that deal essentially with characters presented by their creators as aware of what they are doing and of the potential consequences of these actions and fictions that deal essentially with characters envisioned by their creators as altogether at the mercy of such forces as "environment, heredity, instinct and chance."[2]

The distinction is certainly useful and important. What it neglects is what the critics of naturalism except for Lukács have consistently neglected—the fact that although the menacing and vulnerable Other is incapable of acting as a self-conscious, purposeful agent, he can only be observed and analyzed by such an agent. Sometimes this perspective is inscribed in the text through a character, sometimes it is embodied only by the narrator or implied author. But although we explore determinism, we are never submerged in it and ourselves become the brute.

Implicit in French's remark, for that matter, are a "creator" and an audience who are self-conscious and can resist even though they are not necessarily exempt from "such forces," who even read James and compare him with Dreiser. The assumption of a common ground between certain characters, the narrator and implicitly the author, and the audience of naturalism is not uncommonly overlooked; because it is the ground under our feet we look over it, look past it, and do not see it. For example, at one point in his careful account of *Sister Carrie* Pizer comments that "because we ourselves are also creatures of place—that is, we are middle-class —we can sense the tragic import for our own lives in the fall of a Hurstwood."[3] He repeats the gesture of naturalism, gathering privileged readers (regardless of what their class position may empirically be) around him to stare anxiously at the specter of proletarianization. Such a gesture cannot compel acquiescence; readers' actual appropriation of texts is such a various and complex phenomenon that we have scarcely begun to grasp it. But the conventions of a genre inscribe an invitation to meaning that includes specific relations to narrator and characters.[4] As Fredric Jameson writes, "the shifting in our distance from the characters, the transformations of the very categories through which we perceive characters, are among the most important indices of . . . generic expectation."[5] There is a fundamental difference between empathy and observation, between treating an other (whether character or person) as a producer of signs or as a sign. The determinants of this choice are powerfully local and individual—to use a simple example, I am likely to take a somewhat stronger interest in a character if I learn that he hails from my home town. But they are also formal; and the construction of two polarized categories of characters— one of sign-producers, one of signs—is one of the most distinctive elements of naturalism.

The narrator, in naturalist novels as in others, is generally the "character" who is closest to the reader. This is all the more true in a novel narrated from a third-person omniscient point of view closely equating the narrator and implied author, so that the narrator's presence is effaced although it is no less important.[6] Stephen Crane's *Maggie*, for example, juxtaposes unreasoning characters and a highly sophisticated narrator; the incongruity of Homeric language in a description of urchins fighting in the street provokes the reader to think, but also widens the chasm between the ignorance and brutality of the slum dwellers and the literary sensibilities of the narrator and reader. The narrator makes no direct statements, but within the strict constraints of ironic implication achieves a subtlety of meaning utterly beyond the reach of the characters, whose meager vocabulary, distorted syntax, and impoverished range of reference and idea mark them as the unaware, inarticulate characters French describes. They are indeed quite incapable of self-analysis; their experiences and the contrast between their words and actions imply something to their observers, but not to them—they come no closer to understanding than Jimmie does in this passage in which he ruminates on his sister's "ruin": "he wondered vaguely if some of the women of his acquaintance had brothers. Nevertheless, his mind did not for an instant confuse himself with those brothers nor

106

Form
and
History
in
American
Literary
Naturalism

his sister with theirs." Equally heavy irony is directed at the charac-ters' social pretensions: "He was extremely gracious and attentive. He displayed the consideration of a cultured gentleman who knew what was due. 'Say, what d' hell? Bring d' lady a big glass! What d' hell use is dat pony?' "[7] Not only content and vocabulary but orthog-raphy itself locates these characters as irredeemably Other; their speech is an exotic dialect, virtually a foreign language in compari-son with the "standard English" that is the medium of communica-tion, the common ground of narrator and reader.

Dreiser's more outspoken narrators also constantly reveal to the reader what his characters do not know about themselves, and especially in his early work Dreiser sometimes writes the role of the thoughtful observer into the narrative. "Nigger Jeff" (1901), for example, is narrated from the perspective of a newspaper reporter who by virtue of his role is defined as not participating in, but only chronicling and commenting on, events. The journalist Davies leaves his own urban milieu to cover the story of a lynching and explores a new terrain that he finds both exciting and threatening: "He could scarcely realize that he, ordinarily accustomed to the routine of the city, its humdrum and at least outward social regu-larity, was a part of this."[8] (In *Sister Carrie* the city is the strange terrain, but such relations are structural: the Outside is where the Other is.) We see the events of the story through Davies's eyes, for even when "shaken to the roots of his being," he retains "all the cool observing powers of the trained and relentless reporter" (p. 101). The tale consists both in those events and in the reporter's reaction to his encounter with the brute in the forms of the criminal and the mob. His reaction is ambivalent, double, for he becomes emotionally involved yet remains to the last a spectator: "with the cruel instinct of the budding artist that he already was, he was beginning to meditate on the character of story it would make—the color, the pathos. . . . 'I'll get it all in!' he exclaimed feelingly, if triumphantly at last. 'I'll get it all in!' " (p. 111). Davies's mixed feelings toward the actors of the story replicate the narrator's and reader's ambivalent relation to Davies himself. He embodies our point of view, and we share his sympathy and his spectatorship; but his powers of observation are still developing, his understanding is incomplete, and his reaction itself is to be observed and under-stood. Through the observing character, as is so often the case in naturalist texts, we encounter the limits of spectatorship. Davies is on his way to becoming the narrator, yet he is implicated in his own story and necessarily appears as himself subject to forces and not quite free.

In another early story, "McEwen of the Shining Slave Makers" (1901), a man sitting on a park bench watching ants hurrying by somehow merges into the awareness of one of them. He is plunged into their world of hunger and violence, fights and dies among them, and then returns to himself and, from his human perspective, looks at the battle in which he has just "died." This story too is constructed as the foray of an observer into an exotic realm; Mc-Ewen brings the reader a report on truly alien experience. And like Davies he is simultaneously involved and uninvolved; he is both a tiny, struggling mite in a universe of force—a description applicable to ants, but also to human beings—and a consciousness contemplating that universe. The disjuncture produces the sensations of awe, pity, fear; it produces that spectator's sense of the "mystery and wonder and terror of life" that is so characteristic of Dreiser's work.[9] In these tales the presence of the observer both offers a location for the articulation of theme and, by framing the action, defines the shape of the narrative.

French uses Dreiser's *Sister Carrie* to exemplify naturalist characters' lack of self-awareness and helplessness, and indeed we have seen that Carrie, Drouet, and Hurstwood are profoundly vulnerable and inarticulate. Yet we have also seen that Carrie has a vague sense that a wider vision than her own is possible, and she is constantly drawn toward a better life, which for her consists in two attributes that seem to belong to a "higher" class—wealth and wisdom. As she rises Carrie not only makes money but begins to analyze herself, responding eagerly when Ames speaks to her of her "disposition" and her face's capacity to express desire: "Carrie thrilled to be taken so seriously. . . . Here was praise which was keen and analytical. . . . This was what her heart craved." The manuscript adds, "He was dwelling upon her as having qualities worthy of discussion."[10] Ames offers Carrie the possibility of seeing herself as the narrator and reader have always seen her.

Ames's broader perspective also includes a more analytic view of society. Carrie can observe and admire the scene at Sherry's, studying "the company with open eyes. So this was high life in New York. It was so that the rich spent their days and evenings. Her poor little mind could not rise above applying each scene to all society." But Ames intrigues her by being critical: " 'Do you know,' he said, turning back to Carrie, after his reflection, 'I sometimes think it is a shame for people to spend so much money this way.' Carrie looked at him a moment with the faintest touch of surprise at his seriousness. He seemed to be thinking about something over which she had never pondered." Ames's freedom from want frees him to think such thoughts, but his superiority is also intellectual. The wealthy Vance, in contrast, is absorbed and contained by his milieu: " 'It doesn't do any harm,' said Vance, who was still studying the bill of fare, though he had ordered." Carrie recognizes something new and valuable in Ames, suspecting that "he was better educated than she was—that his mind was better. . . . This strong young man beside her, with his clear, natural look, seemed to get a hold of things which she did not quite understand, but approved of." She con-

108
Form
and
History
in
American
Literary
Naturalism

cludes: "This man was far ahead of her. He seemed wiser than Hurstwood, saner and brighter than Drouet."[11] Ames becomes the new representative of that better life to which Carrie always aspires.

Although Ames represents another step on Carrie's ladder of success, he is qualitatively different from Hurstwood and Drouet.[12] He not only represents Carrie's aspirations but begins to explain aspiration itself to her. His self-conscious, analytical perspective brings Ames very close to the narrator and reader. His special position also derives in part from his access to the privileged ground of literary appreciation; his pronouncements on popular novels of the period, for example, help to convince Carrie that his judgment is more to be trusted than her own:

> Carrie turned her eyes toward him as to an oracle.
> "His stuff is nearly as bad as 'Dora Thorne,' " concluded Ames.
> Carrie felt this as a personal reproof. She read "Dora Thorne," or had a great deal in the past. It seemed only fair to her, but she supposed that people thought it very fine. Now this clear-eyed, fine-headed youth, who looked something like a student to her, made fun of it. [chap. 32, pp. 236–37]

It is on his recommendation that, at the end of the novel, Carrie is reading Balzac. The perspective to which Carrie aspires, and which Ames already shares, is that of the reader of realist and naturalist novels.

Ames does try to teach Carrie: "He was thinking to start her off on a course of reading which would improve her. Anyone so susceptible to improvement should be aided."[13] He fears that she is wasting her potential in comedy and suggests that she " 'turn to the dramatic field. You have so much sympathy and such a melodious voice. Make them valuable to others' " (chap. 46, p. 356). Ames is not only calmly indifferent to his own particular situation, objective, and altruistic, but he encourages Carrie to be altruistic. She has always felt for others and grieved "for the weak and the helpless. She was constantly pained by the sight of the white-faced ragged men who slopped desperately by her in a sort of wretched mental stupor. The poorly clad girls who went blowing by her window evenings, hurrying home from some of the shops of the West Side, she pitied them from the depths of her heart" (chap. 15, p. 107). These unfortunates, of course, suggest Hurstwood's and Carrie's respective nadirs; Carrie's sympathy, unlike Ames's, derives at least in part from her sense of involvement and vulnerability. Under the influence of *Père Goriot* at the end of the novel, however, she seems to have a different perspective on the poor, speaking in more abstract and distant terms of " 'the people who haven't anything tonight' " (chap. 47, p. 364). She has begun to look at poverty less as a frightening prospect than as an ethical and social problem; she has begun to look at it in the light that Ames and the reader do.

Charles Child Walcutt examines the way in which naturalism puts ethical and social problems to the reader. He asserts that although the premises of the naturalist novel "strip the protagonist of will and ethical responsibility . . . will is not really absent from the naturalistic novel. It is, rather, taken away from the protagonist and the other characters and transferred to the reader and to society at large. The reader acknowledges his own will and responsibility even as he pities the helpless protagonist."[14] This vital insight, drawing our attention to the inscription of the audience in the novel, nevertheless continues to neglect characters like Ames who also assume will and responsibility, thinking not just of their own desires but of what ought to be. He considers the significance of the social phenomenon represented by the luxurious restaurant, for example, taking for granted his right and indeed his duty to judge it. Carrie's improvement is itself a kind of cause to Ames, and that is why he lectures her: "He was so interested in forwarding all good causes that he sometimes became enthusiastic, giving vent to these preachments" (chap. 46, p. 357). As an ethically responsible character, and even in some general sense a reformer, Ames shares the ground of the narrator and reader.

Donald Pizer finds Ames an unsuccessful character; he is, Pizer writes, "too much the prig," "almost entirely a spokesman . . . [without] depth or identity except as an instructor of Carrie."[15] Ames seems to have wandered in from another novel—if not exactly from a Henry James novel, at least from one more closely akin to *Roderick Hudson* than to *Maggie*. Self-aware, energetic, and "interested in forwarding all good causes" as he is, Ames somehow fails to act in the novel, standing awkwardly out of the mainstream of events. He is uncomfortably inhibited even in his effort to "stir [Carrie] up" (chap. 46, p. 357), as the differences between the manuscript of *Sister Carrie* and its published text attest. The revisions significantly reduce Ames's role; in the manuscript he develops his opinions at considerably greater length, and we have a correspondingly stronger sense of the prospects they open for Carrie. And in that first version of the novel Ames is attracted to Carrie as a woman: "What Mrs. Vance had told him about her husband's having disappeared, together with all he felt concerning the moral status of certain types of actresses, fled. There was something exceedingly human and unaffected about this woman—a something which craved neither money nor praise. He followed [her] to the door—wide awake to her beauty."[16] The exclusion of this unbending is not, it seems to me, simply a matter of censorship—or rather it is complexly a matter of censorship, for the speakable and the unspeakable are negotiated through both internal and external constraints. When

110

Form
and
History
in
American
Literary
Naturalism

this respectable representative of the narrator and reader yields to or even acknowledges a sexual interest in a "fallen" woman, he not only offends conventional morality but makes himself vulnerable within the novel's own system of meanings. His desire could take him one step too far from his privileged ground and plunge him, as Hurstwood was plunged, into the contingent, hazardous realm of forces. Ames cannot fully come to life in the novelistic drama of causality without losing his footing on the narrative plane of understanding.

In the published text Ames is more aloof and passive than he is in the manuscript, but in both versions he strikes a discordant and telling note. He succeeds in stirring Carrie up, yet to little practical purpose—"the effect of this was like roiling helpless waters" (chap. 46, p. 357). Although he is a practical, professional man (and we will see the significance of that fact more clearly later in this chapter), he prompts Carrie not to act but to brood: "Carrie troubled over [his words] in her rocking-chair for days" (chap. 46, p. 357). Her reflections on her own prospects and on the contrast between comfort and misery suggest no active program for effecting change; although she cannot articulate it, Carrie's apprehension of her own and humanity's perpetually unfulfilled potential is very much Dreiser's: "In your rocking-chair, by your window, shall you dream such happiness as you may never feel" (chap. 47, p. 369). Ames seems to be, and Carrie seems to be striving to become, a self-conscious, purposeful agent; but the gap between contemplation and performance, between understanding and action, can never quite be crossed.

The recurring image of the rocking chair also suggests the dissonance and ambivalence focused in the figure of the spectator, for Hurstwood as well as Carrie rocks and dreams, Hurstwood as well as Ames sits back and judges the passing scene. Reading the newspapers in his corner by the radiator, Hurstwood has a peculiar sense of exemption: "There was something quite knavish in the man's attitude. His eye seemed to be cocked with a twinkle upon the fortunate, expecting their defeat. His own state seemed a thing apart—not considered" (chap. 36, p. 263). When he ventures out into the world of effort and event and gets caught up in the streetcar strike, he meets with one difficulty after another—learning to run a car is not so simple as it looked when he was observing the motorman from his comfortable seat as a passenger, the cold is unbearable, he is attacked by strikers and even shot at. But then he returns to the warm apartment, gets something to eat, and sits "down in his comfortable rocking-chair. It was a wonderful relief." Experience recedes into image: "'Strike Spreading in Brooklyn,' he read. 'Rioting Breaks Out in all Parts of the City.' He adjusted his paper very comfortably and continued" (chap. 41, p. 313). The newspapers, those "Lethean floods of telegraphed intelligence" (chap. 34, p. 252), offer a surrogate experience that at once conceals and deepens Hurstwood's isolation and immobility.[17] *Sister Carrie's* spectator is a profoundly ambivalent figure, as understanding and exemption constantly threaten to become paralysis.[18]

This paralysis haunts the frontier between the terrains of the spectator and the brute, marking the perpetually challenged and reasserted disjuncture between self and Other. Dreiser represents this division in *Sister Carrie* and in "Nigger Jeff" and "McEwen" with their separate realms of reporter and participant, man and ant, realms whose mutual inaccessibility is broken only by the gaze of the observer. In *Maggie* Crane draws a line between the narrator and the reader and the characters, although perhaps Maggie herself—an extrusion of potential humanity into the alien world of the slums—marks the boundary by her uncompromising passivity, her inscrutable and virtually quietist victimage. In *Before Adam* Jack London unites actor and immobilized spectator in the figure of the atavism, for the self-aware narrator can never so much as offer a piece of advice to his mid-Pleistocene double:

> It is I, the modern, who look back across the centuries and weigh and analyze the emotions and motives of Big-Tooth, my other self. He did not bother to weigh and analyze. He was simplicity itself. He just lived events, without ever pondering why he lived them in his particular and often erratic way. . . . I, the modern, often entered into my dreaming, and in the consequent strange dual personality was both actor and spectator. And right often have I, the modern, been perturbed and vexed by the foolishness, illogic, obtuseness, and general all-round stupendous stupidity of myself, the primitive.[19]

The characters who represent the understanding of the narrator and the reader inevitably find that somehow when they enter the terrain of choices and consequences, they are no longer themselves: they can never put the suggestions of their understanding into effect.

Once we become sensitized to the image of immobility it seems to recur obsessively in naturalism. It occurs at two points in London's *Sea-Wolf* (1904), for example. The novel opens in the apparently safe, civilized setting of a ferry steamer crossing San Francisco Bay. We see the journey through the eyes of Humphrey Van Weyden, who like Ames is an educated, privileged character with much in common with a novel-reading audience—he is even a literary critic. But Van Weyden's complacency and self-importance make him ridiculous, and he immediately meets his comeuppance in the form of a shipwreck. The problem of navigation, which he smugly considers "'as simple as A, B, C'"—as simple, that is, as the manipulation of language—turns out to be rather complex; a fellow passenger who was once a sailor asks him, "'How about this here tide? . . . How fast is she ebbin'? What's the drift, eh?'"[20] Van Weyden gets his

112

Form
and
History
in
American
Literary
Naturalism

first lesson in causality as the steamer collides with another boat in the fog and sinks. The laws of nature are neither so simple nor so easily controlled as he thinks. As in *Vandover and the Brute*, the shipwreck metonymically suggests the intrusion of uncontrollable, contingent forces into the life of a middle-class narrator. Van Weyden's facile clichés about men "groping their way blindly through the unseen" (p. 4) are put to flight as he actually experiences his own vulnerability and that of his class as a whole:

> these were women of my own kind, like my mother and sisters, with the fear of death upon them and unwilling to die. And I remember that the sounds they made reminded me of the squealing of pigs under the knife of the butcher, and I was struck with horror at the vividness of the analogy. These women, capable of the most sublime emotions, of the tenderest sympathies, were open-mouthed and screaming. They wanted to live, they were helpless, like rats in a trap, and they screamed. [p. 7]

An instant can reveal the brute at the heart of civilization.

Van Weyden's experience of shipwreck is above all one of helplessness, as he is confronted with a situation in which he has no control—the first of many such that will follow. In the panic he finds himself in the sea in a life preserver: "How I went over I do not know" (p. 8). He cannot swim. The cold numbs his legs, begins to numb his heart, and he loses consciousness. When he comes to himself again, drifting in the freezing sea in a fog, Van Weyden confronts a landscape we recognize as the Wild: "I was alone, floating, apparently, in the midst of a gray primordial vastness" (p. 9). He panics, and "a blankness intervened. . . . When I aroused, it was as after centuries of time" (p. 9). When a ship appears he is too exhausted and defeated to shout for help, although the crew sees him by chance and tries to find him in the fog: " 'Why in hell don't you sing out?' " (p. 11). Van Weyden's passivity at this point is no longer rationally explicable. His paralysis and the "blankness" he enters mark the disjuncture as Van Weyden passes out of the realm of freedom and into the realm of forces. When he is brought out of his stupor on the ship that rescues him, Van Weyden—who will now become "Hump"—has been precipitated into the brutal world of the seal-hunting ship and must submit to its captain, Wolf Larsen. "Force, nothing but force, obtained on this brute-ship" (p. 45).

Already familiar with the role that the wolf plays in London's symbolic system, we are not surprised to find Wolf Larsen a magnificent brute. He is masculine, beautiful, strong with a "strength we are wont to associate with things primitive, with wild animals, and the creatures we imagine our tree-dwelling prototypes to have been—a strength savage, ferocious, alive in itself, the essence of life in that it is the potency of motion" (p. 19). But, surprisingly,

Wolf's intellect and imagination are equally powerful, and this self-educated man even tutors Hump in philosophy. Although he does not hesitate to admit that he presses his unexpected passenger into service because he wants the extra hand, Wolf also claims to be able to judge the consequences of his action—he tells Hump that his refusal to put him ashore is " 'for the good of your soul' " (p. 26). And his proletarian adventure does indeed prove vitalizing and masculinizing for Hump. Through the operation of narrative formulas that I will examine in the last chapter, Van Weyden even finds a way to escape the laws of determinism and find his way back to law and order. At the end of the novel he has added Wolf's potency to his own civilized nature and, like Weedon Scott in *White Fang*, returns triumphant from the Wild. But Van Weyden's passivity is transferred to Wolf. At the beginning of the novel it is Hump who is helpless and womanlike; at the end it is Wolf.[21]

From one perspective Wolf Larsen's end merely illustrates the accuracy of his own pessimistic materialism. He has always believed that the " 'big eat the little that they may continue to move, the strong eat the weak that they may retain their strength. The lucky eat the most and move the longest, that is all' " (p. 50). This is *White Fang*'s law of the meat, and by it, logically, inevitably, Wolf is vulnerable to physical afflictions and, more, eventually must weaken and be destroyed. But it is when he is at the height of his powers that his turn to be weak suddenly and inexplicably arrives. Wolf's deterioration is anything but a determinist illustration of the working out of causal factors; its physiological basis is extremely sketchy. Wolf says, " 'There is no accounting for it. I was never sick in my life. Something's gone wrong with my brain. A cancer, a tumor, or something of that nature,—a thing that devours and destroys. It's attacking my nerve-centres, eating them up, bit by bit, cell by cell' " (p. 343). The disease that enfeebles, blinds, finally paralyzes him is simultaneously a completely contingent circumstance and an inevitable fatality. It is possible to see him as simply unfortunate. It is also possible to see Wolf's illness as Van Weyden does: "There was the awfulness of retribution about it" (p. 344). It is only poetic justice that allows Hump at the end of the novel to give Wolf the same unceremonious burial at sea that Wolf gave a dead sailor at its beginning, and only poetic justice that prevents brutality from triumphing completely in *The Sea-Wolf*. Wolf's paralysis, although assigned a cause, is both utterly arbitrary and structurally necessary to the novel.

Wolf is a brute (the word is used of him again and again), an atavism. Yet he is also a man with a wide understanding who argues his views eloquently. He has both great force and great intellect and seems uniquely qualified to act in the world. This synthesis of energy and understanding proves an unstable combination, and the disjuncture between the two realms reasserts itself in Wolf's paraly-

114

Form
and
History
in
American
Literary
Naturalism

sis. The "seat of [his] trouble" is in his brain (p. 343), and although like Vandover he is devoured from within, the disease does not erode his will and brutalize him but, on the contrary, deprives him of his brutal strength:

> It was the old, indomitable, terrible Wolf Larsen, imprisoned somewhere within that flesh which had once been so invincible and splendid. Now it bound him with insentient fetters, walling his soul in darkness and silence, blocking it from the world which to him had been a riot of action. No more would he conjugate the verb "to do" in every mood and tense. "To be" was all that remained to him—to be, as he had defined death, without movement; to will, but not to execute; to think and reason and in the spirit of him to be as alive as ever, but in the flesh to be dead, quite dead. [p. 345]

Action and self-awareness are once again severed as the magnificent brute Wolf Larsen is reduced to a spectator.[22]

The recurrent images of blocked action and enforced spectatorship in American naturalism suggest that Lukács's characterization of the genre in terms of observation and description embodies a profound insight into the nature of the form. Others have also noted Zola's obsession with observation; without further study we cannot be sure of its full significance, yet the affinity is striking. The editor of an issue of *Yale French Studies* on Zola notes, for example, that out of ten essays "themes of voyeurism and enclosure" underlie six.[23] In one of those essays Leo Braudy finds the author and reader figured in Zola's *Thérèse Raquin* by an image of paralysis as literal as the one we encounter in *The Sea-Wolf*. Braudy contends that Madame Raquin, "sitting immovably between the two murderers, unable to do anything to punish them, forced to watch their arguments and violence . . . becomes the novel's image of the author himself, whose scientific detachment prevents him from acting to change conditions, or an image of the voyeuristic reader, who has decided that he can enter this world of horror with neither obligation nor responsibility. Mme. Raquin sees, understands, but cannot act."[24] Thus in Zola too we encounter both the radical disjuncture between understanding and action and the obsessive inscription of the observer into the narrative.

In the same collection Phillip Walker supports this view by demonstrating that in Zola's imagery the "window, the mirror, the eye—all those things which intervene between the observer and the object observed, which obstruct light, frame, filter, bend, transform it or interpret the data it transmits—are, indeed, among the most central, recurrent, and characteristic motifs of his art. . . . his universe is first and foremost a spectacular universe, a universe dominated by the eye."[25] And Naomi Schor, studying Zola's use of windows, examines the psychic functioning of the Other (what is seen through a window often turns out to be sexual or aggressive behavior), the distancing effect of treating something as a "spectacle," and the particular significance of the spectacle of mob violence and revolution, concluding that the "window is a neuralgic point where Zola's aesthetic, sexual and political concerns intersect." Schor outlines, too, the way in which the topography of the window defines the characters' capacities and incapacities: "The glance of the observer-voyeur creates an invisible wall which reinforces the visible ones. To be seen, to be spied on is to be imprisoned. . . . Topography, history and biology all condemn Zola's characters to a life where free will is powerless to act, to bring about change."[26] These readings suggest that both the victims of determinism and the immobilized observer are to be found in the novels of Zola as well as in American naturalism.

Windows play an important role as well in the specular and spectacular universe of *Sister Carrie*. Dreiser introduces a reference to them as part of his depiction of the urban milieu: "The large plates of window glass, now so common, were then rapidly coming into use, and gave to the ground floor offices a distinguished and prosperous look. The casual wanderer could see as he passed a polished array of office fixtures, much frosted glass, clerks hard at work, and genteel business men in 'nobby' suits and clean linen lounging about or sitting in groups" (chap. 2, p. 12). Not only production but consumption is turned into theater; for Carrie's first taste of prosperity "Drouet selected a table close by the window, where the busy rout of the street could be seen. He loved the changing panorama of the street—to see and be seen as he dined" (chap. 6, p. 44). On the other side of that Chicago window we may place Hurstwood tramping the streets in New York: "Once he paused in an aimless, incoherent sort of way and looked through the windows of an imposing restaurant, before which blazed a fire sign, and through the large, plate windows of which could be seen the red and gold decorations, the palms, the white napery, and shining glassware, and, above all, the comfortable crowd. . . . 'Eat,' he mumbled. 'That's right, eat. Nobody else wants any'" (chap. 47, p. 362). As Philip Fisher writes of *Sister Carrie*, the "window creates a polarized world of inside and outside, actor and spectator, rich and poor."[27] The window offers a location for defining the self and the Other; it also invites one to consider the boundary. It is by her window that Carrie habitually rocks and dreams, from her first evening in Chicago to her last appearance in the novel at her hotel in New York and the image with which Dreiser ends the published text of the novel. Such images focus and figure the confrontation between the turbulent forces of causality and the observing, immobilized consciousness.

Following the inseparable yet discontinuous naturalist preoccupations with the spectator and the brute through the novels leads

116
Form
and
History
in
American
Literary
Naturalism

us both to the characteristic structural elements of the genre and to its recurrent discomforts. The tensions between sensationalism or romanticism and quotidian realism, and between determinism and reformism, that are so often noted by critics of naturalism are inescapably implied by the outlines I have traced. Yet even the most perceptive critics have tended to reinscribe these dynamic oppositions in static formulations and thus to erase the discomfort of the contradictions naturalism figures so urgently. Arguing that Zola is "deeply aware of the pitfalls of observation—which can at worst degenerate into indifference, sadism or paralysis," Schor seems finally to write from within the possibilities envisioned by naturalism: "Zola seems to suggest that at best it can lead to the creation of a work of art which alone can transcend the anguish of enclosure and perhaps even bring about revolutionary change" (p. 51). The critic of American naturalism Charles Child Walcutt, as we have already seen, similarly affirms that the naturalist by portraying "with loathing and bitterness the folly and degradation of man is also affirming his hope and his faith, for his unspoken strictures imply an equally unspoken ideal which stimulates and justifies his pejorative attitude toward the world about him"; "the act of criticism," Walcutt suggests, is "an exercise of creative intelligence" which itself gives grounds for hope (p. 29). The gesture is not unlike the one in which Davies, horrified by the suffering he sees in "Nigger Jeff," comforts himself with a cruel compassion possible only to the author-voyeur: " 'I'll get it all in!' he exclaimed feelingly, if triumphantly at last" (p. 111). Schor and Walcutt, dissimilar in virtually every other way, are both willing to appeal to a magical transformation of society by the will signified in and by a work of art. This will, when transposed from word to deed, from narrative perspective to dramatic action, finds itself immobilized; it can locate no other point of contact with a determined world than the one figured by a window.

In their efforts to come to terms with the most comprehensive reforming project of naturalism as a whole, Schor and Walcutt remind us that its author and reader, and the characters who represent them, take on not only questions of individual destiny but the state of society in general. Despite the fact that critics have often labeled naturalism's reformism a contradiction of its program, the fact that a novel confronts social problems is one of the most important markers readers react to when they identify it as naturalist. Exercising will means not simply acting for oneself but shaping society to considered ends. In many cases the novelists' public statements underscore this commitment to social change perceived in their fiction—from Zola to London to Dreiser to Farrell, naturalists have been allied with or part of the political left. What appears in their fiction, however, is not the direct expression of a program for change, for such authorial opinion is necessarily mediated by form. The narrative may reveal an immanent ideology whose tendency is not quite what the writer would claim (Farrell, for example, would hardly have been pleased by being called a reformist). And even where there is no biographical evidence that a naturalist intended his work as social criticism, contemporary reactions consistently considered them as such. For example, Frank Norris, his first biographer tells us, was "interested in stories, not reforms. He was comparatively untouched by suffering and misery" and intended in *The Octopus* only to portray a segment of American society and the workings of economic forces.[28] Yet it was read as a reform novel, an assault on the Southern Pacific Railroad.[29] This is not so much a failure of control on Norris's part as the most pointed illustration that the tension between determinism and reform is intrinsic to naturalism. Perhaps for that reason, in *The Octopus* one can clearly trace the dynamic that constitutes the form's immanent ideology.

The character we are closest to in *The Octopus* is Presley, who plays a particularly complex and revealing role in the novel.[30] From beginning to end Presley is a spectator. His nature suits him for the role of observer rather than actor: "One guessed that Presley's refinement had been gained only by a certain loss of strength. . . . Though morbidly sensitive to changes in his physical surroundings, he would be slow to act upon such sensations, would not prove impulsive, not because he was sluggish, but because he was merely irresolute."[31] Frequent references are made to "Presley's morbidly keen observation" (2:173) and to "his constitutional irresoluteness" (2:275). The central action of the novel deals with the struggle between the wheat farmers of Tulare County, California, and the Pacific and Southwestern Railroad, and Presley's status as an observer is confirmed and underscored by the fact that he is only a visitor on Magnus Derrick's ranch. He is close to several of the ranchers and his visit is an extended one: "Some eighteen months before this time, he had been threatened with consumption, and, taking advantage of a standing invitation on the part of Magnus Derrick, had come to stay in the dry, even climate of the San Joaquin for an indefinite length of time" (1:71). But Presley is necessarily an outsider to the battle between ranchers and railroad. He is chronicler, commentator, even advocate, but not participant. Just before an important confrontation between the ranchers' league and the agents of the P. & S.W., for example, he is told by Derrick: "'Presley . . . I forbid you to take any part in this affair.' 'Yes, keep him out of it,' cried Annixter. . . . 'Go back to Hooven's house, Pres, and look after the horses. . . . This is no business of yours'" (2:224–25). And Presley looks after the horses and watches as his friends kill and are killed.

Presley, like Ames and Humphrey Van Weyden, is a privileged, educated character who shares with the narrator and reader the ability to understand and appreciate literature. He has "graduated

118
Form
and
History
in
American
Literary
Naturalism

and post-graduated with high honors from an Eastern college, where he had devoted himself to a passionate study of literature" (1:7). Presley aspires to write a great poem about the West. At first economic conflict seems to him an inappropriate topic for art:

> These matters, these eternal fierce bickerings between the farmers of the San Joaquin and the Pacific and Southwestern Railroad irritated him and wearied him. . . . In the picture of that huge romantic West that he saw in his imagination, these dissensions made the one note of harsh colour that refused to enter into the great scheme of harmony. It was material, sordid, deadly commonplace. . . . The romance seemed complete up to that point. There it broke, there it failed, there it became realism, grim, unlovely, unyielding. [1:10]

Although "it was the first article of his creed to be unflinchingly true," Presley also has a desire to see life "through a rose-coloured mist" (1:10) that is one of several false notions he is shown to hold at the beginning of the novel; his thinking is certainly not so affirmatively presented as Ames's in *Sister Carrie*. Yet he learns as the novel progresses, and his growing understanding is shared by the reader. We are not confined to Presley's point of view, but it opens and closes and thus frames the novel, and throughout is adopted more frequently than any other. Presley's is the most comprehensive perspective offered in *The Octopus* and by its conclusion coincides very closely with the narrator's. In fact, the events that Presley observes teach him to be a naturalist. Inspired both by a painting and by the iniquities of the railroad (in particular by Dyke's catastrophe), Presley creates the same synthesis of romance and realism to which Norris aspires. He makes his art out of the same materials Norris uses, taking as the topic of his successful "Socialistic poem" (2:108) "The Toilers" the very conflict between the farmers and the railroad that once wearied him and that is the central action of *The Octopus* itself.

The gulf between the artist-observer Presley and the ordinary denizens of naturalism is established at the opening of the novel when Presley encounters Hooven, a German immigrant and tenant farmer who accosts him with these words: " 'Yoost der men I look for, Mist'r Praicely, . . . Yoost one minute, you wait, hey? I wanta talk mit you' " (1:3). Presley, on the other hand, speaks the same language the narrator does; no idiosyncracies of pronunciation are reflected in the spelling of his remarks: " 'Well, you must be quick about it, Bismarck. . . . I'm late for dinner, as it is' " (1:3). Hooven belongs to the unlovely, unyielding realism the poet wants to reject, and Presley finds him alien and unsettling: "These uncouth brutes of farm-hands and petty ranchers, grimed with the soil they worked upon, were odious to him beyond words. Never could he feel in sympathy with them, nor with their lives, their ways, their marriages, deaths, bickerings, and all the monotonous round of their sordid existence" (1:3). This passage effectively evokes the brutal Other who has become familiar to us in the previous chapter, the victim of determinism condemned endlessly to act out the same bestial drives without any possibility of rising to an appreciation of beauty or an understanding of self and surroundings. Although he is more comic than fearful, we recognize the brute in Hooven because we recognize the significance of the categories that are invoked, however briefly, to describe him. One of the important things Presley learns is to feel more sympathy toward people like the Hoovens, as we will see. But substituting pity for contempt does not change the structure of the relationship; equality and reciprocity between them are never conceivable.

Already in this opening chapter not only Hooven but the railroad itself (a term that can indicate either the machine or the company) is a kind of brute; and indeed throughout *The Octopus* the Other is represented almost obsessively in a variety of images. At the end of the first chapter a locomotive shatters the peace of the pastoral scene, slaughtering sheep who have strayed onto the track: "It was a slaughter, a massacre of innocents. The iron monster had charged full into the midst, merciless, inexorable. To the right and left, all the width of the right of way, the little bodies had been flung; backs were snapped against the fence posts; brains knocked out. . . . Presley turned away, horror-struck, sick at heart, overwhelmed with a quick burst of irresistible compassion for this brute agony he could not relieve" (1:47). The helpless sheep are brutes, and so surely is the iron monster. Presley—not for the last time—finds himself helplessly contemplating a horrific scene and flees: "He hurried on across the Los Muertos ranch, almost running, even putting his hands over his ears till he was out of hearing distance of that all but human distress. Not until he was beyond earshot did he pause" (1:48). The chapter ends with a powerful image of the locomotive as engine of destruction:

> Again and again, at rapid intervals in its flying course, it whistled for road crossings, for sharp curves, for trestles; ominous notes, hoarse, bellowing, ringing with the accents of menace and defiance; and abruptly Presley saw again, in his imagination, the galloping monster, the terror of steel and steam, with its single eye, Cyclopean, red, shooting from horizon to horizon; but saw it now as the symbol of a vast power, huge, terrible, flinging the echo of its thunder over all the reaches of the valley, leaving blood and destruction in its path; the leviathan, with tentacles of steel clutching into the soil, the soulless Force, the iron-hearted Power, the monster, the Colossus, the Octopus. [1:48]

120
Form
and
History
in
American
Literary
Naturalism

This image, used repeatedly in the novel, is one of the crucial elements that enables readers to interpret *The Octopus* as an unequivocal denunciation of the Southern Pacific and the trusts, and therefore as an unequivocal reform novel.

The first chapter also introduces the Other—here the term is Norris's as well as mine—in the form of the brutal rapist of Angéle Varian: "The Other had withdrawn into an impenetrable mystery. There he remained. He never was found; he never was so much as heard of. A legend arose about him, this prowler of the night, this strange, fearful figure, with an unseen face, swooping in there from out the darkness, come and gone in an instant, but leaving behind him a track of terror and death and rage and undying grief" (1:36). Thus sexuality and violence as well as more abstract social forces are incorporated in the novel's image of the Other. We never learn who the criminal is, yet his act reminds us of the existence of these dark forces. The dissonance of the loose end itself suggests that this Other is a projection of those outcast impulses that return in the wild man from the outer darkness. Annixter's complex feelings for Hilma, for example, reveal a kindred lust and aggression that are manifested in his proposition that she become his mistress, a cruelty for which he later berates himself in a familiar idiom: "Brute, beast that he was, he had driven her away" (2:79).

The resistance the railroad engenders is itself imaged as an uncontrollable and terrifying force, and, in a striking correspondence, even as a brute and a mechanical engine. Norris evokes the ideological discourses surrounding the idea of the "mob" in his description of the scene during which the ranchers' league is formed: "The reverberation of the shouting was as the plunge of a cataract. It was the uprising of The People; the thunder of the outbreak of revolt; the mob demanding to be led, aroused at last, imperious, resistless, overwhelming. It was the blind fury of insurrection, the brute, many-tongued, red-eyed, bellowing for guidance, baring its teeth, unsheathing its claws, imposing its will with the abrupt, resistless pressure of the relaxed piston, inexorable, knowing no pity" (1:271).[32] In *The Octopus* the brute combines both the perceived threats discussed at the beginning of Chapter 3: it is both the soulless corporation and the insurrectionary mob.

The political forces embodied in this uprising are as elusive and variable as the content of the image of the brute. Just as any threat to order can be projected onto the brute, the league condenses several contradictory elements. The language of this and other passages treats the resistance of the wheat farmers as a radical mass movement. A novel about "the uprising of The People" would seem to promise a concern with, and indeed probably responds to, the agrarian radicalism so important in American life in the decades leading up to *The Octopus*: populism. It evokes, minimally, the events in the Mussel Slough district of California on which it was partially based. Yet the characters we *see* in *The Octopus* are agriculturists on a scale never attempted by the farmers who resisted the railroad at Mussel Slough. Hooven is asked to leave the meeting at which the league is organized, for he is not a landowner but a tenant. The small farmer and former engineer Dyke is asked to leave; so is the saloon-keeper Caraher, a stereotypical radical who is always ranting that the only thing the railroad trust will listen to is "six inches of plugged gaspipe" (2:71). But Presley and his friend the mystical shepherd Vanamee, who however improbably is also college-educated, are permitted to remain as observers; there is no question but that a class distinction is what is at stake.

Not the "uncouth brutes of farm-hands and petty-ranchers" who disturb Presley but the gentlemen-ranchers, employers of farm-hands who, far from being "grimed with the soil," scarcely get their hands dirty are the actors in this political drama. (Derrick, as we have seen, does soil his in a different way.) Although their efforts to make the biggest possible profit do indeed bring them into conflict with the railroad, they are certainly not the "toilers" of Presley's Socialistic poem. Yet the rhetoric used to describe the league is that associated (by middle-class observers, at any rate) with a revolutionary movement and specifically with a movement of the urban proletariat. In his speech to the league at a later point, for example, Presley rhapsodizes: "'Liberty is the Man In the Street, a terrible figure, rushing through powder smoke, fouled with the mud and ordure of the gutter, bloody, rampant, brutal, yelling curses, in one hand a smoking rifle, in the other, a blazing torch'" (2:261–62). There is a critical slippage in what "The People" represent. This condensation permits a wide range of political unrest and resistance to be figured as a few men in an irrigation ditch defending their property rights; it rewrites the red-eyed, many-tongued brute as a less incomprehensible, far less formidable Other. Yet the historical contradictions that shape this figuration of the brute are preserved in its compressed dissonance.

Although the image of the Other never loses its emotional power and its contradictory complexity, *The Octopus* writes threatening agencies out of the narrative as persistently as it reinscribes them. The concern with causality that is so central to naturalism can itself accomplish such a gesture of comprehension and containment, abolishing—but always marking the exclusion of—the Other. The head of the railroad, Shelgrim (throughout the novel, his is a name to conjure with), tells Presley:

"Believe this, young man . . . *that railroads build themselves.* Where there is a demand sooner or later there will be a supply. Mr. Derrick, does he grow his wheat? The Wheat grows itself. What does he count for? Does he supply the force? What do I count for? Do I build the Railroad? You are dealing with

122
Form
and
History
in
American
Literary
Naturalism

forces, young man, when you speak of Wheat and the Railroads, not with men." [2:285]

This assertion that only impersonal forces act discloses the fetishism of commodities and the mystery of the market, which means it also reveals the erasure of the laborer. Magnus Derrick did not grow his wheat—the toilers who are pushed to the margins of the text did. Nor did Shelgrim build his railroad—Chinese workers who appear nowhere in *The Octopus* did.[33] Yet these excluded others leave their mark, for *The Octopus* remembers them in its moments of dissonance and indeed in its very form.

The denial of human agency figured in the form as well as the philosophy of naturalism denies effective activity to Presley as well. He wants to act, tries again and again to act—but again and again finds himself frustrated. When "The Toilers" succeeds, Presley is asked to tour as a lecturer, and he thinks of trying to turn his influence to practical political account. "He would declare himself the champion of the People in their opposition to the Trust. He would be an apostle, a prophet, a martyr of Freedom." But nothing comes of this project, somehow; whether or not this self-aggrandizing vision could be realized is never even tested: "Presley was essentially a dreamer, not a man of affairs. He hesitated to act at this precise psychological moment" (2:109). He is merely an observer during the climactic gunfight at the irrigation ditch on Derrick's ranch, Los Muertos (the name itself, incidentally, embodies both a kind of fatality and a reminder of a Spanish-speaking population that finds no place in the novel except as an example of degenerated blood). After the deaths of Magnus's son Harran, Annixter, Hooven, and other friends, Presley makes an impassioned speech to the mass meeting of the league: "the madness of the moment seized irresistibly upon Presley. He forgot himself; he no longer was master of his emotions or his impulses" (2:259). It is at this point that Presley invokes the image of revolution quoted earlier, the idea of the "Red Terror," and denounces political corruption and the power of the trusts ("ruffians in politics, ruffians in finance, ruffians in law, ruffians in trade" [2:261])—in the rhetoric of the period, the powerful as well as the powerless can be brutes.

The narrator writes of how the audience "took fire" at Presley's words, of the hush that fell as he spoke, "more significant than mere vociferation" (2:260). He is on the verge of affecting the course of events—but his action is blocked. Somehow, after we thought it had succeeded, his speech misses fire:

> Presley knew that, after all, he had not once held the hearts of his audience. He had talked as he would have written; for all his scorn of literature, he had been literary. The men who listened to him, ranchers, country people, store-keepers, attentive though they were, were not once sympathetic. Vaguely

they had felt that here was something which other men—more educated—would possibly consider eloquent. They applauded vociferously but perfunctorily, in order to appear to understand.

Presley, for all his love of the people, saw clearly for one moment that he was an outsider to their minds. He had not helped them nor their cause in the least; he never would. [2:262]

All the energies of the league somehow cannot produce an effective resistance to the railroad, and when it comes to the point only Presley's friends are at the irrigation ditch. All Presley's sincerely felt vehemence cannot cross the boundary between the literary man and "The People." Desperate, he again attempts to intervene by adopting Caraher's program—the dynamite bomb, that clichéd symbol of mob violence. His attempt to murder the railroad agent by bombing his house is also mysteriously blocked: "By a miracle, S. Behrman himself remained untouched" (2:270). In causal terms Behrman's escape is inexplicable, a "miracle"; in generic terms it is inevitable. Presley's paralysis strikes a discordant note in which the structure of the form declares itself.

The reader does not accompany Presley on his murderous adventure but sees it only retrospectively, through his memories. Nor is his responsibility for the crime ever publicly known—the bomber, like the rapist, remains a faceless Other. But, intolerably, this is an Other who also occupies the privileged ground of the narrator and reader. Presley's effort to understand *and* act, to unite the artist-observer and the dynamiter, puts a pressure on the character that produces an instability not unlike Wolf Larsen's in *The Sea-Wolf*. "Once only he had *acted*" (2:275). And to act proves to be tempting madness—afterward he remembers only the explosion and being "flung headlong, flung off the spinning circumference of things out into a place of terror and vacancy and darkness. And then after a long time the return of reason, the consciousness that his feet were set upon the road to Los Muertos, and that he was fleeing terror-stricken, gasping, all but insane with hysteria. Then the never-to-be-forgotten night that ensued, when he descended into the pit, horrified at what he supposed he had done, at one moment ridden with remorse, at another raging against his own feebleness, his lack of courage, his wretched, vacillating spirit" (2:276). Presley, as he reports it, " '[goes] to pieces.' " His trouble, like Wolf's, is in the brain—" 'nerves mostly . . . , and my head, and insomnia, and weakness, a general collapse all along the line, the doctor tells me. "Over-cerebration," he says, "over-excitement." I fancy I rather narrowly missed brain fever' " (2:271). Only by retreating to the role of observer can Presley regain his stability.

The sequence of events in the San Joaquin valley ends with the

124

Form
and
History
in
American
Literary
Naturalism

report of the bombing of S. Behrman's house. At this point not only Presley but the narrative breaks down—the chapter ends, and in the next the story is taken up again a month later looking back at the catastrophe. The opposition between the planes of the spectator and the actor is marked by a discontinuity in the text as well as by the disruption in Presley's consciousness. Yet Presley, after all these defeats and distresses, is still seeking a way to act:

> there had come to Presley a deep-rooted suspicion that he was—of all human beings, the most wretched—a failure. Everything to which he had set his mind failed—his great epic, his efforts to help the people who surrounded him, even his attempted destruction of the enemy, all these had come to nothing. Girding his shattered strength together, he resolved upon one last attempt to live up to the best that was in him, and to that end had set himself to lift out of the despair into which they had been thrust the bereaved family of the German, Hooven. [2:276–77]

Charity, surely, should be within his range—but this effort too is doomed to failure. Prostrated by his nerves, Presley learns of the Hoovens' departure for San Francisco too late to find them. He encounters Minna, the oldest daughter, only after she has become a prostitute; and suddenly (although not surprisingly when we remember the danger that Flossie represented in *Vandover and the Brute*) the girl presents yet another aspect of that unendurable Other:

> "Well, but—but how are you getting on?" he demanded.
> Minna laughed scornfully.
> "I?" she cried. "Oh, *I've* gone to hell. It was either that or starvation."
> Presley regained his room at the club, white and trembling. [2:298]

In the break between those last two paragraphs, in Presley's terrified flight, another fissure opens in the text. Presley, and the narrator and reader, can contemplate the working girl's unleashed sexuality only from the haven of a gentlemen's club.

Presley virtually realizes his own situation: "A superstitious fear assailed him that he was, in a manner, marked; that he was foredoomed to fail. Minna had come—had been driven to this; and he, acting too late upon his tardy resolve, had not been able to prevent it. Were the horrors, then, never to end? Was the grisly spectre of consequence to dance forever in his vision?" (2:298). The answer would seem to be yes, for certainly Presley is never able to redeem himself by acting effectively. He has set himself to rescue Mrs. Hooven, but she dies of exposure and starvation as he is attending a sumptuous dinner party at the home of a P. & S.W. vice-president.

The juxtaposed scenes, like those of Hurstwood, Carrie, and other characters at the end of *Sister Carrie*, provoke reflections on the contrast between prosperity and misery; in both cases the brutal reality of suffering is acknowledged yet contained as part of a panorama. By the end of the novel Presley has regained the role of the spectator, forgotten his vulnerability, and reconciled himself to what has passed. Gazing at the California coast from the sea, he contemplates the vista of scenes and events as if it were a novel he has just finished: "Already it was far distant from him; but once again it rose in his memory, portentous, sombre, ineffaceable. He passed it all in review" (2:358). And from that distance he finds an impersonal order at work. "Greed, cruelty, selfishness, and inhumanity are short-lived; the individual suffers, but the race goes on. Annixter dies, but in a far-distant corner of the world a thousand lives are saved. The larger view always and through all shams, all wickednesses, discovers the Truth that will, in the end, prevail, and all things, surely, inevitably, resistlessly work together for good" (2:361). This philosophical optimism, affirming that a benevolent order is immanent in nature, assures the spectator that there is indeed no *need* for action.

The paralysis of the observer, like the apparition of the brute, recurs repeatedly in naturalism; it inheres not only in such dissonant moments as those I have noted in *The Octopus* but in the form itself. The tensions between determinism and reformism, between quotidian realism and the exotic setting inhabited by the Other, reveal the structure of the genre. It is perfectly logical for readers and critics to ask how, if society is such a close-knit causal fabric, one can appeal for change. Schor and Walcutt, relying on a familiar ideology of the privilege of art, attempt to provide a logical answer by proposing that the act of writing itself overcomes the paradox. In the sense that the production of narrative is itself an act in which the naturalists reshape ideological and literary materials in a fashion that continues to engage and affect readers well into the second half of the twentieth century, they are correct. But that statement implies a wholly different model of causality than the notion that the exercise of creative intelligence and the communication of author and reader transcend determinism, which depends precisely on the radical disjuncture between action and understanding that the novels figure as paralysis. The insight and good intentions of the author and reader, or of a character who represents the author and reader, can be envisioned as affecting causal processes and determined events only through a vague, virtually magical process. All Presley's attempts to descend from the privileged level of observation and intervene in events—to go slumming in determinism, we might call it—are failures. In his emancipation from causal processes he is as ineffectual as Derrick or Dyke; he may in his mo-

126
Form
and
History
in
American
Literary
Naturalism

ments of insight be almost omniscient, but he is always almost impotent.

The exemption from determinism thus itself becomes a disturbing confinement; the barrier that separates the privileged spectator from the helpless actor, the free from the unfree, seems to imprison both. And when the spectator does become involved in events, his privilege seems alarmingly precarious. Presley's failures actually jeopardize his immunity. Again, if we follow determinist ideas to their logical conclusion, readers and critics may reasonably ask how anyone can get outside the fabric of causality. Are the possibilities for self-awareness not themselves contingent—surely *all* the characters of naturalism and indeed we ourselves must be vulnerable to impersonal forces? From some broader perspective might our own understanding not seem as partial and conditional, even as simple and selfish as that of a brute? And more immediately, especially in the world of these novels, might we not be brutalized at any moment by some disaster? If our understanding is incomplete, may we not even now be making the choices that will lead to catastrophe? Both in their abstract logic and their narrative sequence naturalist novels, persistently as they assert the contrary, imply that the barrier that separates the classes and the two kinds of characters is pierced by proletarianization as well as observation, opening a scandalous possibility that threatens the very gesture of control the genre also implies.

This gesture of control affirms the existence of a perspective that is detached, unconditioned, objective—a perspective that corresponds to the epistemological premises and aesthetic program of naturalism and the claim to convey "facts" delineated in Chapter 1. It affirms the possibility that an adequate understanding can envision and may be able to effect changes that will make society better, more rationally organized, more humane. Schor and Walcutt, looking past the dissonances of the novels and formal tensions of the genre to affirm naturalism as, if not a viable, at least an honorable and reasonable, program for reform, *complete* that gesture of control. The task of my own analysis is rather different: it does not affirm or negate the project of naturalism but is oblique to it, as I rewrite the assertions and antinomies of naturalism in terms of historical contradictions and reconstruct its historical conditions of possibility and its intervention in those conditions. To do so is of course to engage in my own project—I do not claim to be merely a spectator myself—but to give the assertions of the texts I examine a rather different place in that project. In Chapter 3 I examined some of the ideological discourses that were taken up into naturalism. Those stereotypes, propositions, pleas, and laments were relatively limited and local discourses; in this chapter I will propose an affinity between naturalism and a more comprehensive ideological formation. Not surprisingly, the most revealing jux-

taposition is between naturalism and one of the political programs
for social change that took shape during what Richard Hofstadter
calls "The Age of Reform" from populism to the New Deal.[34] The
populist movement from the late 1870s through the 1890s was in
fact roughly contemporary with the formative period of American
literary naturalism, and its impact is registered in the texts.[35] But
the form I have analyzed is fundamentally incompatible with this
mass democratic movement, for it imagines the "toilers" as brutalized, disruptive Others and identifies reform rather with a privileged
perspective that is middle class and yet somehow emancipated
from its conditioned location into a realm of understanding and
free will. In this imaginative structure populism can be represented
only as another dangerous force, and indeed it is thus that agrarian
activism appears in *The Octopus*.

Naturalism anticipates progressivism, a very different movement
which, although it has roots in the 1890s and earlier, developed
after the turn of the century. The emergence of professional social
science and the elaboration of the ideology of professionalism belong to the same period and can be understood in the same frame
of reference. Of course, none of these changes "causes" or is
caused by the others; in order to juxtapose them what we must do
is trace each back, not to causes, but to limiting conditions, which
we may formulate in the most general terms as the social and
economic history that has already been evoked and the gradual
transition, inseparable from changing social and economic conditions, from a laissez-faire to a corporatist ideology. From this perspective, too, the analysis of the immanent ideology of naturalism
appears not as an antiquarian project but as part of an effort to
understand our history and ourselves, for we live today in a world
shaped by these transformations.

The progressive movement that came into being and decisively
changed American politics and the American state between 1900
and the First World War was an immensely complex and is an
immensely controversial phenomenon. Any broad account, and
particularly any brief account, of progressivism is vulnerable to
the danger of overgeneralization; progressivism was a force in municipal, state, and national politics and took specific forms at
each level of organization, in each region, in each period. But historians generally agree that the goals most progressives shared
were to end political corruption and increase public participation
in government, and to extend government activity in order to allevi-
ate social and economic distress.[36] The progressives present themselves as disinterested, virtuous individuals who—in contrast to
other political actors, who are the agents of interest groups—want
to reform society for the good of all. The opposition to reform, and
the forces that endanger the American way of life, are attributed to

128
Form
and
History
in
American
Literary
Naturalism

two self-interested and selfish sources: the large corporation and the various political forces representing the working class—primarily socialism, organized labor, and urban political machines. *The Octopus's* two central images of the brute as the railroad and the insurrectionary mob and the two pressing ideological concerns identified at the beginning of Chapter 3—concisely, the amoral economic order and class struggle—are crucial to progressive thought as well.

Historian George Mowry, using as his specific example a political situation to which *The Octopus* has already indirectly introduced us, describes "the progressive mind" like this:

> the California progressive reacted politically when he felt himself hemmed in, and his place in society threatened by the monopolistic corporation on the one side, and by organized labor and socialism on the other. . . . In the opening speech of the progressive crusade against the Southern Pacific in Los Angeles, Marshall Stimson voiced a fundamental principle. The three choices which confronted the voters of the city, he said, were between, "a government controlled by corporate interests, Socialism, or if we have the courage, unselfishness and determination, a government of individuals."[37]

The high moral tone Stimson takes, his affirmation of the role of the disinterested individual in politics, and his assumption that the government can and should be a neutral instrument of the public good are essential elements of progressivism. The affinity between this hemmed-in progressive calling for a government of unselfish individuals and the naturalist spectator already suggests a structural similarity between the two systems.

It is much easier to report what the progressives said they were doing than it is to establish what they thought they were doing, why they wanted to do it, and what in the end they actually accomplished. I cannot, as I have said before, engage fully with the many controversies of historical interpretation that are summoned up by my analyses. Clearly, the backgrounds and subjective intentions of the progressives were diverse; equally clearly, it would be informative to generalize about them. But for my purposes the central questions are, first, How did the progressives imagine society and their own place in it?, and second, What were the effects of progressive reforms? The answers to these questions are closely related, for the writing of progressive thought into social reality provides a sharp image of its structure.

We may set against the progressives' own claims certain historians' assertion that whatever the needs or intentions of reformers, the objective results of progressive reforms were conservative. Progressives certainly did at times come into conflict with the interests of business. Nor, for that matter, can one speak of the "interests of

business" as if those interests were always clear to the parties concerned and were always homogeneous; groups within the corporate
elite often waged fierce battles, both for measures profitable to
particular sectors and for their own visions of how social stability
was to be achieved.[38] But progressive agitation consistently served
to channel unrest into movements which did not challenge the
fundamental order of society, that is, which reproduced the relations of production; and one can argue that their reforms strengthened the position of the powerful by extending the influence of state
apparatuses that they controlled. But the concrete is richer than the
abstract; let me open this question by evoking a historical tableau
in which the allegiances and ambiguities of progressivism are figured. Mowry describes how the same progressives who in 1906
began an attack on the Southern Pacific with the words just quoted,
in 1911 allied themselves with the machine in order to defeat a
Socialist who had won a primary election and stood a good chance
of becoming mayor of Los Angeles:

> When the implications of Harriman's victory became clearer, a
> panic swept through the business elements of the city. Almost
> immediately regulars and reformers joined forces to down this
> threat of "the lawless elements," as Earl of the *Express* called
> them. . . . According to the Fresno progressive, Chester Row-
> ell, "Churches and saloons, partisans and nonpartisans, Re-
> publicans, Democrats, and Independents, reformers and per-
> formers, Otis and Earl, Parker and Lissner, men who hate and
> distrust each other [were] united against the menace of class
> rule." . . . This was the church militant of middle-class capital-
> ism drawn up against "the forces of evil."[39]

The rhetoric of "lawlessness" and "evil" is by now familiar. Faced
with a threat from the Other, at this critical moment the progressives' concern for a morally ordered society collapses into a concern simply for an ordered society.

At this municipal level progressives tended to concentrate on (to
put it in their own language) "cleaning up city politics"; the image
in John Hay's *Breadwinners* of men with foreign names and without
ethics running the town government for their own profit while the
educated citizens neglect their civic duties suggests how middle-
class reformers saw the situation. The commission and manager
charters proposed by progressives tended, James Weinstein argues,
to increase the influence of business on city government and de-
crease public participation in decision-making. He notes that the
Socialist party opposed them for three reasons: "the elimination of
ward representations, which meant the end of minority representation; the extreme concentration of power in the hands of the commission, which meant quick decisions and little time to mobilize
opposition; and the 'fallacy' of the nonpartisan ballot, which meant

130
Form
and
History
in
American
Literary
Naturalism

the elimination of three-way contests for office and an emphasis on personality, rather than party."[40] Also, because of his training and his mandate, the city manager often approached running a city as if it were a business and was sympathetic to business interests (pp. 111–12). Weinstein sums up his analysis of municipal progressivism like this: "Developed and led by business groups, the movement fulfilled the requirements of progressivism by rationalizing city government and institutionalizing the methods and values of the corporations that had come to dominate American economic life. The end result of the movements was to place city government firmly in the hands of the business class" (p. 115).

Complementing Weinstein's analysis of progressive reform in the cities, Gabriel Kolko argues that federal regulation of business was not an attempt to limit the power of corporations but an effort to "rationalize" the economy. He writes: "Progressivism was initially a movement for the political rationalization of business and industrial conditions, a movement that operated on the assumption that the general welfare of the community could be best served by satisfying the concrete needs of business."[41] In the most radical reinterpretation of progressivism, Kolko asserts both that the political process that resulted in the enactment of progressive reforms was dominated by business interests and that the results of such reforms objectively benefited those interests. The first point is the more controversial; although Kolko's thesis has been widely criticized, David Kennedy points out that if questions of tone are set aside, much of that criticism has contended that "Kolko really said nothing new when he remarked the basically pro-capitalist character of progressivism."[42] Such a revelation of the interested nature of the progressive movement does not exhaust its significance, as we will see, but it does suggest the uses of the rhetoric of neutrality.

For Kolko what progressivism accomplishes is, in the broadest analysis, to initiate something he calls "political capitalism": "the utilization of political outlets to attain conditions of stability, predictability, and security—to attain rationalization—in the economy" (p. 3). Like the antimonopoly, anticorporate attitudes (such as the attacks on the Southern Pacific) more vociferously announced by progressives, such a program clearly reflects a felt need to control the forces at work in economic processes. Government intervention in the economy is, according to Weinstein, one of the "two essential aspects of the liberal state as it developed in the Progressive Era" (p. x). The other—intimately related to the first, as evidenced in the repetitious appeals to stability and rationality—is the replacement of the ideology of laissez-faire by (in Weinstein's words) "an ideal of a responsible social order in which all classes could look forward to some form of recognition and sharing in the benefits of an everexpanding economy. Such a corporate order was, of course, to be based on what banker V. Everitt Macy called 'the industrial and

commercial structure which is the indispensable shelter of us all'"
(p. x). Both the "non-partisan," more "efficient" commission and
manager forms of city government and federal regulation of the
economy simultaneously served the interests of business and pro-
claimed their neutrality and social responsibility.

As Weinstein puts it, the "key word in the new corporate vision of
society was responsibility" (p. x). Social welfare programs, like reforms of municipal government, maintained the power of the privileged classes by channeling unrest and consolidated it by extending social control apparatuses. Weinstein shows, for example, that
"company workmen's compensation plans were designed to reduce
the need for independent political action by labor, as well as the
appeal of unionism in the large corporations" (p. 47). Kolko's analysis of political capitalism in fact makes a place for such management of conflict when he writes that by "security" he means "protection from the political attacks latent in any formally democratic
political structure" (p. 3). But we need not, in recognizing this
effect, necessarily challenge the sincerity of progressive activists
who proposed humanitarian reforms. As Weinstein writes,

> Of course some middle-class reformers, like *New Republic*
> editor Herbert Croly, understood that progressive democracy
> was "designed to serve as a counterpoise to the threat of
> working class revolution." But even for them the promotion of
> reform was not an act of cynicism: they simply sought a way
> to be immediately effective, to have real influence. Their pur-
> pose was not only to serve as defenders of the social system,
> but also to improve the human condition. In the most pro-
> found sense they failed, and badly; yet they were a good deal
> more than simply lackeys of the capitalist class. [p. xi]

What we are concerned with is not only sincerity—which after
all assumes the unity of an individual's subjective intent in a way
no longer particularly credible in either historical analysis or critical theory—but something much more important: the horizons of
imagination. In the broadest sense I am suggesting that naturalism
and progressivism share what Althusser might call a problematic.
Charles Child Walcutt, as we have seen, finds in the novels an
image of the "scientist-reformer" who must prove "that the state of
man needs to be improved, and that human conditions are determined by the operation of material causes which can be traced,
recorded, understood, and, finally, controlled" (p. 24). It is a very
short step from naturalism's gesture of control to progressivism's,
from the sympathy and good intentions of the naturalist spectator to
the altruistic and ultimately authoritarian benevolence of the progressive reformer.

The mingling of compassion for the poor and alarm over their
disruptive potential that characterizes progressive reform (and that

132
Form
and
History
in
American
Literary
Naturalism

is, of course, continuous with the ideological discourses of class and crime examined in Chapter 3) is appropriately exemplified in an anecdote published in 1890 by journalist and reformer Jacob Riis:

> A man stood at the corner of Fifth Avenue and Fourteenth Street the other day, looking gloomily at the carriages that rolled by, carrying the wealth and fashion of the avenues to and from the big stores down town. He was poor, and hungry, and ragged. This thought was in his mind: "They behind their well-fed teams have no thought for the morrow; they know hunger only by name, and ride down to spend in an hour's shopping what would keep me and my little ones from want a whole year." There rose up before him the picture of those little ones crying for bread around the cold and cheerless hearth—then he sprang into the throng and slashed about him with a knife, blindly seeking to kill, to revenge.
>
> The man was arrested, of course, and locked up. To-day he is probably in a mad-house, forgotten. And the carriages roll by to and from the big stores with their gay throng of shoppers. . . .
>
> Nevertheless the man and his knife had a mission. . . . They represented one solution of the problem of ignorant poverty *versus* ignorant wealth that has come down to us unsolved, the danger-cry of which we have lately heard in the shout that never should have been raised on American soil—the shout of "the masses against the classes"—the solution of violence.
>
> There is another solution, that of justice. The choice is between the two. Which shall it be?[43]

Riis is the moral citizen, concerned for the welfare of this unfortunate man—quite genuinely, one feels, although he represents the poor only in the most clichéd terms—and also concerned for the welfare of society as a whole. Such class antagonism should never have arisen in America, he laments. To resolve it he appeals not to those who *have* a problem, the poor—indeed the poor themselves *are* the problem—but to the privileged, to those he assumes have the understanding and the power to choose the direction America will take. Riis looks over the shoulder of the man with the knife to awaken the comfortable to, in his profoundly significant title, *How the Other Half Lives*. The relations between the author, the reader, and the character whose actions we contemplate are structured quite precisely as they are in the naturalist novel.

Riis's book also draws on racial and class stereotypes already familiar to us. To take just one of many examples, he writes that the tenement dwellers in one area "share such shelter as the ramshackle structures afford with every kind of abomination rifled from the dumps and ash barrels of the city. Here too, shunning the light, skulks the unclean beast of dishonest idleness. 'The Bend' is the home of the tramp as well as the rag-picker" (p. 49). In New York or San Francisco, it is also Vandover's ultimate home. Although the attack of "the man with the knife" presages the impending blood-bath of class war evoked most directly in *The Breadwinners*, the image of the Other that dominates Riis's work is that of the victim; again the tensions embodied in this double image of the brute are already familiar.

The man's "little ones" are particularly appealing as objects of assistance, for they share their father's victimage but are only vulnerable and not menacing as well. The second book Riis wrote in his campaign against the housing conditions of the slums was in fact called *The Children of the Poor*, and many reformers addressed their efforts to improving the lot of working-class children. Robert Wiebe writes that if "humanitarian progressivism had a central theme, it was the child. He united the campaigns for health, education, and a richer city environment, and he dominated much of the interest in labor legislation. . . . The most popular versions of legal and penal reform also emphasized the needs of youth."[44] The paternalism and sentimentality associated with the image of the child are less prevalent in naturalism than in progressivism, but we will see that they are not entirely absent.

Such paternalism was not only directed at children, however. Los Angeles reformer Charles Dwight Willard, writing in 1912, provides an example of how the "keyword" responsibility is used to figure social relations in terms of the roles of almoner and dependent: "There is . . . a manifest disposition on the part of the people to demand that more and more enterprises of the charitable sort be taken over by public authority. This illustrates the growing sense of responsibility that society feels for the care of its own unfortunates."[45] Willard also deals with the question of criminality, explicitly rejecting the image of the criminal as vicious brute in favor of the image of the victim: "The popular idea concerning the inmates of prisons is that they are all wild beasts with more than human cunning. This description fits only an insignificant percentage of them. Nearly all are below par mentally, and great numbers of them are sick. What they need most of all is something they have had little of in their lives, namely, kindness" (p. 7). The criminal here certainly has not been advanced to full humanity and reciprocity— Willard still credits the existence of that small percentage of vicious brutes, and the other inmates are dull brutes. As criminologist Anthony Platt points out, progressive reformers "shared the view of more conservative professionals that 'criminals' were a distinct and dangerous class, indigenous to working-class culture, and a threat to 'civilized' society. They differed mainly in the procedures by

134

Form
and
History
in
American
Literary
Naturalism

which the 'criminal class' should be controlled or neutralized."[46]
The criminal remains an Other to be controlled, although through
apparently more benevolent means.

When Willard writes that "society" feels responsible for unfortunates, he writes from the point of view of the disinterested progressive who represents society, who considers the good of all citizens
including those who are (and I use the word precisely) the objects
of that benevolence. He arrogates to himself, as "society," the power
of diagnosing a social problem and deciding how to solve it; the
measures he advocates assume the intervention of members of one
class in the lives of another. He reports, for example, that "the most
successful work ever done in Chicago in dealing with men tramps
and getting the truth out of them was done by a woman, a subordinate in the Associated Charities. She was young, unmarried and
rather attractive in appearance, and for a number of years her sole
business was to talk to tramps, make them tell her the truth, advise
with them and help them to get a fresh grip, if there was any good
left in them" (p. 7). The problem is defined as inducing the "unfortunate" to transform his life according to the values of the reformer,
so that not only society as a whole but these particular defectives
can be reformed and improved. Humanitarians never seem to suspect that clients might have ideas and desires of their own about
what their problem, if any, is, and what ought to be done about
it. The passage registers the independence and resistance of the
tramps, however, in the need to "make them tell the truth," a phrase
that manifests not only the stereotype of dishonesty but the impact
of the men's refusal to open themselves to the definition and control of the reformer. We are reminded that the interests of the two
groups are in fact *not* the same, no matter how fervently one invokes the good of "society" and the good intentions of the reformer.

The imputed passivity and victimage of the criminal opens the
door to progressive reforms, for the criminal and other unfortunates
are seen not as evil but as "sick" and hence potentially curable.
Historical criminologist Ronald Boostrom writes: "Because of the
efforts of Progressive reformers, correctional criminology was institutionalized as the legitimate approach to the social problem of
crime. It became useful as a policy science for elite groups in
rationalizing the creative management of 'problem populations' in
the new corporate state. Unlike regulatory efforts that were supposed to keep 'criminaloid robber barons' in line, these mechanisms could not be controlled by the target population—the poor,
the alien, and the social outcast."[47] The rhetoric of neutrality and
responsibility cannot be separated from a practice in which the
problem and the solution are attributed to two different classes.
Like naturalism, progressivism marks out two asymmetrical roles
for its cast of characters, enacting a gesture of control in which the
rational (and privileged) manage the brutal (and powerless).

Weinstein writes of the progressives rationalizing city government, Kolko of their rationalizing the economy, Boostrom of their rationalizing the apparatus of social control. Of the last Platt generalizes: "The Progressive reformers saw criminal justice as a problem of 'social engineering.' Believing that United States society had become both more complex and more subject to disruption by the end of the nineteenth century, they advocated more restraint and regulation. But unlike earlier specialists in social control, they viewed the criminal justice apparatus as an institution for *preventing* disorder and *harmonizing* social conflicts, as well as simply *reacting* with brute force."[48] Maintaining order—that is, maintaining the existing social relations—is taken for granted as the only rational political goal. And how could we doubt the benevolence—however authoritarian—of reformers who act, not in their own interests, but as neutral representatives of an essentially undivided America, using their reason to ensure that society functions in an efficient, orderly, rational way? The notions of "reason" and "rationality" carry as much normative baggage as those of "reality" and "realism."

Wiebe notes the emergence early in the twentieth century of a political theory whose advocates "were convinced that the process of becoming an expert, of immersing oneself in the scientific method, eradicated petty passions and narrow ambitions, just as it removed faults in reasoning. The product was the perfect bureaucrat, whose flawlessly wired inner box guaranteed precisely accurate responses within his specialty. . . . At this level, the theory purported to describe government by science, not by men" (p. 161). Such a theory of the expert and the state tended to transform issues from questions of political policy into questions of feasibility. Weinstein notes a similar attitude in the National Civic Federation, an organization through which businessmen worked for reform; its members preferred to keep "social questions out of the arena of public debate, . . . [and] started with the assumption that problems were essentially technical, that the framework of the political economy need only be rationalized and that 'experts' applying their skills in the assumed common interest could best do the job" (pp. 30–31). The axioms underlying many programs of reform were that efficiency and order are by definition desirable and that society could and should be managed by experts who possess specialized knowledge that enables them to act effectively to achieve ends beneficial to all. This ideology is at least as much an unconsciousness as an opinion, for it circumscribes the questions that can be shaped: one never asks *what* or *why*, only *how*.

The notion that such experts are "social engineers" is a powerful legitimation. The engineer is someone with "know-how," someone who takes hold of and manipulates objects and forces to accomplish a clear-cut task. In the new conditions of industrial capitalism

136
Form
and
History
in
American
Literary
Naturalism

during the late nineteenth century, in fact, engineering itself was transformed and emerged as a newly professional and prestigious field. Alan Trachtenberg writes:

> The schools, the professional societies, the new roles of responsibility within corporate hierarchies, fostered a new quality of mind and outlook: disciplined, systematic, administrative. Trained to combine the findings of formal science with economic, legal, and logistical considerations, the new engineers brought into industry an apparently detached, objective, and highly specialized approach to solving problems. But whether designing the flow of work in factories or rating the output of machines, the engineer served finally a chronic need of the industrial system: to impose system and order, through improved machinery, for the sake of assuring a reliable return on investments.[49]

My point is not that other experts modeled themselves directly on engineers or naively thought that human behavior and social forces could be regulated in the same way as machines. As Wiebe suggests in *The Search for Order*, the causal networks of human society are frequently recognized as virtually infinite in their complexity and the most influential social principles resembled "orientations much more than laws, stressed techniques of constant watchfulness and mechanisms of continuous management" (p. 145). But the image of social engineering does suggest the widespread fascination with the apparently pure instrumentality and the practical effectiveness of engineering. It is worth noting that two of the most self-assured and successful characters in naturalism, Weedon Scott in *White Fang* and Ames in *Sister Carrie*, are engineers.

The movement for "scientific management" demonstrates the process of rationalization and its concomitant concentration of power in the hands of an elite applied to the labor process. Frederick Winslow Taylor, the most articulate initiator of this movement, provided a succinct expression of its principles.[50] Taylor asserts first of all that scientific management works for the common good; it "has for its very foundation the firm conviction that the true interests of [employers and employees] are one and the same," and he insists repeatedly that while his system increases profits it makes the worker more prosperous too.[51] But in the interest of their united prosperity, management and labor must divide their tasks, for according to Taylor "in almost all the mechanic arts the science which underlies each workman's act is so great and amounts to so much that the workman who is best suited actually to do the work is incapable (either through lack of education or through insufficient mental capacity) of understanding this science" (p. 41). Therefore, efficiency requires the separation of mental and manual labor. The knowledge of a particular task that defined the skilled workman is gathered and centralized in the hands (or rather, minds) of experts who then prescribe, quite literally, the employee's every motion. The individual worker theoretically becomes more efficient, and he or she is also reduced from an independent actor to the mere support of a procedure determined elsewhere.

When Taylor launches into his famous story about the introduction of scientific management in handling pig iron, his mild comment on workmen's mental incapacity, based on the assumption that brains and brawn are attributes of different groups, metamorphoses into the image of a very dull brute indeed. The most suitable pig-iron handler is "a man of the type of the ox,—no rare specimen of humanity, difficult to find and therefore very highly prized. On the contrary, he was a man so stupid that he was unfitted to do most kinds of laboring work, even" (p. 62). Predictably, the man chosen for the first experiment is not only extraordinarily unintelligent and inarticulate, but speaks with an accent: " 'Vell, I don't know vat you mean'" (p. 44). Like another German immigrant, Hooven, Schmidt is a comic figure who nevertheless recognizably evokes the brute. Taylor's attempt to sever the understanding of a task from its execution, to create two separate categories of autonomous thought and automatic action, casts the "scientific" manager and worker in roles that once again strongly resemble naturalism's spectator and brute —although beside the complete control of the labor process imagined by Taylorism, naturalist novels tend to seem irresolute indeed.

Scientific management establishes control of information and, in Harry Braverman's words, makes *"use of this monopoly over knowledge to control each step of the labor process"* (p. 119). For the manager, the engineer, the expert on social and economic forces, possession of a specialized and exclusive body of knowledge is power. Thomas Haskell, examining the emergence of professional social science during this period, adds to the developing pattern the suggestion that a "profession has many of the qualities of a self-perpetuating monopoly—in this case, a monopoly in authoritative opinion about the nature of man and society."[52] The key word here is authoritative, for although many scholars and laymen in the mid-nineteenth century were engaged in social investigation, they did not constitute an "ongoing, disciplined community of inquiry" (p. 24) like that of professional academic social science, whose emergence in America was "underway in the 1880's and in full swing by the 1890's" (p. 25).

Haskell traces the rise of professional experts on society to the rapidly increasing interdependence of life in industrializing, urbanizing, modernizing America. He suggests that "reflective individuals experienced a general recession in the perceived location of the important events, people, and institutions that influenced their lives" (p. 40). Interdependence, he argues, fostered both a

138
Form
and
History
in
American
Literary
Naturalism

preoccupation with causality—a suggestion that is certainly borne out by the concerns of literary naturalism—and a hunger for expert guidance: "Professional social science could not exist as long as human affairs seemed readily and self-evidently explicable. . . . But when the more articulate members of the public experience a recession of causation . . . they look upon the inquirer as a man of extraordinary importance. For his task is to pursue causation, to track it down. . . . As causes recede and growing interdependence introduces more and more contingency into each chain of causation, the realm of inquiry must expand and the conditions of satisfying explanation must change. Common sense fails and the claim of expertise gains plausibility" (p. 44). The result is the institutionalization of a prestigious "community of competence" that contemporary professionals saw as "a major cultural *reform*, a means of establishing authority so securely that the truth and its proponents might win the deference even of a mass public, one that threatened to withhold deference from all men, all traditions, and even the highest values" (p. 65). Haskell's history of this movement is fascinating in its own right, but useful here particularly for the light it casts on the developing ideology of professionalism and the affinity between the "vicarious, deliberate, rational manner of the social researcher—presumably always master of his data, holding society at arm's length as a mere object of examination—but also in the immediate, haphazard, unaware manner of the voter, lover, consumer, and job-seeker who is himself an object and onrushing element of the social process" (p. 16), and the naturalist spectator.

Haskell focuses our attention on the institutions and ideology of the professions as important phenomena that emerged during this period and that remain extremely influential today. Burton Bledstein indeed makes "the culture of professionalism" virtually coextensive with modern American society when he asserts that it "has been so basic to middle-class habits of thought and action that a majority of twentieth-century Americans has taken for granted that all intelligent modern persons organize their behavior, both public and private, according to it."[53] Bledstein paints a pessimistic portrait of the effect of expert advice on its consumers; his professionals construct a world that looks very much like naturalism's brutal realm of force:

> Professionals not only lived in an irrational world, they cultivated that irrationality by uncovering abnormality and perversity everywhere: in diseased bodies, criminal minds, political conspiracies, threats to the national security. An irrational world, an amoral one in a state of constant crisis, made the professional person who possessed his special knowledge indispensable to the victimized client, who was reduced to a condition of desperate trust. The culture of professionalism

exploited the weaknesses of Americans—their fears of violent, sudden, catastrophic and meaningless forces that erupted unpredictably in both individual and mass behavior. [p. 102]

I would go further and suggest that the tendency of professionalism is particularly conservative when, as in the progressive model, the expert is cast as the disinterested agent of a neutral state. In the name of the good of all, power over most is exercised by some; the disabling voice of the expert diagnoses and prescribes.[54] The assumption that decisions affect our lives—whether about arms control, remedies for unemployment, or one's own medical treatment—are to be made by professionals is, it seems to me, only more pervasive today.

The meaning of "middle class," a central category in Bledstein's analysis, is of course notoriously difficult; and Bledstein draws very broad consequences from his concrete evidence (he admits both difficulties, offering his book as "not definitive but exploratory, probing" [p. xi]). But even more than Haskell's, Bledstein's work asks us to consider the significance of the professional in American ideology and experience. And such consideration in its turn suggests that the structure of thought immanent in naturalism is by no means so antiquated as critics' ritual ridicule of determinism would suggest.

In the ideology of professionalism the expert seems to offer the solution to social problems—Anthony Platt notes that progressive reformers advocated "professionalizing the police and other agencies of social control" (p. xxvii) as the way to eliminate corruption and incompetence in the criminal justice system. But professionalism is also a solution to individual problems; Boostrom comments that those reformers were "meeting their own needs for professional status and prestige while sincerely rationalizing their need to be public servants acting in the public welfare."[55] Bledstein's description of the competitive, status-conscious world of the professional brings matters very close to home indeed. Pizer's observation that "because we ourselves are also creatures of place—that is, we are middle-class—we can sense the tragic import for our own lives in the fall of a Hurstwood" (p. 81) takes on a fuller significance in this context. It implicitly centers author and reader in a particular location, which is a "community of competence," and it also accurately captures the anxiety shared by naturalism's potential victim of proletarianization and the professional literary critic. Self-esteem, social status, and financial security depend on professional success and on the prestige of the professional role. Like the literate spectators we have met in naturalism, professionals are constantly at risk; their understanding, whatever its impact on the world outside the window, above all constructs the privileged ground that they occupy (including the university and disciplinary organiza-

140
Form
and
History
in
American
Literary
Naturalism

tions). As Haskell puts it, "the common aim of the men and women who participated in the movement [to establish authority] was to construct safe havens for sound opinion" (p. 64).

Naturalism not only manifests structural affinities with professionalism in general and professionalizing social science in particular, but offers itself as a kind of social science. It concerns itself with objective facts conveyed by an objective researcher. Like the anthropologist, the naturalist ventures into an exotic land to bring back reports on the savage inhabitants. Like the sociologist, he provides a portrait of society in which causal processes are visible, comprehensible, potentially open to intervention. Positivism and determinism figure in the philosophical sources of social science as well as naturalism, but the authors' frequently naive ideas and inevitably amateur status as social inquirers quickly disqualify them in the eyes of the "real" professionals.

In another arena, however, the naturalists might more practically aspire to professionalism. Christopher Wilson has recently examined the belief in authorship itself as a "professional ideal" that a "newly expanded literary marketplace" fostered in the American naturalists. He reports that "popular naturalists like David Graham Phillips, Jack London, Upton Sinclair, and Frank Norris described literary endeavor as a skill based in professional dedication. They said that authorship was not a matter of inspiration, but of rigorous work habits, a watchful eye on market demand, and a sense of one's responsibility to the public."[56] The elaboration of this value system is, as Wilson shows, extraordinarily complex; he notes in passing, for example, the affirmation of the masculinity of the narrative voice. The normative perspective from which the Other is defined and authority is asserted is, in naturalism as elsewhere, essentially masculine, and a full understanding of the ideology of professionalism should eventually include an analysis of how it is bound up with gender identity. But Wilson is primarily concerned with the naturalists' ambivalent relation to the marketplace and commercialism. (The topics of gender ideology and popular fiction will recur, once again in close conjunction, in Chapter 5.) Wilson examines the tensions produced by the fact that their fiction aspires to be both sincere and saleable. Like the work of the progressive reformers and other professionals, the work of the naturalists provides them simultaneously with a legitimate way to serve society and an avenue to personal success. In this sense the act of creating the naturalist novel does itself supply the solution to a problem, although this is scarcely what Walcutt meant by proposing the notion. Defining the Other demarcates the boundary of the self and asserts power and privilege—but even better, portraying proletarianization could, quite literally, enable the naturalist to avoid it.

Not all American naturalists, by any means, subscribed to the professional ideal of authorship that Wilson discusses. Nor did they necessarily subscribe to progressivism, when they lived to see it. Nevertheless, the diverse ideological formations described in this chapter manage and figure the same set of historical contradictions in strikingly similar ways. Just as Wilson finds the popular naturalists' credo inherently unstable, these "solutions" are not static substance but dynamic articulations of difference. The texts of naturalist novels are not perfect realizations of the gesture of control that expresses the form's immanent ideology, as the recurring image of the spectator's immobility reminds us. That paralysis can make it difficult to generate a plot, and we will see that the strategies by which naturalist texts produce a narrative sequence in which someone acts, something happens, and closure is achieved persistently disrupt the novels. In many ways—in unique ways in each novel—naturalist texts are not homogeneous and purely naturalist but specific and various. Those narrative strategies, and those disruptions and discontinuities, are the topic of Chapter 5.

5 Documents, Dramas, and Discontinuities: The Narrative Strategies of American Naturalism

Both the naturalists' imperative to convey "a true picture of life, honestly and reverentially set down" (the phrase is Dreiser's)[1] and the paralysis of the spectator discussed in Chapter 4 suggest the descriptive rather than narrative tendency of the genre. Yet naturalist novels emerge only very gradually and never fully disengage themselves from a novel tradition in which the reader can expect to encounter not only consistent characters moving in a coherent world, but also reported events forming an intelligible series and apparently conveying some significant insight—that is, a novel tradition that is still organized by plot and theme. In naturalism we find a *bricolage* of strategies for generating meaningful sequence and closure. This chapter will examine those strategies and consider the significance of the diverse solutions naturalists invent to resolve this problem of form.[2]

The descriptive program of naturalism can itself provide an organizing principle. Perhaps the most distinctively naturalist strategy consists in a group of devices for arranging essentially static material according to a documentary logic. The strategy I call the plot of decline or fatality, which structures a narrative as the anatomy of a progressive deterioration, also enables construction of an intelligible series and, above all, catastrophic closure. These strategies for generating a narrative syntax complement the immanent ideology outlined in the previous chapters. But there are other strategies as well. When cast in narrative form that gesture of control not only inscribes its own disruption, but must coexist with heterogeneous and even contradictory materials derived from other genres. One principle of the genre criticism I advocate in the first chapter of this study is the inevitable articulation of different generic discourses in a specific text, and such generic discontinuities are particularly marked in this form. Naturalist novels frequently incorporate conventional elements from popular literary genres like the adventure story and the domestic novel and in general have a complex relation to mass culture. And, of course, naturalism exists in constant dialogue with realism.

We have arrived, by a rather different path, at a characterization of naturalism that strongly recalls Lukács's contrast between realism as a narrative and naturalism as a descriptive form. Naturalism's distinctive handling of the reader's distance from characters, its separation of free will and self-awareness from effective action, indeed prohibit the "direct involvement of characters in events" and "general social significance emerging in the unfolding of characters' lives" that Lukács associates with realism. If we rewrite his prescription that significance should emerge through action in more traditional literary categories—losing much, such as the focus on social significance to which I will return in a moment, but not misrepresenting his theory—we find that what he advocates can be seen as a kind of unity of plot and theme. This is a remarkably powerful and persistent idea. For example, when Jonathan Culler rewrites structuralist narrative theory as a synthesized "poetics of the novel," he recommends a surprisingly similar unification:

> the goals towards which one moves in synthesizing a plot are, of course, notions of thematic structures. If we say that the hierarchy of kernels [units of action—the term is Roland Barthes's] is governed by the reader's desire to reach a level of organization at which the plot as a whole is grasped in a satisfying form, and if we take that form to be what Greimas and Lévi-Strauss call the four-term homology, Todorov the modification of a situation, and Kristeva the transformation, we have at least a general principle whose effects at lower levels can be traced. The reader must organize the plot as a passage from one state to another and this passage or movement must be such that it serves as a representation of theme.[3]

Although for Culler plot and theme must be constructed from the separable units of the text, they still aspire toward a coherent, unified figure of action and significance. Culler presents this observation as relevant to the novel in general, yet we may wonder if this is not another case in which the norms of realism insinuate themselves as the natural, necessary procedures of narrative.

At any rate, when Lukács equates realism with the successful correlation of event and meaning, it is scarcely surprising that he goes on to claim that special satisfactions inhere in the realist form. The recognition of an unexpected pattern, the resolution of apparent multiplicity into unity can indeed yield profound psychological satisfaction—the most astute analysis of such pleasure is Freud's work on wit.[4] But surely such recognitions and resolutions play a role in all literature and at all levels of the text. They cannot be the property of any single genre, nor are they the only or even the primary generic markers that identify realism, as work like George Becker's makes clear. I am haunted by the suspicion that realism's successful synthesis of plot and theme is enabled only by the con-

144

Form
and
History
in
American
Literary
Naturalism

trast with an other—in Lukács's case, naturalism or modernism, but there are many less subtle versions of this normative schema—that proposes a different correlation of event and significance and thus "fails" to achieve such unity. If we actually look at the novels of Balzac or Eliot or Howells, do we not find that they construct a kind of closure without ever erasing the marks of their own production and achieving some seamless unity? Is not such evanescent coherence one of the first specters to disappear when we study concrete reading rather than an ideal, normatively "competent" reader modeled on the image of the empirically existing critic? Yet as I have said the image of the unification of plot and theme has proved a powerful one and must be given its due. The opinion that realism produces a particularly satisfying narrative resolution is widespread, and indeed it is precisely its attempt to establish unity and order and its movement toward closure that offend poststructural critics of realism. We are a long way from the satisfactory poetics of narrative that would allow us to discuss this issue rigorously. Nevertheless, the generic text forcefully suggests that the correlation of action and meaning must be considered an element of realism, although it is an element we do not yet fully understand.

It seems to be Culler's acceptance of the category of "plot" that introduces realist norms into his account of the novel (postmodern narrative, surely, requires a different category to comprehend its "events," and so for that matter does *Moby-Dick*). "Plot" suggests a conflict between characters and thus purposeful action, a connected series of incidents and thus a coherent web of causality. It places us in that fabric of society which Lukács explicitly evokes. For Lukács realism correlates not only action and meaning, but *individual* action and *social* meaning. The characters' destinies figure historical truth, in what Jameson calls "an analogy between the entire plot, as a conflict of forces, and the total moment of history itself considered as process."[5] We might think, for example, of how courtship in Jane Austen's novels becomes the focus for complex issues of personal identity and social order and how its conclusion resolves a multiplicity of significant choices into the unifying figure of a wedding.[6] According to Lukács modernism and naturalism sever the connection between the individual and the social and thereby render both unintelligible. He contends that modernism abandons the social for the solitary and subjective, depriving itself of any stable, objective ground on which to organize the personality and transforming reality into a nightmare; naturalism, on the other hand, focuses obsessively on the objective and, lacking a coherent perspective from which to view it, reduces it to chaos.[7]

If we refrain from rejecting this system out of hand as unjustifiably normative and nostalgic and consider it instead as descriptive literary history, we can examine the possibility that Lukács's mod-

ernists and naturalists are writers for whom the historical opportunity to correlate individual action and social meaning in a single,
unified figure has closed.[8] Based on what we have seen in previous
chapters, so too has it closed for the American naturalists. They are
writers who refuse to give up the attempt to imagine the social, yet
fail to propose meaningful correlations between individual choices
and social processes. We may take Haskell's "recession of causation" in an interdependent society as one evocative although imper-
fect image of the historical forces at work here; from the vantage
point of the naturalists the effective causes of events are becoming
less and less immediate, their sense and significance more and
more abstract. There is, of course, a tremendous distance between
this suggestion, which indicates one of the ultimate limiting conditions of the genre, and the more immediate difficulties of the heterogeneous materials out of which the naturalist generates narrative (and in making that observation I reveal myself as a victim of
the same recession). But at the most practical level of plot construction such correlation is difficult because for naturalism the
social means, above all, social problems; hence the problem of
individual action presents itself as the problem of effecting social
change. Yet conventions that derive from realism require that events
remain within the bounds of the "real," and the depiction of profound social change, which would propel us from the present into a
parallel or a future world and thus into utopian or science fiction, is
generically proscribed. The choices that remain to the characters
may be imbued with personal or metaphysical meaning, but they
can never be adequate to the central, social themes of the novel.

Yet naturalism constantly strives for plot. Indeed, it may achieve
the correlation of plot and theme; "unity" is a vague enough term
that in realism and naturalism alike it can always be a matter for
argument. Critics who claim that this or that novel by an author
commonly considered a naturalist (they most often choose Dreiser)
is actually realistic usually demonstrate only the novel's congru-
ence with their own norms and their ingenuity at selecting evidence
and weaving an argument for a work's unity; their claims are made
at the expense of the distinctive formal qualities of either realism or
naturalism. Nevertheless, it is true that naturalism can never be
fully disengaged from realism and that it never discards although it
may violate realistic conventions. We need accept neither Lukács's
valorization of realism nor his denigration of naturalism to find his
distinction between the genres important and insightful. We need
not accept the ideal of the logically consistent and formally unified
text to see that the antinomy between determinism and reformism
does indeed pose problems for a storyteller. As Charles Child Walcutt, working inductively from his analyses of American naturalist
novels, puts it, "naturalism involved a continual *search* for form."[9]
Naturalist novels are not failed realist novels, but they are narratives

146

Form
and
History
in
American
Literary
Naturalism

haunted by realistic expectations; and they are narratives that cobble together a variety of strategies for generating coherence and closure and that, therefore, not infrequently foreground their own contradictions.

The aesthetic ideology of naturalism, as voiced most explicitly and elaborately by Zola, itself militates against the resolution of empirical multiplicity into essential unity. Naturalist representation offers itself not as a correlation of event and significance but as a slice of life, "une tranche de vie." Such representation does not even aspire to totality; after all, whatever slice of life one takes, the next slice and the one after it are not present in it—each part remains itself, and partial. The naturalist's very principle of accuracy, embodied in his allegiance to the irreducible individuality of objects, people, and places, implies a truth found in dispersion rather than in synthesis. The aesthetic ideology of naturalism proposes a relation to reality that is not primarily metaphoric but metonymic; the text is to convey facts themselves, it is to be *continuous* with the world. In this ideology the significance of those facts can be suggested as an abstract idea, however; Lukács complains that in naturalism "metaphor is over-inflated in the attempt to encompass reality. . . . Zola himself confessed to such intentions, declaring: 'In my work there is a hypertrophy of real detail. From the springboard of exact observation it leaps to the stars. With a single beat of the wings, the truth is exalted to the symbol.' "[10] The metonymic narrative can include metaphors that promise to unify it as meaning without reference to event.

And indeed in the practice of American naturalism the claim that something is true is often enough to give it a place in the narrator's discourse. We may take as a representative if unusually striking example of this fascination with the fact the moment in *Sister Carrie* when, in the midst of Hurstwood's flight from Chicago, the action is halted briefly to inform us that Hurstwood makes a call from "one of the first private telephone booths ever erected."[11] The only apparent reason for this piece of historical information to be inserted is an interest in sheer fact; it must be self-sufficiently relevant, for it is never integrated into a thematic structure and has no implications for the novel's plot. Any link we might suggest between naturalism and late nineteenth-century innovations in communication belongs to another level of analysis; more immediately, the detail fits because it describes. It belongs to the documentary logic that is one of the most important narrative strategies of the naturalist novel.

Every narrative, of course, must have some strategy for placing detail. Such strategies are generically specific—descriptive particulars function rather differently in, say, *The Odyssey*, *The Faerie Queene*, *Moby-Dick*, *Ulysses*. Roland Barthes has made the influential suggestion that in realism the circumstantial detail announces the text's reference outside itself, constituting what he calls the "reality effect": "the laugh, the glove, are effects for the sake of reality, notations whose very insignificance authenticates, signs, signifies 'reality.' "[12] For such a procedure to operate as a consequential part of any narrative apparatus a way of thinking that prizes the empirical for its own sake must already have come into being; the reader must already live in a world in which information has to some degree been detached from a context in which it conveys an immediate human meaning or an implication for action. Fredric Jameson links the development of the novel itself to a "fundamental change in the character of social life itself in the great industrial cities of the late nineteenth and early twentieth centuries. . . . [This] new social material . . . no longer seems to offer any 'laws' or *moeurs* or prescribed behavior patterns to describe." He suggests, in fact, that "the older social novel or novel of *moeurs* has some claim to be considered an ancestor of phenomenological or ethnomethodological sociology."[13] But naturalist narrative gives the detail an especially privileged position, including and going beyond the "reality effect." In naturalism details are facts, *data* which when subjected to the proper scrutiny can produce knowledge. That knowledge is seen as not deprived but independent of immediate, interested meaning and as a way of making objective sense out of puzzling social material. The prestige of fact in the naturalist project is perhaps most familiarly figured in the image of the naturalist as researcher: Zola or Upton Sinclair with notebook in hand gathering material for a new novel. In naturalism the detail signifies not only reality but the rigorous investigation of reality.

The aesthetic ideology and documentary project of naturalism link it to other practices like sociology that depend on the separation of the object of knowledge and the knowing subject, the transparency of perception and language, and the self-sufficient authority of fact. John Berger comments that during the nineteenth century "positivism and the camera and sociology grew up together. What sustained them all as practices was the belief that observable quantifiable facts, recorded by scientists and experts, would one day offer man such a total knowledge about nature and society that he would be able to order them both."[14] The development of realism belongs to this period and shares many of the impulses and ideas identified here. But it is in naturalism—that most positive and sociological transformation of realism—that this belief in the development of knowledge as a means of control is invoked most directly, and in naturalism that the formal consequences of a fascination with fact are worked out. As we have already seen and as Berger goes on to suggest, the sequel of the project is unexpected: "the unachieved positivist utopia became, instead, the global system of late capitalism wherein all that exists

148
Form
and
History
in
American
Literary
Naturalism

becomes quantifiable—not simply because it *can be* reduced to a statistical fact, but also because it *has been* reduced to a commodity" (p. 99). In naturalism too the fact takes on a life of its own, not only in the fetishism of the commodity we have seen in *Sister Carrie*, but in the narrative strategy of description.

The organization that naturalists devise to accommodate a discourse conveying such urgent information is an extremely various and flexible strategy that is invoked to give place and purpose to everything from the fragmentary fact to the structure of sequences in a given novel to the series of novels documenting different aspects of society. Zola's colossal genealogical fantasia *Les Rougon-Macquart* is of course the classic example of that last, most general project. Among the American naturalists only Upton Sinclair wrote so many novels and clearly aspires to such a totalizing portrait of society. But there are a number of important novel sequences in American naturalism, if none so comprehensive as Zola's; we may think of Dreiser's *Trilogy of Desire*, Dos Passos's *U.S.A.* trilogy, Farrell's *Studs Lonigan* trilogy. Norris's *Octopus*, in fact, is the first volume of a projected "epic" trilogy of the Wheat (*The Pit* is the second). The series was to be united not by common characters or continuous events but by a concept—by one of Zola's inflated symbols, in Norris's phrase "an idea as big as all outdoors."[15] The most general logic of *The Octopus*, into which Derrick's and Dyke's deteriorations are subsumed, is its relation to this abstraction: "These novels, while forming a series, will be in no way connected with each other save only in their relation to (1) the production, (2) the distribution, (3) the consumption of American wheat. When complete, they will form the story of a crop of wheat from the time of its sowing as seed in California to the time of its consumption as bread in a village of Western Europe."[16] *The Octopus* is also, as its subtitle tells us, "A Story of California"—as *McTeague* is "A Story of San Francisco," and *Maggie* is (in the 1893 edition) "A Story of New York." The portrayal of a place or milieu provides a similarly general and abstract ordering principle for naturalist novels. Thus *Sister Carrie* and *Studs Lonigan* are partly "about" Chicago, and about "the city"; the telephone booth is placed not by its relation to any event but by its location and its relation to an idea. The detail is fixed in the gaze of the spectator; it is related to other details by the circuit through that central perspective. The documentary project organizes the narrative according to a unity not of action but of topic, thus transforming naturalism's descriptive and even static tendency into a strategy for ordering the text.

Even such description involves a kind of action, however, and continues to be coordinated with plot. Barthes once again offers a useful way of thinking about the discrete units of the text. In *S/Z* he suggests that we construct sequence out of kernels operating in the "proairetic code": "whoever reads the text amasses certain data under some generic titles for actions (*stroll, murder, rendezvous*), and this title embodies the sequence; the sequence exists when and because it can be given a name, it unfolds as this process of naming takes place, as a title is sought or confirmed" (p. 19). Such generic titles, frequently presenting themselves as natural constituents of everyday experience, constitute immensely complex, culturally and historically specific vocabularies of human experience that are an important part of that already-shaped material out of which narrative is generated. A wide range of such titles is mobilized in any narrative, and naturalist novels are no exception. But what is most striking about the action of naturalist novels is the constant recurrence of one particular named sequence or "proairetism": the act of looking.

The reiterated gesture of the look is inseparable from the documentary strategy and is dramatized at every level of the text. For example, early in *Sister Carrie* Dreiser surveys Drouet's appearance and character in order to document him as the "type" of—in the slang terms Dreiser cites—the "'drummer'" and the "'masher'" (chap. 1, p. 3). We are provided with the proper categories under which to range the evidence, and then our gaze is carefully directed to informative detail. The gesture produces a kind of metonymic organization: the eye travels from one object to another as in a progression organized by proximity we examine Drouet's suit, shirt, cuff links, rings, watch-chain, shoes, hat. Then, in a less literally metonymic and spatial but equally surveying and successive style, we review his methods of approaching women. The purpose of all this is explicitly documentary: "Lest this order of individual should permanently pass, let me put down some of the most striking characteristics of his most successful manner and method" (chap. 1, p. 3). The same sequencing by proximity and topic can organize an account of a scene or a milieu as well as an individual. The following passage unfolds under the title of the gaze at least as much as the stroll:

> The walk down Broadway, then as now, was one of the remarkable features of the city. There gathered, before the matinée and afterwards, not only all the pretty women who love a showy parade, but the men who love to gaze upon and admire them. . . . Women appeared in their very best hats, shoes, and gloves, and walked arm in arm on their way to the fine shops or theatres strung along from Fourteenth to Thirty-fourth streets. Equally the men paraded with the very latest they could afford. A tailor might have secured hints on suit measurements, a shoemaker on proper lasts and colours, a hatter on hats. [chap. 32, p. 226]

Carrie's movements are subsumed into the pattern of her destiny, but also into a progressively more detailed map of the modern city.

150
Form
and
History
in
American
Literary
Naturalism

Observation is replicated at every level of the text. Carrie too is looking at Drouet: "He was, for the order of intellect represented, attractive, and whatever he had to recommend him, you may be sure was not lost upon Carrie, in this, her first glance" (chap. 1, p. 3). On Broadway everyone is looking at everyone else—the parade is quite self-consciously a spectacle, its purpose seeing and being seen, just as Drouet likes to see and be seen as he dines. The gestural unity of the gaze is also inscribed in relationships among the characters. Thus "Nigger Jeff" and "McEwen of the Shining Slave Makers" are structured by the act of looking: the man on the park bench watches the ants, the reporter watches the lynching and Jeff's mother's mourning. The observers contain and frame the events of the stories; their points of view provide coherence to action that otherwise might seem mere chaotic suffering. Presley's retrospective look over the scenes of *The Octopus* even more markedly attempts to suggest coherence, containment, and therefore closure:

> Well, it was all over now, that terrible drama through which he had lived. Already it was far distant from him; but once again it rose in his memory, portentous, sombre, ineffaceable. He passed it all in review from the day of his first meeting with Vanamee to the day of his parting with Hilma. He saw it all— the great sweep of country opening to view from the summit of the hills at the headwaters of Broderson's Creek; the barn-dance at Annixter's, the harness room with its jam of furious men. . . .[17]

And so on. In a similar strategy, the juxtaposition of brief glimpses of the characters at the end of *Sister Carrie* images the whole of the action and the represented society *as* a whole, evoking an inclusive panorama as a gesture of closure. Thus the role of the spectator and the unity of topic are dramatized in the recurrent gesture of the look.

The spectator's gaze can define the Other without offering itself to view and opening the possibility of a mutual naming. In this sense the naturalist look is Sartre's "regard," the look that denies reciprocity. The brutes who inhabit determinism are treated as objects rather than as self-aware subjects; they are merely components of the spectacle displayed to the reader. When we understand that Drouet is attractive "for that order of intellect," the qualification inevitably invokes the wider perspective and privilege of a reader and narrator who must belong to a superior order. They are not among "the children of endeavour . . . [who] try and are hopeful" but among those who "knowing, smile and approve" (chap. 17, p. 127). The narrator's lofty tone habitually insists upon that distance.

Yet we do participate to some degree in Carrie's yearning. Dreiser

conveys the complex emotional resonance of her longing for the
jacket Drouet can give her, if not exactly for him. He sees, and makes the reader see, the glamor that the kaleidoscope of desire casts on first one object, then another. But just as Carrie ultimately finds nothing that is adequate to her desire, Dreiser immediately reveals each object as meaningful only within a particular system of desire. Thus Carrie regards the opulent scene at Sherry's with admiration until Ames criticizes it; then—as indeed she must if she is not to be reduced to an object by his regard—she stands away from her own desire and tries to adopt his perspective. Dreiser is perhaps the most powerful novelist of a world that offers no stable position from which to view it, a world in which not only the realm of the Other, but the most intimate interactions have become mysterious and alien and must be studied as a series of codes in a foreign language. Reading Dreiser, not just the slums but the whole social order can seem exotic. Dreiser is a kind of perpetual stranger who peers into and yet never loses himself in any milieu, who moves through each point of view and portrays every character from within but remains with none and so sees every character from without as well. The reader's position in relation to the window of observation is constantly shifting; we, and the narrator, are both inside and outside (which may explain why Dreiser is the only naturalist to portray female characters in convincing interior detail). Dreiser's study of the play of intersubjective meanings does indeed make him a kind of sociologist, although he resembles the ethnomethodological students of daily life more than their positive predecessors. For Dreiser, both meaning and identity are structural, positional, and not substantial.

The profound yet partial, painful empathy that constantly distinguishes Dreiser's fiction itself manifests the characteristically naturalist tension between spectatorship and participation. Although this protean vulnerability emerges with particular force in *Sister Carrie*, ambivalent relations to some characters are already implied by the specter of proletarianization and the plot of decline. This narrative strategy (examined in more detail in Chapter 3) is based on biographical sequence—one of the most fundamental and powerful categories of storytelling—and through the inexorable progress of a deterioration and the inevitable disaster that closes it quite successfully generates consequent and coherent narrative. The tale of decline at once risks and rescues the reader, for it figures the fascinating, repellent possibility of a privileged character being swallowed up by brutality; yet the very fatality of the procedure always suggests that the character somehow inevitably belonged to the realm of forces and not the realm of freedom. The interpenetration of the documentary and reforming projects of naturalism and the plot of decline also manages the risk represented by the dizzying prospect downward by constantly affirming the existence of

152
Form
and
History
in
American
Literary
Naturalism

disinterested intelligence. The existence of the discrete, observable fact is inseparable from the existence of the objective observer, although the role of the latter may be elided by the focus on detail—which only renders it the less open to question.

The specter of proletarianization itself implies the need for the spectator to slum in determinism in order to learn through vicarious experience what that repellent yet fascinating world of the Other is like. The spectator must try out the role of the brute in order to control it. Thus one of naturalism's documentary strategies takes the form of a virtually anthropological expedition into the alien territory of the working class and the underclass. The journey of exploration, following an impulse we have already seen toward mapping the social order and especially the city, provides a clear organizing principle for a narrative. Once again we follow a metonymic sequence, as the observer's feet and eyes stray from one spot to another and new regions are filled in on his chart. Such a map is comprehensive not because it is complete—another detail could always be added—but because it includes extreme contrasts, setting rich and poor side by side in the text to evoke the discontinuity of their terrains and providing an abstract and cognitive, although not necessarily concrete and crossable, bridge across the chasm that separates them. Although the realms of the free and the unfree cannot be resolved into a unified figure of plot and theme, they can be contained within the borders of a single map; the gesture of closure is the same one evoked by the image of the panorama. In each case, we encounter not a unity of action but a unity of topic and observation.

Although Hurstwood and Vandover are unable to return from the outer darkness, not all explorers are so unlucky. Humphrey Van Weyden, although he wears the clothes and does the work of a sailor, eventually escapes the realm of brutal force. And in *The People of the Abyss* (1903), Jack London's descriptive account of his experiences in the slums of London, the naturalist transgresses the boundary between classes with impunity. He identifies his expedition as a dangerous one by alleging that respectable Londoners find it incredible; they see an adventure into the heart of the civilized city as at least as dangerous and less worthwhile than visiting more exotic scenes: "O Thomas Cook & Son, pathfinders and trail-clearers, living sign-posts to all the world, and bestowers of first aid to bewildered travellers—unhesitatingly and instantly, with ease and celerity, could you send me to Darkest Africa or Innermost Thibet, but to the East End of London, barely a stone's throw distant from Ludgate Circus, you know not the way!"[18] The privileged can propose only one avenue of communication with the aliens of the slums: they suggest he contact the police. In this map of London's social order the only mediator between classes is the agency of social control—or, of course, the intrepid author-explorer. London buys some old clothes and, playing at proletarianization, plunges into the slums.

Proletarianization, as we have seen in other novels' images of the sea and shipwreck, provokes a fear of being submerged and losing oneself in the swirling forces of determinism: "the fear of the crowd smote me. It was like the fear of the sea; and the miserable multitudes, street upon street, seemed so many waves of a vast and malodorous sea, lapping about me and threatening to well up and over me" (p. 8). But London is relatively safe in his role of dauntless investigator, with a typewriter to record his observations hidden away in a secret refuge, and soon he writes: "The vast and malodorous sea had welled up and over me, or I had slipped gently into it, and there was nothing fearsome about it—with the one exception of the stoker's singlet" (p. 15). London's mind and his skin remain more sensitive than those of the brutalized slum-dwellers, and the smart of this "rough and raspy" (p. 13) garment—the stoker's singlet—is a constant reminder of the boundary between the prosperous and the poor, the free and the unfree, a boundary that is here coextensive with the body of this swimmer in the rough seas of the East End.

Here as in *Sister Carrie* clothing carries the code that most directly signifies class position, and it is his costume that enables London to claim that he is telling the story of the abyss from its own depths. "All servility vanished from the demeanor of the common people with whom I came in contact. . . . My frayed and out-at-elbows jacket was the badge and advertisement of my class, which was their class. It made me of like kind, and in place of the fawning and too respectful attention I had hitherto received, I now shared with them a comradeship" (p. 14). The risk he runs in joining the dangerous classes is represented as quite literal, although it does not come from the direction his respectable friends would have anticipated; when he crosses a street crowded with vehicles he finds himself in danger of being run over, and "it was strikingly impressed upon me that my life had cheapened in direct ratio with my clothes" (p. 15). As this remark reveals, London's purpose in this book is to expose social injustice. But as always we must recognize that such a purpose is cast into narrative form in a fashion that reveals not only conscious intent but immanent ideology, and we find that the "people of the abyss" have much in common with the "abysmal brute" we have already met. In the East End London moves among "twisted monstrosities . . . inconceivable types of sodden ugliness, the wrecks of society, the perambulating carcasses, the living deaths—women, blasted by disease and drink till their shame brought not tu'pence in the open mart; and men, in fantastic rags, wrenched by hardship and exposure out of all semblance of men, their faces in a perpetual writhe of pain, grinning idiotically, shambling like apes, dying with every step they took and

154

Form
and
History
in
American
Literary
Naturalism

each breath they drew" (pp. 286–87). These are the "inefficients" (p. 201), brutalized, pitiable failures; they may talk of "bloody revolution" (p. 78), but they are always the objects of a demonstration and never the subjects of history.

In *The People of the Abyss* London piles one horror on another; every step in his exploration adds more evidence. He imbues his personal testimony on the misery in which the other half lives with all the authority and emphasis specificity and italics can give:

> I thought it was cigar and cigarette stumps they were collecting, and for some time took no notice. Then I did notice.
> *From the slimy sidewalk, they were picking up bits of orange peel, apple skin, and grape stems, and they were eating them. The pits of green gage plums they cracked between their teeth for the kernels inside. They picked up stray crumbs of bread the size of peas, apple cores so black and dirty one would not take them to be apple cores, and these things these two men took into their mouths, and chewed them, and swallowed them; and this, between six and seven o'clock in the evening of August 20, year of our Lord 1902, in the heart of the greatest, wealthiest, and most powerful empire the world has ever seen.* [p. 78]

London's sequences are metonymic and accretive. He constantly asserts that his information is factual, for his strategy is above all documentary as he buttresses the claims of his own observation by quoting statistics, newspaper articles, court reports (for examples, see p. 41, pp. 187–91, pp. 202–6 and following, throughout the last hundred pages of the book). One can scarcely go further in implementing naturalism's descriptive project as a narrative strategy.

Indeed, one cannot go further because at this point description has been almost completely severed from narration. Fact enjoys a particularly privileged status in *The People of the Abyss* because, although it continues to manifest many of the qualities of literary naturalism, the book is not a fictional text but presents itself as an account of the "real" Jack London's "real" experiences. Here the documentary strategy no longer coexists with plot, and we are no longer reading a novel but a piece of journalism, amateur sociology, political essay, or, simply, documentary. No single name yet exists to indicate the literature of fact that is an increasingly vital and prominent genre in contemporary culture. The rise of the documentary or nonfiction novel has been widely noted, but the implications of this reinvention of mimesis are, I think, not yet well understood, and certainly such experimentation has not been fully accommodated in contemporary generic categories. A range of unclassifiable innovation can be invoked by the names Agee, Capote, Mailer, Haley, Terkel, Reed, Doctorow, Kingston, Berger.[19] Photographic, film, and television documentary, as well as literary nonfictions like *The People of the Abyss*, have frequently continued naturalism's disjunction between the observer and the observed. But today one can see the possibility for a more widespread and systematic disruption of that stance than has hitherto been achieved.[20] And it must be a disruption and not simply a modification, for documentary necessarily exists in relation to the literary history I begin to sketch in this study. Forms, of course, do not "evolve"—the model implicit in that biological metaphor is utterly incompatible with the view of genre advanced here. But texts are synchronic unities of differing generic strands that are, diachronically, separable. Naturalism combines a particularly complex group of generic messages, including both residual forms and the important emergent form of documentary.

In fact, the claims of fictional forms like realism and naturalism to tell the truth and report the facts are necessarily, from the perspective of logic, peculiar and paradoxical. But a productive ambiguity about the relation of history and narrative, story and verity characterizes the novel from its beginnings. Conventions about the relation between fiction and fact are always important generic markers; one can see them in transition, for example, when Dreiser at his publishers' insistence changes the names of real persons and places to fictional ones.[21] Today, particularly, the distinction between fiction and nonfiction—often figured in the spatial organization of a bookstore or a library and institutionalized rather bluntly in the Dewey decimal system—is virtually inescapable; readers always want to know whether a book "is" fiction or nonfiction. This ambiguity is precisely what is tantalizing about the "nonfiction novel"; it foregrounds the question of reference and often, although not always, works to transform the terms of the discussion.

The fluid distinction between fiction and nonfiction in American naturalism is illustrated by the close relationship between an article titled in part "Curious Shifts of the Poor," which Dreiser published in *Demorest's Magazine* in 1899, and material in the concluding chapters of *Sister Carrie*, one of which has the same title. Ellen Moers, studying the manuscript of the novel, comments on how carefully Dreiser works sections of the article into the novel, how natural it seems to be for him to "transform journalism into literature."[22] She notes, too, Dreiser's debt to Crane's Bowery sketches, which originated in his writing for newspapers. Almost all the American naturalists, in fact, worked as journalists at some point in their careers. That biographical connection indicates the deeper structural connection between the specular world of naturalism and the specular world of the newspaper.

Not only the predicament of the naturalist spectator, but more specifically Hurstwood's dazed passivity are illuminated by Alan Trachtenberg's analysis of the big-city daily newspapers and journals of the late nineteenth century. He treats the growth of mass

156
Form
and
History
in
American
Literary
Naturalism

communications as one of the new modes of human experience that emerged as human relations were transformed in the increasingly impersonal marketplace of the city: "In technologies of communication, vicarious experience began to erode direct physical experience of the world. Viewing and looking at representations, words and images, city people found themselves addressed more often as passive spectators than as active participants, consumers of images and sensations produced by others."[23] In a world of receding causality and insistent spectacle individuals can experience a radical estrangement from the conditions of their own lives, an estrangement that, as Trachtenberg eloquently reports, journalism both expresses and effects: "Thus, the dailies dramatized a paradox of metropolitan life itself: the more knowable the world came to seem as *information*, the more remote and opaque it came to seem as *experience*. . . . Yet, in providing surrogate experience, the newspaper only deepened the separations it seemed to overcome— deepened them by giving them a precise form: the form of reading and looking" (p. 125). The most evocative figure of this absorption in vicarious experience remains Hurstwood in his comfortable rocking chair, lost in his newspapers, slipping into immobility. The gesture of reading and looking interposes the same glassy pane between information and activity that we have seen in naturalist narrative. The circumstantial detail occupies a place among the functions of fact not only in naturalism but in a wide range of emerging cultural institutions.

Upton Sinclair's *The Jungle*, a novel whose veracity actually became a topic of federal investigation, provides another interesting example of the complex relation between fact and fiction and between naturalism and other literary and nonliterary discourses. *The Jungle* in many ways presents the appearance of a conventional novel: it has character, event, theme. Yet it is also profoundly shaped by the documentary strategy. Although the novel is organized biographically, the course of the protagonist Jurgis Rudkus's life follows a path which ensures that he will observe phenomena that interest Sinclair; he is conducted through a series of experiences that are not only representative but comprehensive, for this account of the meat-packing industry and the conditions of life for immigrant workers attempts to be encyclopedic. When the Rudkuses arrive in Chicago the first thing they do is tour the packinghouses, giving occasion for sentences like this one: "The chutes into which the hogs went climbed high up—to the very top of the distant buildings; and Jokubas explained that the hogs went up by the power of their own legs, and then their weight carried them back through all the processes necessary to make them into pork."[24] As Jurgis and other members of his family take jobs in various parts of the plants, the different operations—slaughtering, processing, canning and so on—are described in more detail.

Jurgis also works in a harvester factory and a steel mill, passing through periods of prosperity and of unemployment and want; eventually almost every vicissitude of working-class life befalls Jurgis or one of his relatives. Jurgis himself begins as a strong and successful wage earner, but he is injured on a job and has great difficulty supporting himself while recovering, spends time in jail after a conflict with a foreman, tramps in both the country and the city, joins a union but later works as a scab and then as a foreman, reaps the benefits of corrupt machine politics, and finally becomes a Socialist. His wife is sexually exploited by her boss and dies in childbirth without competent medical care. His son drowns in a muddy street in Packingtown. His father dies of an illness caused by a job. His cousin becomes a prostitute. What Jurgis cannot experience at firsthand he learns about from others; for example, his cousin tells harrowing stories of women forced into prostitution and explains why she cannot save any money working in a brothel: " 'I am charged for my room and my meals—and such prices as you never heard of; and then for extras, and drinks—for everything I get, and some I don't.' . . . [S]eeing that Jurgis was interested, she went on: 'That's the way they keep the girls—they let them run up debts, so they can't get away' " (p. 352). Jurgis even rounds out our map of the social order when he "chances" to meet the drunken son of a packing-house owner and is taken into a mansion built by a meat fortune to see how the other half lives. The novel is episodic, even disjointed, if one attempts to organize it in terms of plot; its coherence derives from the documentary strategy. Its events are linked not directly to one another but through their common connection with the abstraction of the "jungle" and their relevance to the topic of the Chicago meat-packing industry and the lives of its "wage slaves."

The Jungle demonstrates the metonymic, accretive nature of the documentary strategy, for despite its aspiration to provide a totalizing map of Chicago its most characteristic procedure is to pile horror upon horror just as London does in *The People of the Abyss*. The action of *The Jungle* is produced less by the characters' choices than by their reactions as one disaster after another bursts upon them. When Jurgis and his family buy a house, they discover that "it was not new at all, as they had supposed; it was about fifteen years old, and there was nothing new upon it but the paint, which was so bad that it needed to be put on new every year or two. The house was one of a whole row that was built by a company which existed to make money by swindling poor people. The family had paid fifteen hundred dollars for it, and it had not cost the builders five hundred, when it was new" (p. 77). They find that they owe not just the monthly payments they have been told of but interest, so that it will be almost impossible for them to keep up the payments, and "when they failed—if it were only by a single

158
Form
and
History
in
American
Literary
Naturalism

month—they would lose the house and all that they had paid on it, and then the company would sell it over again" (pp. 77–78). The house brings other hidden dangers, too; conditions constantly threaten their health and their very lives: "how could they know that there was no sewer to their house, and that the drainage of fifteen years was in a cesspool under it? How could they know that the pale blue milk that they bought around the corner was watered, and doctored with formaldehyde besides?" (p. 89). Even when Jurgis thinks he knows all the tricks of the street, he can be fooled again— the hundred dollars he is given by the packer's son is stolen from him when he tries to change the bill in a bar, and Jurgis winds up with change for a dollar minus the price of his glass of beer. The Rudkuses constantly struggle to rise, only to be knocked down, again and again, by one blow after another.

An inexorable fatality seems to pursue Jurgis and his family, so that *The Jungle* at times seems to be following the logic of the plot of decline. Jurgis's misfortunes come close to turning him into a brute as well as an ignorant victim and destroying him as a human being: "He heard the old voices of his soul, he saw its old ghosts beckoning to him. . . . Their voices would die, and never again would he hear them—and so the last faint spark of manhood in his soul would flicker out" (p. 350). But Jurgis is saved by becoming a Socialist, and the plot of decline is defeated. His political awakening emancipates him not only from helpless victimage but from the sordid life and narrow horizons of the brute. "Jurgis recollected how, when he had first come to Packingtown, he had stood and watched the hog-killing, and thought how cruel and savage it was, and come away congratulating himself that he was not a hog; now his new acquaintance showed him that a hog was just what he had been—one of the packer's hogs" (p. 376). As Carrie reads *Père Goriot*, Jurgis reads *The Appeal to Reason*, the Socialist weekly newspaper in which *The Jungle* was first published as a serial; thus he attempts to join the communicative circuit that unites narrator and reader. Yet when we move from the exposition of a problem to its solution, the story somehow ceases to be Jurgis's. In the final four chapters, he is merely an observer, an auditor of others' speeches and conversations about socialism. The novel's conclusion rather melodramatically envisions the victory of the workers— " 'We shall bear down the opposition, we shall sweep it before us— and Chicago will be ours! *Chicago will be ours! CHICAGO WILL BE OURS!* " (p. 413). But the achievement it actually depicts is the preservation of Jurgis's humanity and the enlightenment of the reader, victories that remain bounded by art and by consciousness.

Portraying a political awakening is one way of suggesting the possibility of profound social change without violating the conventions of realism, and it is a strategy that emerges still more strongly in a later genre that has many affinities with naturalism, the proletarian novel. Jurgis's transformation strikes the reader as such a dissonant and discontinuous element in this novel because it so obviously requires him to leave his native realm of victimage to become a character who exercises free will. There is no pretense in *The Jungle* that the group Sinclair is writing *about* is the same or even has much in common with the group he is writing *for*. In a gesture we have encountered before, we find the narrator and reader clearly marked off from the characters by the very languages they use: Sinclair prefaces one description with the remark that "the reader, who perhaps has never held much converse in the language of far-off Lithuania, will be glad of the explanation that . . . " (p. 2). Although the only things that are recognizably Lithuanian about the Rudkuses are their names (Sinclair even provides a footnote to tell us how to pronounce "Jurgis"), they are certainly foreigners. One might debate the exact degree of irony in that "perhaps"—I think it is considerable—and attempt to measure the exact width of this chasm between classes, but its existence is taken for granted.

Throughout the novel the naturalist plays the role of the readers' guide and interpreter in an alien land. But he is not a native of that land either. Sinclair tells us in his autobiography that his own painful experiences of want—that is, his confrontation with proletarianization, to which his autobiography testifies at length—imbue the book with anguish, but that he is a stranger to the "jungle" of Chicago. The book is based on his research during "seven weeks lived among the wage slaves of the Beef Trust, as we called it in those days. People used to ask me afterward if I had not spent my life in Chicago, and I answered that if I had done so, I could never have written *The Jungle*; I would have taken for granted things that now hit me a sudden violent blow. I went about, white-faced and thin, partly from undernourishment, partly from horror."[25] Despite the novel's affirmation of the possibilities for change, the realms of knowledge and experience, the worlds of the observer and the participant, remain polarized, joined only by the narrator's pity and good intentions.

Nevertheless, *The Jungle* is famous as a novel that changed the world: an important progressive reform, the passage of the Meat Inspection and Pure Food and Drug Acts in 1906, is widely attributed to the public furore over conditions in the meat-packing industry that it created. (It was this that motivated the intense scrutiny of Sinclair's facts.) But as Sinclair himself recognized, the movement for the inspection of meat had originated with the big packers themselves and ultimately benefited them by providing a guarantee of quality at government expense and removing obstacles to meat exporting.[26] And the reforms demanded by the horrified readers of *The Jungle* addressed not the condition of the workers but the menace of the unsanitary practices Sinclair reported—what bothered them was less the claim that men fell into the cooking vats

160

Form
and
History
in
American
Literary
Naturalism

and died agonizing deaths than the revolting idea that "all but the bones of them had gone out to the world as Durham's Pure Leaf Lard!" (p. 117). Sinclair wrote, "I aimed at the public's heart, and by accident I hit it in the stomach."[27] He was neither the first nor the last socialist to set out to write of the iniquities of class society and find himself enmeshed in the mysteries of consumer society. In a characteristic naturalist gesture, Sinclair appeals to his readers to pity the miserable, thwarted lives of the other half; yet he also pays a great deal of attention to unclean meat and does not distinguish the two concerns so clearly as his lament would seem to suggest. The revolting truth about meat revealed an avenue by which the unclean horrors of a world outside the campfire found their way into that well-lighted, respectable circle and exposed a potentially contaminating contact between the disorder of the slaughterhouse district and the haven of the middle-class home. Although it clearly did not capture Sinclair's full intent, the impulse to regulate and rationalize the meat-packing industry was a perfectly consistent response to Sinclair's plea for reform. The connection illustrates the fundamental structural similarity, seen here in miniature and in Chapter 4 at length, between naturalism and progressivism.

In *The Jungle* and in many of Sinclair's other novels plot responds quite directly and unequivocally to the project of describing a given milieu. Sinclair tends to use elements of the naturalist form like the documentary strategy in a particularly straightforward and even schematic way. We may think of his *King Coal*, published in 1917—later than the other novels examined in this study although still relatively early in the author's long career—as punctuating the end of this first moment of American naturalism. The novel was published just as the United States entered the First World War and apparently for that reason was a commercial failure. Sinclair writes that he never published the sequel he wrote because "world war had come and no one was interested in labor problems any more" (p. 217). At least, that interest seems to have required a different expression.[28] For *King Coal* naturalism not only already exists as a recognizable form but is well on its way to becoming a standardized set of literary devices. It is no longer a dynamic solution to a formal problem but a conventional form.

The penetration of a bourgeois observer into the sordid existence of the proletariat is the explicit premise of *King Coal*. Hal Warner is a mine-owner's son who during his summer vacation from college assumes a false name, puts on old clothes and dirties his face, and takes a job in the mines, with "youth in his heart, and love and curiosity; also he had some change in his trousers' pocket, and a ten dollar bill, for extreme emergencies, sewed up in his belt."[29] Influenced by the "muck-rakers," Hal has argued for reform against his conservative older brother and wants to see for himself what conditions are really like in the coal mines. Although Sinclair retains the fictional format, like London in *The People of the Abyss* he sends his protagonist on a perilous journey of investigation. Hal is simultaneously an educated observer documenting a slice of proletarian life and the hero of an adventure story, a brave explorer who puts on a costume and embarks for an exotic land.

The bond between the protagonist and the narrator and reader is constantly emphasized by the fact that in the narration he is always "Hal," but the miners know him as "Joe Smith." Hal never admits—indeed, never conceives—that the workers he wants to help might be capable of comprehending his true identity. The class boundary marks a mutual misunderstanding—but Hal's world comes to contain the miners', even though theirs can never encompass his. The reader's knowledge of that widest world and Hal's double identity is the condition of our participation in the novel. We are always privy to a secret from which the other characters are excluded, the secret that Hal is not what he seems but is a privileged person, a kind of prince in disguise. The ways in which Dreiser, Norris, and London handle such double identity—the contrasts between G. W. Hurstwood of Chicago and G. W. Wheeler of New York, between Van Weyden and "Hump," between Hal Warner and Joe Smith—reveal much about the similarities and differences of these ventures into proletarianization.

In an image that has become familiar in earlier chapters, Hal envisions the realm of determinism as a turbulent sea:

> Hal had come here, as one goes upon the deck of a ship in mid-ocean, to see the storm. In this ocean of social misery, of ignorance and despair, one saw upturned, tortured faces, writhing limbs and clutching hands; in one's ears was a storm of lamentation, upon one's cheek a spray of blood and tears. Hal found himself so deep in this ocean that he could no longer find consolation in the thought that he could escape whenever he wanted to: that he could say to himself, It is sad, it is terrible—but thank God, I can get out of it when I choose! I can go back into the warm and well-lighted saloon and tell the other passengers how picturesque it is, what an interesting experience they are missing! [p. 70]

Hal is aware of the limitations of his role as a tourist, but all his emotional involvement cannot change it. He finds his experiences as an explorer emotionally disturbing, but the truth is that he is utterly safe; ensconced as he is in a virtually formulaic role, no shipwrecks threaten him as they do other protagonists of naturalism. However deeply Hal feels the suffering and injustice he sees, he is always an onlooker, an outsider. For him the events of the novel are just "a summer-course in practical sociology" (p. 158).

King Coal reproduces stereotypes of the working class and par-

162
Form
and
History
in
American
Literary
Naturalism

ticularly of immigrants. Hal's initial reaction to the "shanty-town" of the mining-camp is an inventory of such shopworn images of brutality:

> These homes were beneath the dignity of chicken-houses, yet in some of them a dozen people were crowded, men and women sleeping on old rags and blankets on a cinder floor. Here the babies swarmed like maggots. They wore for the most part a single ragged smock, and their bare buttocks were shamelessly upturned to the heavens. It was so the children of the cave-men must have played, thought Hal; and waves of repulsion swept over him. He had come with love and curiosity, but both motives failed here. How could a man of sensitive nerves, aware of the refinements and graces of life, learn to love these people, who were an affront to his every sense—a stench to his nostrils, a jabbering to his ear, a procession of deformities to his eye? What had civilisation done for them? What could it do? After all, what were they fit for, but the dirty work they were penned up to do? So spoke the haughty race-consciousness of the Anglo-Saxon, contemplating these Mediterranean hordes, the very shape of whose heads was objectionable. [p. 21]

Like Presley's initial view of Hooven, this first response to the miners is revealed as deplorably unsympathetic and is soon corrected: "as always, when one understood the lives of men, one came to pity instead of despising. Here was a separate race of creatures, subterranean gnomes, pent up by society for purposes of its own" (p. 22). But again, the central character's better vision, substituting pity for contempt and fear, differs in emotional tone but retains the same register of characterization. Such pitiable subhumans can exert no claim to self-awareness, self-determination, reciprocal naming, although they can exert a claim on compassion.

Hal and the narrator insist that the miners are not *naturally* inferior but rather that they are brutalized by the conditions of their existence. "It was impossible for any one to work so hard and keep his mental alertness, his eagerness and sensitiveness" (p. 69). Whatever causal sequence produces them, they are irreparably damaged human beings. Even in the midst of struggles on their behalf, Hal does not respect the workers—"It had been a crude and stupid plot, yet Hal realised that it was adapted to the intelligence of the men for whom it was intended" (p. 141). "Hal . . . saw the workers going to their tasks, the toil-bent, pallid faced creatures of the underworld, like a file of baboons" (p. 143). At other times he sees them as "child-like people, whose moods were quick, whose tempers were balanced upon a fine point" (p. 306); several of the working-class characters are presented quite sentimentally. In the writing of this avowed Socialist and advocate for the working class, the miners are represented not simply as different from the middle-class protagonist, author and reader but as alternately bestial and childlike, brutalized and sentimentalized. In *King Coal* the potency associated with the image of the brute has almost vanished. Sinclair based the book largely upon visits to Colorado during and after the great strike of 1913–14, which amounted to a virtual civil war, and he depicts the fears that the miners evoke in middle-class people.[30] But for Hal and for Sinclair the workers are predominantly objects of pity, not fear; the problem is not to control but to rouse and organize them.

Hal is not trapped in his stance of observation as Presley is. He at once becomes involved in movements to improve conditions in the mines, and the miners turn naturally to him as a leader: "At last Hal stood up. It was something he was to experience many times in the future; because he was an American, and educated, he was forced into a position of leadership" (p. 120). Not in its explicit political program but in the way it structures the narrative, *King Coal* implies that middle-class reformers must speak *on behalf of* the working class, that without such assistance the miners will be completely outmatched and unable to resist and will remain sunk in their misery. Hal's privileged upbringing makes him naive—he is constantly taken aback at political realities that others take for granted (the elections are dishonest! the newspapers will not print the truth! the safety regulations are not enforced!), thus providing a vehicle for communicating unpleasant truths to the reader. But his class background also enables him to save situations that otherwise would be hopeless. He has the ability to speak to and challenge the bosses on their own terms, yet he has little enough at stake to dare to do so since he is one of the " 'people who cannot be sent to prison' " (p. 154). When his life is in danger from " 'thugs and gunmen in the company's employ' " (p. 245), he can take refuge in the private railroad car of the owner's son, where a party of his friends is conveniently gathered. And he can shame that son, his schoolmate, into ordering the rescue of men trapped in the mine even though that will endanger the coal—for this irreproachably humanitarian demand, and not the demand for class power, insensibly emerges as the pivotal political struggle of the novel.

Yet even Hal's special powers ultimately accomplish very little; his most effective action is to *stop* a strike when as the messenger of the union he bids the men to wait for a more propitious moment. As he returns home he realizes "the grim truth about his summer's experience—that the issue of it had been defeat. Utter, unqualified defeat! He had caused the bosses a momentary chagrin; but it would not take them many hours to realise that he had really done them a service in calling off the strike for them. They would start the wheels of industry again, and the workers would be just where they had been before Joe Smith came to be stableman and buddy

164
Form
and
History
in
American
Literary
Naturalism

among them" (p. 375). Hal dreams of exposing the iniquities of the Coal King and running for governor, but he quickly comes "down to practical matters" (p. 376) and settles for assisting a few of his worthy friends. For all his busy activity, the sum of his achievements adds up to something that sounds uncannily like those of the humanitarian progressive reformer: Hal has directed unrest into channels that are not immediately disruptive, achieved a few humanitarian reforms, practiced philanthropy, and accumulated a specialized knowledge of the other half, which qualifies him to speak for them and prescribe remedies for social problems. Even though Hal's belief that the solution to all the miners' problems is to inform the public about them has been revealed as naive (p. 196 and following), the project of the book is inevitably the dissemination of information. The only action that seems open to Hal, and to Sinclair, is to return to the stateroom and tell the privileged passengers how the other half lives.

Sinclair bases a considerable part of *King Coal*'s claim to the reader's attention on its accuracy as a depiction of conditions in the coalfields, and he adds a postscript that supports those claims:

> From previous experiences the writer has learned that many people, reading a novel such as "King Coal," desire to be informed as to whether it is true to fact. They write to ask if the book is meant to be so taken; they ask for evidence to convince themselves and others. Having answered thousands of such letters in the course of his life, it seems to the author the part of common-sense to answer some of them in advance.
>
> "King Coal" is a picture of the life of the workers in unorganised labour-camps in many parts of America. The writer has avoided naming a definite place, for the reason that such conditions are to be found as far apart as West Virginia, Alabama, Michigan, Minnesota, and Colorado. Most of the details of his picture were gathered in the last-named state, which the writer visited on three occasions during and just after the great coal-strike of 1913–14. The book gives a true picture of conditions and events observed by him at this time. . . .
>
> The reader who wishes evidence may be accommodated. There was never a strike more investigated than the Colorado coal-strike. The material about it in the writer's possession cannot be less than eight million words, the greater part of it sworn testimony taken under government supervision.
> [p. 384]

Sinclair goes on to give more specific references and quote some authorities, laying particular emphasis on a decision by the Colorado Supreme Court. He comments, "It is not often that the writer of a novel of contemporary life is so fortunate as to have the truth of his work passed upon and established by the highest judicial tribunal of the community!" (p. 385). The standards of evidence by

which naturalism is to be judged interpenetrate with those of other discourses, particularly in the case of these two novels by Sinclair that invoke the powerful legitimation of the law. In this gesture we see how deeply the documentary strategy informs the naturalist novel, giving it purpose and shape.

Naturalist novels continue to be written after the First World War, of course. But the later writers most often identified as naturalists take a rather different direction from Sinclair's. Perhaps because the generic text is more codified, they are more narrowly consistent in their naturalism, and they conform more closely to the conventions of "serious" novels of their times. James T. Farrell's *Studs Lonigan* trilogy (1932–35), for example, combines two characteristically naturalist strategies: it is both the anatomy of a decline and the anatomy of a particular Chicago milieu. And it honors the prohibition of the "intrusive" narrator and the prescription of consistent "point of view" proposed by James and generally accepted in late realism, thus producing a singularly claustrophobic delineation of the realm of forces. However, the qualitatively different realm of the narrator and readers is still present in *Studs Lonigan*, as here when the narrator adopts a literary tone that would never be possible to the novels' limited, inarticulate characters:

> "It's swell here."
> "Yeh," they answered.
> Darkness came, feather-soft. The park grew lonely, and the wind beat more steadily, until its wail sounded upon Studs' ears like that of many souls forever damned. It ripped through the empty branches. It curved through the dead leaves on the ground, whipped bunches of them, rolled them across bare stretches of earth, until they resembled droves of frightened, scurrying animals.[31]

Farrell's style is more frequently terse, minimizing the contrast between the narrator's and the characters' language, but it is never vacuous and repetitive as the quoted speeches of the characters are.

In Hubert Selby, Jr.'s *Last Exit to Brooklyn* (1964) the domination of point of view is still stronger, and the narrator's voice is almost entirely merged with the characters'. The orthographic distinction between a standard-English-speaking narrator and the dialect of characters is elided: "They sprawled along the counter and on the chairs. Another night. Another drag of a night in the Greeks, a beatup all night diner near the Brooklyn Armybase. Once in a while a doggie or seaman came in for a hamburger and played the jukebox. But they usually played some goddam hillbilly record. They tried to get the Greek to take those records off, but hed tell them no.

166

Form
and
History
in
American
Literary
Naturalism

They come in and spend money. You sit all night and buy notting."[32] But the informing awareness of an intelligent, articulate narrator persists in the expectations we bring to reading and is inscribed in the text by biblical epigraphs whose relevance would be incomprehensible to the limited inhabitants of this dead-end, determinist slum. The quotations place the novel firmly in an important tradition in American literature, marking it as a kind of jeremiad. Although in this much later period naturalism itself is inevitably a *re*invention, and no doubt serves new purposes, I suggest that critics identify this novel as latter-day naturalism not only because of its pessimism but because it does indeed have crucial structural similarities to naturalist novels of an earlier period.

Since critics not infrequently call Farrell and Selby "naturalists," the generic text identifies them, along with a relatively small number of other twentieth-century writers like Steinbeck and Bellow, as inheritors of the form we have been studying. Certain qualities in a larger group of writers including Dos Passos, Hemingway, Faulkner, are also identified as having some oblique relation to the form—their work has "naturalistic" tendencies. Dos Passos, for example, organizes *U.S.A.* at its most general level very much according to a documentary project. The prelude to the volume that brought the three novels of the trilogy together opens by evoking a journey of observation: "The young man walks fast by himself through the crowd that thins into the night streets." And it concludes with a metonymic, panoramic collection of details:

> U.S.A. is the slice of a continent. U.S.A. is a group of holding companies, some aggregations of trade unions, a set of laws bound in calf, a radio network, a chain of moving picture theatres, a column of stock-quotations rubbed out and written in by a Western Union boy on a blackboard, a publiclibrary full of old newspapers and dogeared historybooks with protests scrawled on the margins in pencil. U.S.A. is the world's greatest rivervalley fringed with mountains and hills, U.S.A. is a set of bigmouthed officials with too many bank-accounts. U.S.A. is a lot of men buried in their uniforms in Arlington Cemetery. U.S.A. is the letters at the end of an address when you are away from home. But mostly U.S.A. is the speech of the people.[33]

In this passage and the novels that follow the narrative strategies and styles of a wide variety of forms, including modernism, are juxtaposed—*U.S.A.* would provide a rich field for an investigation of the resources of generic discontinuity as an explicit technique as well as an inescapable condition of literary production.

Dos Passos is also, it seems to me, an inheritor of naturalism. There is nothing to be gained by arguing for the importance of naturalism for contemporary literature primarily in terms of a con-

tinuing tradition of centrally naturalist works. What is in question is
a quite different system of generic categories in which the formal resources developed by naturalism remain influential. The formal impulses that emerge later in the century as "naturalistic" elements in modernist novels, in the proletarian novel, and in the literature of fact constitute part of the synchronic unity that is American naturalism around the turn of the century. I would also argue that naturalism has strong affinities with a form John Cawelti calls the "best-selling social melodrama." He writes: "There has been a continuing connection between the nineteenth- and twentieth-century tradition of novelistic social criticism or muckraking and the social melodrama. Indeed, a number of quite extraordinary works such as Stowe's *Uncle Tom's Cabin*, Frank Norris's *The Pit*, Lewis's *Main Street*, and Mitchell's *Gone with the Wind* lie somewhere on a continuum between the formulaic social melodrama and naturalistic novels by writers like Dreiser, Hemingway, Faulkner, and Bellow."[34] There is of course much more to be said about the best-seller, and about all these inheritors of naturalism—but that is not my topic here.

The affinity between naturalism and the best-seller returns us to the direction that Sinclair takes. For his novels are popular novels that constantly tend toward the formulaic, not only formalizing naturalism but incorporating the highly formalized residual narrative patterns of melodrama, adventure, and domesticity. In reading *The Jungle* and *King Coal* one is struck by how many narrative strategies are invoked besides the plot of decline and documentary. Although the phenomenon is particularly marked in Sinclair, it is also characteristically naturalist. Fredric Jameson observes the same plurality of narrative strategies in topical novels by the English naturalist George Gissing: "Starting from such an abstract and global subject matter, which in itself proposes no traces or hints of narrative articulation, the novelist inevitably finds himself forced back upon the older readily available stereotypical narrative matrices."[35] During the formative moment of American naturalism the portrait of a deterioration and the exploration of a milieu rarely stand on their own and produce a coherent, satisfyingly sequenced narrative; we must go on to examine generic discontinuity as an essential element of naturalist narrative.

Just as the formal choices of naturalism are developed in later forms, traces of older forms are sedimented in naturalism. Understanding the crucial place of these generic discontinuities in naturalism presents a particularly complex problem because we must penetrate a moment in which not only literary form but the very conditions of literary form in the social institutions of culture are in transition. The functions of such conventionalized codes as melodrama, adventure, and sentiment, which are the strongest evi-

168
Form
and
History
in
American
Literary
Naturalism

dences of generic discontinuity in naturalism, are understandable only in the context of this transformation. Not only generic codes and generic systems but the *nature* of generic operations is specific, and the emergence of mass culture constitutes a profound transformation of the very categories through which genre works.

By "mass culture" I do not mean merely cultural forms that appeal to large numbers of people or to "the masses" as opposed to an elite. Every social community has its cultural practices, elaborated as a kind of collective discourse in dialogue with other communities; it is in this sense that genres are, as Jameson calls them, "socio-symbolic messages."[36] Folk cultures must be distinguished from mass culture in which the relation between cultural producer and audience is mediated by mass production and by an impersonal marketplace. Mass culture is produced as a commodity for an atomized mass audience, for a "public" composed not of a community but of a series of "private" individuals. We have already looked at one of the mass media developing in the late nineteenth century—the newspaper, an institution of which Trachtenberg writes that "each individual paper, a replica of hundreds of thousands of others, served as a private opening to a world identical to that of one's companion on a streetcar, a companion likely to remain as distant, remote, and strange as the day's 'news' comes to seem familiar, personal, and real" (p. 125). As the multiple connections of newspapers and naturalism suggest, the specular world and descriptive strategy of the genre in some sense already belong to the world of mass culture.

But almost everything remains to be learned about the emergence and, for that matter, the present functioning of mass culture. Studies of its genesis and its ongoing penetration into all regions and classes are urgently needed as are studies of its articulation with the cultural production of residual or emergent collectivities and its reappropriation by consumers as the vehicle of their own meanings. For we should not mistake the evocative image of the utterly atomized, utterly homogenized mass culture such as Trachtenberg's, which represents the *tendency* of mass culture, for its more varied empirical reality.[37] Such studies can be productive only if they abandon the condescending depreciation of mass cultural forms pervasive in literary criticism and, equally, the valorization of "popular culture" common in the field which takes that name. Departments of English generally take as their object of study the literature of the past and the high culture of the present, a culture now inescapably defined *against* mass culture and taking the form of what we can (albeit too simply) call modernism and postmodernism. High cultural forms resist or parody commodification and hence resist generic classification; it is this transformation of the institutions of cultural production that is the necessary ground of the theoretical critique of genre theory that I have outlined. In mass

culture, on the other hand, genre is more important than ever, constituting as it does a kind of labeling system that consumers use to
guide their choice of product. The aficionado of mysteries who
buys a book called *Murder in the Library* only to discover that it is a
Western or a romance is likely to be very annoyed and indeed to
feel that he or she has been taken in by fraudulent packaging.

The novels of the formative moment of naturalism, it seems to
me, have not yet yielded to the differentiation of mass and high
culture and for that very reason have proved difficult for literary
critics to classify and understand. The tendency of traditional genre
criticism to typologize in purely formal and often ahistorical terms
has rendered this tension within naturalism virtually invisible. We
see it registered, however, in discussions of the conformity or non-
conformity of specific novels to taken-for-granted aesthetic criteria
inevitably drawn from high cultural norms; such discussions can
unconsciously map the discontinuities between codes current in
very different cultural institutions that are operating simultaneously
in the heterogeneous naturalist text. Ultimately, I would argue, it is
the coexistence of such contradictory codes in a single body of
work that produces the ambiguous status of an author like Jack
London, whose claim to literary merit is passionately argued by
some critics and dismissed by others. Sinclair's standing as a "serious" author is even more precarious. Perhaps the other side of the
critical denigration of the naturalists is the fact that they have for
many years been among the most widely read American authors in
Europe and the Soviet Union and that—in my experience at least—
they are enormously successful in the classroom. The juxtaposition
of codes that have now unmistakably emerged as mass and high
cultural conventions is not the only, but it is an important, source of
the popular taste and critical distaste for naturalism.

I do not want to claim that naturalism is unique in compounding
elements of mass and high cultural codes; indeed such interpenetration is constant and inevitable. Mass and high culture constitute a kind of antinomy, and the terms of an antinomy do not prescribe separate, essential, and substantial meanings but provide
the ground for structural oppositions and meaning. But naturalism
has particularly strong affinities with journalism and with the newly
invented "best-seller" and with the conventionalized narrative patterns that become institutionalized in mass culture as formulaic
subliteratures.[38] Some of those connections, like the fact that so
many naturalists worked as reporters, are biographical. As a young
man Upton Sinclair wrote juvenile stories for the Street & Smith
"fiction factory."[39] During the ten years that intervened between
the publication of *Sister Carrie* and his second novel, Theodore
Dreiser edited dime novels and a pulp magazine for Street & Smith
and became a successful editor of women's fashion magazines.
Frank Norris wrote not only naturalist works but the adventure story

170

Form
and
History
in
American
Literary
Naturalism

Moran of the Lady Letty and the sentimental courtship tale *Blix* (to oversimplify the generic attributions, since the two novels have many elements in common and indeed elements in common with Norris's better-remembered works). Norris's *The Pit* presents an even more complex problem, uniting as it does a descriptive study of "the Wheat" with a love story and occupying a prominent place on the early best-seller lists. And, of course, the works and career of that tireless and uninhibited generic experimenter Jack London are inextricably involved with codes and institutions of mass culture.

London found that his very success in the literary marketplace—and, of course, his desire to repeat that success—constrained his literary production in certain ways. According to Christopher Wilson, " 'a man does one thing in a passable manner,' Jack London once lamented, 'and the dear public insists on his continuing to do it to the end of his days.' "[40] Repetition offers different satisfactions at different historical moments and in different genres, of course. When Norris tags each of the characters in *The Octopus* with an epithet, he does not duplicate but alludes to and reappropriates Homeric epithets and their function in classical poetic diction. Neither use of repetition bears much resemblance to Gertrude Stein's. In mass culture repetition ensures the satisfaction of the reader who wants a particular kind of product to consume: surely no conventionalized narrative patterns before mass production offered quite the same reiterated pleasure as consuming "Agatha Christies" or "James Bonds."

Repetition is also important to the function of the highly conventionalized narrative patterns embedded in naturalist novels. These readily available formulas, precisely because they follow a predictable sequence, provide a stable, reassuring narrative order. After encountering such a formula, the reader in a sense already knows what will happen; possible outcomes are confined to the safe and familiar world of convention rather than remaining vulnerable to the impact of new and potentially unpleasant "facts" signaling the presence of the "real." Thus repetition itself contributes to a novel's sequential coherence and closure. But the presence of formulaic plots also necessarily opens a seam of dissonant generic discontinuity in the text, for both such predictability and its content are utterly incompatible with the aesthetic ideology of naturalism. However petrified and predictable they may appear now, the conventionalized narrative patterns we find in naturalism are transmogrified versions of genres that in their own time and place carry their own sociosymbolic messages. Those messages become part of the new form in ways that may be either disruptive or stabilizing and are likely to be both.

We can see this mixing of messages very clearly in the "best-selling social melodrama," which Cawelti defines as a novel characterized by an interweaving of the patterns of melodrama with a particular set of current events or social institutions, the result being a complex double effect: the social setting is often treated rather critically with a good deal of anatomizing of the hidden motives, secret corruption, and human folly underlying certain events or institutions; yet the main plot works out in proper melodramatic fashion to affirm, after appropriate tribulations and sufferings, that God is in his heaven and all's right with the world. The sympathetic and the good undergo much testing and difficulty, but are ultimately saved. Evil rides high but is, in the end, overcome, at least as far as the main characters are concerned. [p. 261]

As Cawelti comments, "this synthesis combines the escapist satisfactions of melodrama—in particular, its fantasy of a moral universe following conventional social values—with the pleasurable feeling that we are learning something important about reality."[41] It is a compound that has been very successful indeed and that we now encounter in a variety of media.

Winston Churchill, a now almost forgotten novelist whose novels sold immensely at the turn of the century and until the First World War, is for our purposes one of the most interesting practitioners of this genre. Churchill earned his early fame with historical romances but later began writing novels about social questions and eventually about contemporary social problems not unlike those that concern the naturalists. *Mr. Crewe's Career* (1908), for example, deals with the unjust domination of state government by a railroad monopoly. But a family drama and a love story are also important elements of the tale, which relies heavily on its conventional plotting to achieve closure and resolve the tensions it has evoked. Although he works from a very different set of critical assumptions from mine, Charles Child Walcutt discusses Churchill as a kind of naturalist *manqué* and acknowledges the inherent interest of his formal compromises. Churchill's difficulty, Walcutt writes at the end of a long analysis of his novels, is that "if he accepts this traditional form, or any parts of it, he will find his ideas modified by it; and yet he has problem enough to cling to his new ideas without the added burden of devising a new artistic medium through which to express them. Small wonder that a half-hearted pioneer like Churchill failed! He might as well have tried to carry a nine-room Victorian mansion, complete with furniture, over the Rockies in a prairie schooner" (p. 179). We can set aside Walcutt's teleological assumption that a consistent naturalism automatically constitutes success to recognize that he provides us with a vivid metaphor for what I call generic discontinuity.

Although the social melodrama shares with naturalism an impulse toward social criticism, a claim to convey valid information,

172
Form
and
History
in
American
Literary
Naturalism

and a "realistic" atmosphere, it combines those elements with a predictable plot that contravenes the philosophical commitment to an objective, impersonal determinism. In melodrama the fundamental oppositions are not those of causality but those of morality. The "sensationalism" or intensification of affect we associate with melodramatic fiction and drama is necessarily associated with a clearly defined conflict between good and evil. All the formulaic narrative patterns embedded in naturalist novels are in this most general sense melodramatic. Unlikely as the combination may seem, when Sinclair casts socialism as the savior of Jurgis's manhood and potentially of Chicago, he stages political conflict as a melodramatic confrontation between good and evil. The plot of decline also moves toward melodrama when it concentrates on fate rather than forces, on catastrophe rather than causality. In *Vandover and the Brute*, for example, a melodramatic thread twines itself into the fabric of a physiological determinism; we are not fully in the world of melodrama—Dolly Haight certainly does not deserve his misery—but Vandover's vice and indolence do almost merit his degradation. It is a kind of poetic justice that he should literally become a brute, and the tone in which his deterioration is described is sensational indeed. Elements in *The Octopus* that place us in a melodramatic "world that is purportedly full of the violence and tragedy we associate with the 'real world' but that in this case seems to be governed by some benevolent moral principle" (Cawelti, pp. 44–45) sometimes blend less smoothly with Norris's naturalism. The most disturbing moment, I think, is S. Behrman's death: the Wheat has been explicitly described as an impersonal force within a realistic universe of causality, yet when Presley fails it assassinates the railroad agent, acting as a benevolent principle within the morally ordered world of a melodramatic formula that is, however, rapidly becoming unacceptable in "serious" literature.

Clear-cut oppositions between right and wrong in general characterize the conventional narrative strategies embedded in naturalist novels. In the adventure story the hero is assumed to represent the "right," but the focus is not on confrontations between good and evil but on the extraordinary abilities of the protagonist. In his *Dreams of Adventure, Deeds of Empire*, Martin Green defines the adventure tale as "a series of events, partly but not wholly accidental, in settings remote from the domestic and probably from the civilized (at least in the psychological sense of remote), which constitute a challenge to the central character. In meeting this challenge, he/she performs a series of exploits which make him/her a hero, eminent in virtues such as courage, fortitude, cunning, strength, leadership, and persistence." The form has its own immanent ideology, of course—Green calls it "the energizing myth of English imperialism"—and to explore it fully would be a study in itself.[42] But certainly elements of the adventure tale move through some naturalist novels; we can easily recognize the protagonists of Sinclair's *King Coal* and London's *People of the Abyss* as intrepid adventurers into psychologically and socially remote, dangerous regions. We have already seen that the East End of London is more difficult to penetrate than "Darkest Africa or Innermost Thibet." The savage within civilization offers an important point of contact between naturalism and the adventure tale—it is perhaps not wholly coincidental that two of London's geographically remote settings, Alaska and Hawaii, have been incorporated in the American federal system and thus in a sense constitute another kind of internal colony. In both London's and Norris's work a naturalistic ideology of heredity combines smoothly with the "deeds of empire" in a profoundly racist image of Anglo-Saxon superiority. That superiority is most effectively embodied, of course, in the hero. Thus the codes of adventure provide coherence and closure as they enhance the status of the protagonist, distance the Other, and offer the resolution of an ending that not only fulfills a fantasy but is gratifyingly predictable.

Given naturalism's aesthetic ideology and categories of characterization, of course, that capable personage the hero necessarily exists in tension with other elements of the narrative. The setting of *The Sea-Wolf* is appropriate for an adventure story, but Humphrey Van Weyden at first falls far short of being a hero: he must learn the role during the course of the novel. But here we are dealing with yet another set of conventions, for it is with the introduction of the character Maud Brewster that formulaic elements come to the fore and we begin to rely on the happy ending with some assurance. The arrival of a real lady on the masculine "brute-ship" signals the presence of what we may for the moment call the sentimental. Idealization of the feminine has already come in for some criticism in this novel, as it does in *Martin Eden*; during the shipwreck we have seen that ladies too can scream like "pigs under the knife of the butcher," and we have learned that the seal-hunters make themselves into bloody butchers for the sake of those same ladies—"we travelled . . . ravaging and destroying, flinging the naked carcasses to the shark and salting down the skins so that they might later adorn the fair shoulders of the women of the cities."[43] But Maud is always quietly brave and instinctively sympathetic; from the first she belongs to a privileged realm and even an idealized species. Through talking with her the erstwhile "Hump" regains his sense of social and intellectual superiority; in consequence Wolf Larsen betrays his first sign of weakness: "listening curiously to our alien speech of a world he did not know. . . . He rose to his feet and laughed awkwardly. The sound of it was metallic. 'Oh, don't mind me,' he said, with a self-depreciatory wave of his hand. 'I don't count'" (p. 199). Maud's presence in the story shifts its direction and its register of characterization, and Van Weyden changes correspondingly: "The

174
Form
and
History
in
American
Literary
Naturalism

coming of Maud Brewster into my life seemed to have transformed me. After all, I thought, it is better and finer to love than to be loved, if it makes something in life so worth while that one is not loath to die for it" (p. 266). But Hump is metamorphosing into the hero of a sentimental love story, and while the hero must be ready to die—we know that he will not.

The fact that Wolf Larsen continues to command far more narrative energy than the lovers is evidence of the uncomfortable, discontinuous coexistence of naturalism and sentiment in the text. But Wolf is doomed, of course. He is not bound by the sentimental convention that decrees that the heroine is sexually untouchable, crosses the class boundary to lay hands on her—and is immediately struck down by his mysterious, predictable brain disease. Van Weyden, on the other hand, follows the laws of the genre and does no more than tenderly brush Maud's hair with his lips. The conventions of sentiment and London's rhetoric of nature and the atavism blend oddly in descriptions of a love that is both the most civilized and subtle of sensations and a passion that taps their (fortunately Anglo-Saxon) instincts, for Maud is in Van Weyden's words "'my woman, my mate-woman, fighting with me and for me as the mate of a caveman would have fought, all the primitive in her aroused, forgetful of her culture, hard under the softening civilization of the only life she had ever known'" (pp. 339–40). They can declare their love only at the moment when the rule of law is reasserted, as Wolf Larsen's body sinks into the sea and a United States revenue cutter steams in to rescue them from their derelict vessel and also, as Maud says, "'rescue us from ourselves'" (p. 366). The resolution of the novel depends upon generic discontinuity, asserting at one and the same time that Van Weyden and Maud have recovered a primitive principle of potency and that their love remains within the bounds of lawful wedded bliss.

Sentimental fiction is melodramatic in the sense that it assumes the categories of good and evil rather than causality and uses a conventional language of intensified affect, but like the adventure tale it stages the moral drama in a particular kind of setting—here, courtship and the family. The category of sentimentalism is itself controversial; Nina Baym observes that the critics who designate popular women's novels of the mid-nineteenth century as "sentimental" generally mean to imply that they evade reality and exaggerate emotion, and she argues that the term is both inaccurate and inappropriately normative. She demands a more historical understanding of the values these novels advocate:

> The "cult of domesticity" that pervades this fiction is not
> equivalent to a later generation's idea of such a cult, as a simple injunction for woman willingly to turn the key on her own
> prison. The fiction does excoriate an unhappy home as the

basic source of human misery and imagines a happy home as 175
the acme of human bliss. It assumes that men as well as Narrative
women find greatest happiness and fulfillment in domestic re- Strategies
lations, by which are meant not simply spouse and parent, but
the whole network of human attachments based on love, support, and mutual responsibility. Domesticity is set forth as a
value scheme for ordering all of life, in competition with the
ethos of money and exploitation that is perceived to prevail in
American society.[44]

Baym may well be right to assert that the crusade for domesticity
and the domestic novel served the needs of women; surely, they
could never have been so successful if they had not responded to a
real need, although we might ask if that need is filled by a real or
a false—or at least contradictory—satisfaction. A similar debate
takes place about the contemporary women's fiction of the mass-
produced romance; we not infrequently find ourselves trapped, in
such discussions, in a fruitless polemic between those who dismiss
such fiction as escapist or blatantly manipulative and those who
valorize it as an authentic popular culture. The principle that mass
culture *unites* a utopian impulse and an ideological tendency—and
even, sometimes, manipulation—moves us a necessary step forward. (Baym seems to be moving in the same direction, although
this would certainly not be her language.) But Baym is writing
about a specific genre of novels in a specific period, a particular
group of novels written "by and about" and primarily for women,
and to enter fully into these questions would, again, require a study
in itself. What concerns us is the way in which formulas developed
in these and related fictions are taken up into American naturalism.

And despite the fact that it was the American realists who began
the attack on the sentimental that Baym is still resisting, despite the
direct contradictions between the ideas associated with naturalism
and the assumptions of domestic fiction, those formulas do frequently appear as part of the naturalist novel, from the first to the
most recent examples of the genre. Harold Frederic was an admirer
of Howells and a self-identified realist, and his *Seth's Brother's Wife*
(1887) is one of the earliest of the novels critics commonly consider naturalist.[45] Frederic writes out of an aesthetic ideology that is
not specifically naturalist, he has not yet taken up the larger questions of reform, and the novel's generic heterogeneity is so profound that we might want to call it protonaturalist. But the question
of where one draws the boundary of the genre is less interesting
than the way in which *Seth's Brother's Wife* sketches out ideological and formal tensions and solutions that will appear, in different
combinations, in later works.

Seth's Brother's Wife begins as a portrait of the blighted lives of
inhabitants of rural New York, but by the end of the novel Frederic

176
Form
and
History
in
American
Literary
Naturalism

has fallen back on a highly conventionalized narrative strategy and provided a happy ending. Passages from the beginning and the conclusion of the book suggest the discontinuity between the text's different voices:

> "Ef ther' ain't a flare-up in *this* haouse 'fore long, I miss *my* guess," said Alvira, as she kneaded the pie-crust, and pulled it out between her floury fingers to measure its consistency. "Ole Sabriny's got her back up this time to stay."
>
> "Well, let 'em flare, says I. 'Taint none o' aour business, Alviry."
>
> "I knaow, Milton; but still it seems to me she might wait at least till th' corpse was aout o' th' haouse."
>
> "What's thet got to dew with it?"

> One closing scene we may glance at—a pretty room, with modern furniture, and wide, flower-clad windows looking upon one of the best of Tecumseh's residential streets. Annie, grown brighter-faced and yet no older in looks, despite the nearly four years of married life which have gone by, stands at the window with a baby in her arms, and laughs as she tosses the infant forward toward the panes, in greeting to the paternal parent, who is coming up the front steps. . . .
>
> "O Seth, her first tooth has come through!"[46]

Alvira and Milton, the "hired folk," cannot pronounce a sentence without reminding the reader of their geographical and class origins, and Milton's talk reveals his brutality. Seth and Annie are somewhat better-educated inhabitants of the same rural areas; as we might expect, however (or perhaps for the sake of illustration I should write haowever), their transcribed speech never reflects any accent and through its normative standard English asserts that they share the ground of the narrator and reader. The dichotomized register of characterization is familiar from our study of later naturalism, but this early example demonstrates clearly that different kinds of characters are constructed within different generic codes.

Different as they are, on second glance both the quoted passages prove to be concerned with the same topic: the family. *Seth's Brother's Wife* is constantly concerned with sexuality and aggression among close kin, from the feud under discussion in the first quotation to Seth's political and personal conflicts with his brother and his flirtation with his brother's wife. The shadows of fratricide and incest that hang over Seth are dispelled only when his brother is murdered—by someone else. Milton is not only a murderer but lusts after Annie, staring at her with "a look to frighten an honest young woman—an intent, hungry, almost wolfish look, unrelieved by so much as a glimmer of the light of manliness" (p. 25). The displacement of disturbing forces onto the hired man, the move from one generic discourse to another, makes possible the idyllic domestic scene at the end of the novel.

We have already encountered many texts in which naturalism is articulated with the conventions of domestic fiction. Melodrama and sentiment often merge into each other; in both *The Jungle* and *King Coal*, for example, an important aspect of Sinclair's melodramatic portrayal of the evils of capitalism is its destruction of its victims' families. When Jurgis strives to resign himself to brutality after the death of his son, it is his love for his family that represents his humanity and that he feels he must eradicate:

> He had wasted his life, he had wrecked himself, with his accursed weakness; and now he was done with it—he would tear it out of him, root and branch! There should be no more tears and no more tenderness; he had had enough of them— they had sold him into slavery! . . . This was no world for women and children, and the sooner they got out of it the better for them. Whatever Antanas might suffer where he was, he could suffer no more than he would have had he stayed upon earth. And meantime his father had thought the last thought about him that he meant to; he was going to think of himself, he was going to fight for himself, against the world that had baffled him and tortured him!
>
> So he went on, tearing up all the flowers from the garden of his soul, and setting his heel upon them. [pp. 253–54]

And certainly domestic values are a vital part of the best-selling social melodrama—Winston Churchill is fascinated by precisely the conflict Baym identifies between the values of the home and of the market, and more than one of his plots turns on a woman's effort to come to terms with the exploitive, immoral behavior of a beloved man. We have already seen that the affirmation of domestic ideology reappears as the solution to a seemingly catastrophic immersion in natural forces in so recent and unlikely a text as *Altered States*.

The naturalists who have been central to this study are far more ambivalent about mass culture in general and domestic ideology and sentimental conventions in particular. But they also sometimes fall back on this formula. Jack London embraces but resists his popular success, relies on but tirelessly transforms the formulaic genres of mass literature, criticizes bourgeois ideals of femininity and domesticity but kills off Wolf Larsen and permits Humphrey Van Weyden and Maud Brewster to live happily ever after. Perhaps the sharpest and strangest image of London's powerful, contradictory articulation of naturalism and the domestic formula is the conclusion of *White Fang*, in which the domesticated wolf is not only guardian of the human household but, in a bizarre parody of the ideal family, is himself head of a canine household.

178
Form
and
History
in
American
Literary
Naturalism

In *Sister Carrie* Dreiser also occasionally advocates domestic values. He writes, for example:

> A lovely home atmosphere is one of the flowers of the world, than which there is nothing more tender, nothing more delicate, nothing more calculated to make strong and just the natures cradled and nourished within it. Those who have never experienced such a beneficent influence will not understand wherefore the tear springs glistening to the eyelids at some strange breath in lovely music. The mystic chords which bind and thrill the heart of the nation, they will never know.
> [chap. 9, p. 63]

But these sentimental reflections describe what it is that the Hurstwoods' home *lacks*, and the topic of the novel is not the vitality but the failure of the family. "Sister" Carrie, as I have noted, leaves her home on the first page of the novel and merely passes through the Hansens' flat on her way to adventures in a larger world. Although she contracts alliances in which she becomes "Mrs. Drouet" and "Mrs. Wheeler," she never returns to the family by actually marrying or irrevocably committing herself to a household. The well-worn coin of sentimental language is handed about, and the form of marriage is observed, but these formalities are as empty as the Hurstwoods' and Hansens' homes. The family is important in *Sister Carrie*—but only as a point of departure.

The domestic survives most vitally in *Sister Carrie* precisely as form, for the novel constantly reflects on and remakes such conventional codes. Cathy and Arnold Davidson have made a detailed study of the relationship of *Sister Carrie* to formulaic literature, finding prototypes for Carrie as heroine in four types of popular fiction that they believe Dreiser draws on, transforms, and even parodies: the "working girl" novel, the sentimental "costume" romance, the domestic novel centering on matrimony, and the Horatio Alger tale of success. They contend that the novel "mirrors the conventional fiction of its time, for Theodore Dreiser employed well established plot devices to examine the same manners and mores prescribed by his now forgotten contemporaries. But the moral image reflected in various widely read turn-of-the-century novels is, in Dreiser's work, refracted and distorted."[47] *Sister Carrie* not only plays with these devices but dramatizes their significance in the text itself, using characters' taste in literature to locate them in social and intellectual hierarchies.

It is in fact not uncommon for the naturalists to incorporate a self-reflective consideration of the modern artist and thus their own contradictory roles as cultural producers—Presley and Martin Eden face very different but equally uncomfortable situations, for example. The naturalists are caught up in an expanding and changing literary marketplace and, as I have suggested in considering

the significance of formulaic narrative strategies in naturalism, are
deeply ambivalent about the status of the literary work as a commodity. The developing division between mass and high culture is itself unevenly correlated with gender and class. The authorial ideology of naturalism, characterized by both an aggressive masculinity and professionalism, is another terrain on which these complex problems are worked out, not only to make a place for the writers but in order for them to understand the possibilities and social significance of the various available forms. *Sister Carrie* remains one of the most evocative explorations of this network of problems.

Frank Norris both wrote some wholly or predominantly sentimental tales and incorporated domestic formulas in virtually all his work. In his "Man Proposes" sketches, he constructs characters as polarized and generically bound as those of Frederic's *Seth's Brother's Wife*. In *Vandover and the Brute*, he embodies the forces of sexual passion in the prostitute Flossie and the saving grace of the good woman in Turner Ravis; we can see the vocabulary that complements the melodramatic descriptions of Vandover's decline in the quintessentially sentimental speech in which Turner asks him to be virtuous " 'if not for your own sake, then for the sake of that other girl that's coming into your life some time, that other girl who is good and sweet and pure, whom you will really, really love and who will really, really love you.' "[48]

In *The Octopus* Hilma Tree succeeds where Turner Ravis fails in teaching Annixter to beware the brute within and awakening his better self. Once Hilma is married and with child, she exerts an elevating influence not only on Annixter but on everyone around her; at the jackrabbit drive she sits with her back against a tree "as on a throne, raised above the rest, the radiance of the unseen crown of motherhood glowing from her forehead, the beauty of the perfect woman surrounding her like a glory. And the josh died away on Osterman's lips, and unconsciously and swiftly he bared his head" (2:215). Immediately after this scene Annixter is killed and their household destroyed, so that Hilma's story would seem to come to a pessimistic conclusion. But her suffering serves to bring her to "her perfect maturity; she had known great love and she had known great grief, and the woman that had awakened in her with her affection for Annixter had been strengthened and infinitely ennobled by his death." She still has the same uplifting effect on a sensitive man, rousing Presley to wish "to be strong and noble because of her, to reshape his purposeless, half-wasted life with her nobility and purity and gentleness for his inspiration" (2:338). The discontinuity between the sentimental and the naturalist is much less apparent in *The Octopus* than in *Vandover and the Brute* because the love story takes its place as part of the panorama of life in the San Joaquin. And the novel's philosophical optimism attempts

180
Form
and
History
in
American
Literary
Naturalism

to build a conceptual bridge between the affirmation of virtue and the theory of causality; the beneficent results of Hilma's and Annixter's love serve as one more proof that, as the novel's conclusion asserts, all forces work together for the good.

There is no such sentimental subplot in *McTeague*, in which Norris resolutely rejects domestic values. McTeague's marriage to Trina is motivated by a sexual attraction, and far from refining their sentiments and actions it contributes to their misery. The prostitute Flossie, unnerving as she is to Dolly Haight and the narrator, is at least comprehensible in terms of a confrontation between virtue and wickedness—one can resist or try to reclaim her. The amoral world of forces that we see in *McTeague*, on the other hand, presents a deeper threat because it challenges the sentimental image of human nature and relationships and changes the ground of meaning. In *The Octopus* Minna is still unnerving, but she is clearly a victim of forces beyond her control rather than an evil temptress; Crane's *Maggie*, too, questions the relevance of moral categories to human behavior.

The terrain of meaning is indeed different in domestic fiction and in strictly naturalist portrayals of courtship and the household, for it is as always in the slums that we see forces rather than freedom at work. In the degraded world of *McTeague* and *Maggie* the family is no safe enclave in which humanity, affection, and virtue can assert themselves; instead, brutality, passion, and indifferent causality predominate. The family itself becomes a nightmare; the bonds between family members are not only ambivalent, as in *Seth's Brother's Wife*, but manifestly burdened with sexual and aggressive impulses. Both *McTeague* and *Maggie* comment ironically on the courtship plot and the image of the family as represented in sentimental formulas and the domestic novel, revealing life as it "really" is—at least in another part of the city. The portrait of the family as the scene of sexualized rage reaches its fullest, most painful development in Selby's *Last Exit to Brooklyn*: "The fuckin bitch. Why cant she just leave me alone. Why dont she goaway somewhere with that fuckin kid. Id like ta rip her cunt right the fuck outta her" (pp. 119–20). In the slums the family is not a haven but only the most intimate arena for the forces of destruction.

The generic discontinuity between naturalism and the domestic formula can be contained in various ways and can even resolve other formal and ideological dilemmas, but it necessarily opens a potentially disruptive fissure in the text. Both its stabilizing and its disruptive force depend on the complex interpenetrations of form and meaning that constitute the text, for all its elements are both generically defined and inescapably bound up with extraliterary ideological discourses. The conditions under which this transmutation of form into content and content into form take place are the historical changes in the family during the modern period and

the increasingly hegemonic bourgeois conception of the family—
two phenomena that are, I should perhaps underscore, distinct although certainly not unrelated. Our contemporary usage of "family," with its unproblematized conflation of kinship and household, itself depends on those developments. The representations of the family deployed in the literary texts we have been examining are continuous with the general ideology of the period. Trachtenberg writes of "the spectacle of contrast performed in the press, between 'home' and 'slum'" (p. 128). When Riis wants to win sympathy for his unfortunate "man with the knife," he writes of his "little ones crying for bread around the cold and cheerless hearth"; when a magazine writer wants to warn of the menace of the corporation, he writes of its profit-seeking "fingers feeling where our children play."[49] The privacy of the middle-class home is the inverse of the dangerous streets of the slum and the impersonal battlefield of the economy.

The contrast between the idyllic scene of middle-class domesticity in *Seth's Brother's Wife* and the sordid family drama of *Last Exit to Brooklyn* sketches out the naturalists' dynamic articulation of representations of class and family. Baym's description of women's fiction suggests a rather different articulation of the economic and the domestic, but she acknowledges that after 1870 the significance of the domestic changes: "Home now became a retreat, a restraint and a constraint, as it had not appeared to be earlier; to define it as woman's sphere was now unambiguously to invite her to absent herself permanently from the world's affairs" (p. 50). Jane Austen as well as Baym's popular novelists strove to unify economic values and the traditional order of kinship and reciprocal obligations, taking marriage as the privileged ground of that negotiation. But the fictions that inherit the conventions of mid-nineteenth-century domestic fiction refuse these wide-ranging, increasingly mysterious connections in favor of a passionate, even obsessive defense of the limited relations of the family. To support that burden those intimate connections must now be represented as unconditionally loving and self-sufficiently satisfying. And as a residual element in various sorts of fiction, the formula does indeed begin to take on the emotional exaggeration and vociferous optimism commonly associated with the sentimental. In naturalism the conventionalized image of the domestic becomes precisely the claustrophobic retreat Baym describes. But it is an enclave that can never seem wholly safe, for it is penetrated by the very impulses that are attributed to the wild man outside the campfire and is only tenuously independent of the pitiless economic jungle that looms outside the hearth. The sentimental formula must refuse the powerful psychological forces and public affairs that on another page of the same narrative are the very topic of naturalism, and its gesture of exclusion always reminds us of the text's heterogeneity.

182

Form
and
History
in
American
Literary
Naturalism

The domestic formula completes but does not close the list of the narrative strategies of naturalism, leaving our description of the genre open to many kinds of generic discontinuity. Each text arrives at a unique and unpredictable although never arbitrary combination of elements. As the first chapter of this study argues, genre inevitably enters into every work but no work is contained by genre. The diversity of topics considered in this chapter appropriately complements the generalized model of naturalism emerging from the preceding discussions; we rise from the abstract to the concrete. However, the array of narrative strategies examined in this chapter—documentary organization, the plot of decline, the incorporation of melodramatic and sentimental formulas—consistently recur in association with the semantic field and the register of characterization already identified as characteristically naturalist. The genre cannot, and should not, be delimited, but its distinctive array of features and the narrative dynamic established by their coordination can be described.

This account of naturalism as a genre opens the way for a more just assessment of the naturalists. Questions of value have not been a central concern in this study, and to take them up in any detailed way would require laying yet another theoretical groundwork. But I hope it has been apparent that I enjoy and esteem these novels and that I think they are generally underestimated. Although I am drawn to the naturalists by a shared interest in social conflict and social change, in studying them I have not, as critics so often do, chosen authors whose ideas and values resemble my own. The naturalists are not particularly congenial to contemporary intellectuals. But we deceive ourselves if we think we have nothing in common with these writers, and if we refuse to attend to them we lose not only the considerable pleasure and insight that many of their works can produce but knowledge of our own history and our own culture.

Naturalism is not just deterministic fiction or realism in a pessimistic mood. Those characterizations point toward some of the qualities of naturalist novels, but they do not enable us to penetrate analytically the way in which the novels reinvent the possibilities of narrative at their historical moment. The pattern that emerges from this transmutation of form into content, content into form, is distinctive although it can never be wholly abstracted from the heterogeneous literary texts, literary history, and social history in which it takes shape. Analyzed through the concept of the genre, the antinomies of naturalism, its unstable division of spectator and actor, its diverse strategies for generating sequence and closure take on new meaning as elements of the imaginative landscape of late nineteenth- and early twentieth-century America. My goal has been to reinvent that terrain as part of a new literary history.

Notes

Chapter 1

1. See for example Tzvetan Todorov, *The Fantastic: A Structural Approach to a Literary Genre* (1970), trans. Richard Howard (Ithaca, N.Y.: Cornell University Press, 1975), p. 7: "literature now seems to be abandoning the division into genres"; David H. Richter, "Pandora's Box Revisited: A Review Article," *Critical Inquiry* 1 (1974): 453: "The movements in philosophical method which we associate with Kant and Croce coincided with trends in literary criticism that de-emphasized, denigrated, and all but destroyed the idea of genre—cast it off the throne it had occupied during the Neoclassical period and, indeed, since the Middle Ages, and put it into the doghouse. The hegemony of the Romantic, the neo-Kantian, and the 'New' critics has lasted long and is only now beginning to dissolve"; Gustavo Pérez Firmat, "The Novel as Genres," *Genre* 12 (1979): 274: "Nowadays it is readily recognized that genology has been the ugly duckling of twentieth-century literary criticism. Brushed aside first by Croce and his followers, and later by the different schools of formal analysis, only in the last few years has it once again entered by mainstream of critical inquiry" [*sic*]. See also n. 14.

2. Robert Con Davis, "Book Reviews: Introduction," *Genre* 14 (1981): 269. The emphasis is Davis's.

3. Jacques Derrida, "The Law of Genre," trans. Avital Ronell, *Critical Inquiry* 7 (1980): 59.

4. Paul Hernadi, *Beyond Genre: New Directions in Literary Classification* (Ithaca, N.Y.: Cornell University Press, 1972), p. vii.

5. Todorov, *The Fantastic*, pp. 8–9.

6. Hernadi, *Beyond Genre*, p. 166. I should note, however, that Hernadi considers that several modes operate in an individual work, which is a more polycentric position than that of most critics.

7. See Pérez Firmat, "The Novel as Genres," pp. 278–79.

8. In "The Law of Genre" Derrida proposes: "Every text participates in one or several genres, there is no genreless text; there is always a genre and genres, yet such participation never amounts to belonging . . . because of the *trait* of participation itself, because of the effect of the code and of the generic mark. Making genre its mark, a text demarcates itself" (p. 65).

9. John Reichert, "More Than Kin and Less Than Kind: The Limits of Genre Theory," *Yearbook of Comparative Criticism* 8 (1978): 57–79, discusses these issues in detail.

10. Claudio Guillén, *Literature as System: Essays toward the Theory of Literary History* (Princeton, N.J.: Princeton University Press, 1971). See especially p. 390.

11. See Todorov, "The Notion of Literature," *New Literary History* 5 (1973): 5–16.

12. Pérez Firmat, "The Novel as Genres," p. 284. Todorov's suggestion appears in "The Origin of Genres," *New Literary History* 8 (1976): 159–70.

13. Pérez Firmat, "The Novel as Genres," p. 271.

14. "If one groups works together on the basis of observed similarities one does indeed have purely empirical taxonomies of the sort which have helped to bring the notion of genre into disrepute. A taxonomy, if it is to have any theoretical value, must be motivated." Jonathan Culler, *Structuralist Poetics: Structuralism, Linguistics, and the Study of Literature* (Ithaca, N.Y.: Cornell University Press, 1975), p. 136.

15. Gustavo Pérez Firmat, "Genre as Text," *Comparative Literature Studies* 17 (1980): 17.

16. Reichert, "More Than Kin," pp. 58–59.

17. Northrop Frye, *Anatomy of Criticism: Four Essays* (Princeton, N.J.: Princeton University Press, 1957), pp. 247–48.

18. Pérez Firmat, "Genre as Text," p. 24.

19. My contentions here are informed by (although not necessarily faithful to) both Fredric Jameson's genre theory and the study of "literary production" undertaken by Althusserian and post-Althusserian cultural theorists.

20. Fredric Jameson, *The Political Unconscious: Narrative as a Socially Symbolic Act* (Ithaca, N.Y.: Cornell University Press, 1981), pp. 106–7.

21. Raymond Williams, *Keywords: A Vocabulary of Culture and Society* (New York: Oxford University Press, 1976), p. 184.

22. On realism see George J. Becker, "Introduction: Modern Realism as a Literary Movement," in *Documents of Modern Literary Realism*, ed. George J. Becker (Princeton, N.J.: Princeton University Press, 1963), p. 7. On naturalism see Lilian R. Furst and Peter N. Skrine, *Naturalism* (London: Methuen, 1971). The latter is a particularly useful brief account of the "generic text" of naturalism.

23. On Zola and naturalism see for example Harry Levin, *The Gates of Horn: A Study of Five French Realists* (New York: Oxford University Press, 1963) and Charles Child Walcutt, *American Literary Naturalism, A Divided Stream* (1956; reprint, Westport, Conn.: Greenwood Press, 1973). On the question of the direct influence of European naturalism on American naturalism, see Lars Åhnebrink, *The Beginnings of Naturalism in American Fiction: A Study of the Works of Hamlin Garland, Stephen Crane, and Frank Norris with Special Reference to Some European Influences, 1891–1903* (New York: Russell & Russell, 1961).

24. Becker's essay is the Introduction to *Documents of Modern Literary Realism*, which he edited.

25. Williams, *Keywords*, pp. 217–18.

26. This is perhaps the moment to comment that my use of "his" in such formulations is quite deliberate and considered. The location of this perspective is normatively masculine.

27. John Berger and Jean Mohr, *Another Way of Telling* (New York: Pantheon Books, 1982), p. 96. This complex meditation on photography has important implications for any cultural practice concerned with appearances.

28. E. H. Gombrich, *Art and Illusion: A Study in the Psychology of Pictorial Representation*, rev. ed. (Princeton, N.J.: Princeton University Press, 1969), p. 301.

29. See Hayden White, *Metahistory: The Historical Imagination in Nineteenth-Century Europe* (Baltimore: Johns Hopkins University Press, 1973).

30. Émile Zola, "Naturalism in the Theatre." I quote the easily accessible translation in Becker, *Documents of Modern Literary Realism*, p. 208.

31. Zola, "The Experimental Novel," in Becker, *Documents*, p. 168.

32. Frank Norris, "Frank Norris' Weekly Letter" (1901), in *The Literary Criticism of Frank Norris*, ed. Donald Pizer (Austin: University of Texas Press, 1964), pp. 73, 75. The emphasis, which is mine, reproduces the sense of the phrase when read in context.

33. I allude to Roland Barthes, *Mythologies* (1957), trans. Annette Lavers (New York: Hill and Wang, 1972).

34. On the transformed meaning of animals since the beginning of the nineteenth century see John Berger, "Why Look at Animals?," in *About Looking* (New York: Pantheon, 1980), pp. 1–26.

35. Fredric Jameson, "On Goffman's Frame Analysis," *Theory and Society* 3 (1976): 126.

36. I am far from the first person to make this criticism. See for example Frank Lentricchia, *After the New Criticism* (Chicago: University of Chicago Press, 1980), pp. 105–12. I hope it is clear at this point that in rejecting Culler's notion of the reader I do not mean to reduce reading to a subjective process, but rather to overcome the sterile opposition between subjectivity and objectivity and arrive at a situated historical analysis.

37. Jameson, *The Political Unconscious*, p. 141.

38. Ibid., p. 105. See also Jameson's discussion of Lukács in *Marxism and Form*, quoted below.

39. Georg Lukács, *Writer and Critic and Other Essays*, trans. and ed. Arthur D. Kahn (New York: Grosset & Dunlap, 1970), p. 116. Lukács's critique of naturalism is to some degree informed by his hostility to socialist realism which in his view committed similar errors. This does not, however, undermine the seriousness of Lukács's analysis of naturalism. The last section of "Narrate or Describe?," dealing with Soviet socialist realism of the thirties, was omitted from *Writer and Critic* presumably because of a policy of "eliminating from the text polemics pertinent at the time of publication in order, by this pruning, to expose more effectively what is of lasting significance" (Preface by Lukács, p. 8). This omitted material may be found in English in Part 2 of S. Altschuler's translation of the essay as "Narration vs. Description," *International Literature* 7 (1937): 93–98.

40. Fredric Jameson, *Marxism and Form: Twentieth-Century Dialectical Theories of Literature* (Princeton, N.J.: Princeton University Press, 1971), p. 195.

41. Georg Lukács, *Studies in European Realism*, trans. Edith Bone (New York: Grosset & Dunlap, 1964), p. 13.

42. Georg Lukács, *Realism in Our Time: Literature and the Class Struggle*, trans. John and Necke Mander (New York: Harper and Row, 1971), p. 48.

43. Lukács, *Writer and Critic*, p. 47.

44. Ibid., p. 43.

45. Ibid., p. 51.

46. Ibid., p. 131.

47. My reading in this section is based on Jameson's essay on Lukács in *Marxism and Form*. See pp. 161–63 and especially pp. 189–90: "Indeed, we

are tempted to claim that for the Lukács of *History and Class Consciousness* the ultimate resolution of the Kantian dilemma is to be found not in the nineteenth-century philosophical systems themselves, not even in that of Hegel, but rather in the nineteenth-century *novel*: for the process he describes bears less resemblance to the ideals of scientific knowledge than it does to the elaboration of plot."

48. Georg Lukács, *History and Class Consciousness: Studies in Marxist Dialectics*, trans. Rodney Livingstone (Cambridge, Mass.: MIT Press, 1971), p. 135.

49. See Lukács's *Studies in European Realism*, pp. 85–86.

50. Jameson, *Marxism and Form*, p. 204.

51. Jameson, *The Political Unconscious*, p. 148.

52. For examples see Gareth Stedman Jones, "The Marxism of the Early Lukács," and André Glucksmann, "A Ventriloquist Structuralism," both reprinted in *Western Marxism: A Critical Reader*, ed. New Left Review (1977; London: New Left Review/Verso, 1978), pp. 11–60 and pp. 273–314 respectively.

53. Louis Althusser and Étienne Balibar, *Reading Capital* (1965; 2d ed., 1968), trans. Ben Brewster (London: New Left Books, 1977), p. 36.

54. Jameson, "Imaginary and Symbolic in Lacan: Marxism, Psychoanalytic Criticism, and the Problem of the Subject," *Yale French Studies*, no. 55/56 (1977): 389.

55. Althusser and Balibar, *Reading Capital*, p. 43. According to Brewster's Glossary, *Verbindung* means "a complex structure, doubly articulated (in the mode of production, by the productive forces connexion and the relations of production connexion . . .), and one that specifies its content (its 'supports' . . .), which changes with a change in the formation or mode of production analysed" (p. 311).

56. Terry Eagleton, *Criticism and Ideology: A Study in Marxist Literary Theory* (London: New Left Books, 1976), pp. 69–70.

57. Lars Åhnebrink, *The Beginnings of American Literary Naturalism*, cited in n. 23 above.

58. See *The Literary Criticism of Frank Norris*, ed. Donald Pizer, especially "Zola as Romantic Writer," pp. 71–72.

59. Eric Sundquist, ed., Introduction to *American Realism: New Essays* (Baltimore: Johns Hopkins University Press, 1982), p. 4.

60. See Donald Pizer, *Twentieth-Century American Literary Naturalism: An Interpretation* (Carbondale: Southern Illinois University Press, 1982) for an argument that American literary naturalism continues well into the twentieth century.

61. My formulation here is indebted to Jay Martin, *Harvests of Change: American Literature, 1865–1914* (Englewood Cliffs, N.J.: Prentice-Hall, 1967), p. 1.

62. Robert Higgs, *The Transformation of the American Economy, 1865–1914: An Essay in Interpretation* (New York: John Wiley & Sons, 1971), p. 50.

63. Ibid., pp. 18–21.

64. Ibid., pp. 19–20.

65. Howard Zinn, *A People's History of the United States* (New York: Harper Colophon, Harper and Row, 1980), p. 247.

66. Higgs, *Transformation of the American Economy*, p. 46.

67. Ibid., pp. 47–48.

68. Ibid., pp. 39–42.

69. Ibid., p. 34.

70. Burton J. Bledstein, *The Culture of Professionalism: The Middle Class and the Development of Higher Education in America* (1976; reprint, New York: W. W. Norton, 1978), p. 47.

71. Daniel J. Boorstin, *The Americans: The Democratic Experience* (New York: Random House, 1973), pp. 99–100.

72. Ibid., p. 203; see also pp. 200–203.

73. Alan Trachtenberg, *The Incorporation of America: Culture and Society in the Gilded Age* (New York: Hill and Wang, 1982), p. 59. My account of the establishment of the time zones derives from this source, pp. 59–60. Trachtenberg weaves a wide variety of interdisciplinary materials into a cultural history of America from 1865 to 1893, and those not already familiar with this book may wish to consult it for the kind of full account of the period I will not provide in this study.

74. Higgs, *Transformation of the American Economy*, p. 59.

75. Ibid., pp. 48, 23.

76. Melvyn Dubofsky, *Industrialism and the American Worker, 1865–1920* (Arlington Heights, Ill.: AHM Publishing, 1975), pp. 9–10.

77. See Lawrence Goodwyn, *The Populist Moment: A Short History of the Agrarian Revolt in America* (New York: Oxford University Press, 1978); on the persistence of "hard times" see p. viii.

78. Dubofsky, *Industrialism and the American Worker*, p. 19.

79. Ibid.

80. Herbert G. Gutman, *Work, Culture and Society in Industrializing America: Essays in American Working-Class and Social History* (1976; reprint, New York: Random House, 1977), p. 13.

81. For a stern exposition of this point see Althusser and Balibar, *Reading Capital*, pp. 99–105. Although I bracket the theoretical problems of periodization that this recognition entails, in practice my analysis does not assume a uniform historical time.

Chapter 2

1. George J. Becker, "Introduction: Realism as a Literary Movement," in *Documents of Modern Literary Realism*, ed. George J. Becker (Princeton, N.J.: Princeton University Press, 1963), p. 35.

2. Lars Åhnebrink, *The Beginnings of Naturalism in American Fiction: A Study of the Works of Hamlin Garland, Stephen Crane, and Frank Norris with Special Reference to Some European Influences, 1891–1903* (New York: Russell & Russell, 1961), pp. vi–vii.

3. Ronald E. Martin, *American Literature and the Universe of Force* (Durham, N.C.: Duke University Press, 1981), p. 59. Martin, incidentally, writes of Norris, London, and Dreiser as realists and does not take up the generic questions that concern me here.

4. I cite such works throughout this chapter. For more general studies of the period, including but not limited to naturalist authors, see also Warner Berthoff, *The Ferment of Realism: American Literature, 1884–1919* (New York: The Free Press, 1965); Larzer Ziff, *The American 1890s: Life and Times*

of a Lost Generation (Lincoln: University of Nebraska Press, 1966); and Jay Martin, *Harvests of Change: American Literature, 1865–1914* (Englewood Cliffs, N.J.: Prentice-Hall, 1967). Harold Kaplan has recently published a study titled *Power and Order: Henry Adams and the Naturalist Tradition in American Fiction* (Chicago: University of Chicago Press, 1981), in which he argues that Adams coherently expresses the "naturalist imagination" and that "the major literary contribution of naturalist thought is a myth of power and conflict charged with apocalyptic themes of order and chaos, creation and destruction, purgative crisis and redemptive violence" (pp. x–xi). Many of Kaplan's observations about naturalism—for example, his acknowledgment of its reformist and melodramatic components and its "typical division . . . between actors and spectators" (p. 69)—are compatible with my own. However, he generalizes "naturalism," which comes to include not only a naturalist tradition and imagination but a naturalist ethos and a naturalist politics, far beyond what I consider defensible. His interest is ultimately not in genre but in the implications of the themes he discusses for problems in modern ethics and politics.

5. Vernon L. Parrington, *The Beginnings of Critical Realism in America, 1860–1920*, vol. 3 of *Main Currents in American Thought* (New York: Harcourt, Brace & World, 1930), p. 325.

6. Donald Pizer, *Twentieth-Century American Literary Naturalism: An Interpretation* (Carbondale: Southern Illinois University Press, 1982), p. x.

7. Donald Pizer, *Realism and Naturalism in Nineteenth-Century American Literature* (Carbondale: Southern Illinois University Press, 1966), p. 12.

8. Lilian R. Furst and Peter N. Skrine, *Naturalism* (London: Methuen, 1971), p. 22.

9. Charles Child Walcutt, *American Literary Naturalism, A Divided Stream* (1956; reprint, Westport, Conn.: Greenwood Press, 1973), pp. 24–25.

10. Charles Child Walcutt, "Naturalism and Robert Herrick: A Test Case," in *American Literary Naturalism: A Reassessment*, ed. Yoshinobu Hakutani and Lewis Fried (Heidelberg: Carl Winter, 1975), p. 81.

11. Sydney J. Krause, ed., Introduction to *Essays on Determinism in American Literature* (Kent, Ohio: Kent State University Press, 1964), p. 9.

12. Theodore Dreiser, *Jennie Gerhardt* (New York: Harper & Brothers, 1911), p. 401.

13. A. J. Greimas and F. Rastier, "The Interaction of Semiotic Constraints," *Yale French Studies*, no. 41 (1968): 86–105. Greimas and Rastier use this more elaborate diagram for the elementary structure of meaning (p. 88):

"S2" is the *contrary* of s1, that is, a concept which is its opposite. $\overline{s1}$ is s1's *contradictory*, that which is "not s1." $\overline{s2}$ is both the contrary of $\overline{s1}$, and the contradictory of s2. The relation between s1 and $\overline{s2}$, and between s2 and $\overline{s1}$, is one of implication; these are the "deixes." S is the semantic axis which consists of the concept "both s1 and s2"; $\bar{S}$ is "neither s1 nor s2."

This model can refer either to a whole semiotic system or to one of its systematic instances.

Greimas illustrates his explanation of the structure of signification with a "study of the sexual relations of a human group" (p. 93). In the following diagrams from that study the difference between the contrary, that which is forbidden, and the contradictory, that which is simply not prescribed, is perhaps somewhat easier to grasp.

General model (p. 93):

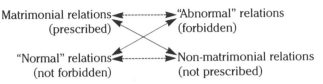

In traditional French society (p. 94):

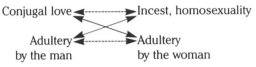

14. The semantic rectangle has been used to analyze literary texts in various ways. In "The Interaction of Semiotic Constraints" Greimas and Rastier set up a series of rectangles and investigate the correlations between them, claiming that a series representing whether a marriage is prescribed, profitable, or desirable (or, for each, any of the other three alternatives) could "furnish an organon adequate to describe interpersonal relations in narrative" (p. 98). Greimas also uses the rectangle to analyze Bernanos in his *Sémantique Structurale* (Paris: Larousse, 1966); and Fredric Jameson uses it in different ways in both *The Prison-House of Language* (Princeton, N.J.: Princeton University Press, 1972) and *The Political Unconscious: Narrative as a Socially Symbolic Act* (Ithaca, N.Y.: Cornell University Press, 1981).

I suspect that the elementary structure of signification lends itself to diverse applications because of its somewhat uncertain status as a theoretical construct, and I want to emphasize that I am aware of its limitations and use it only as a heuristic device. Given the perspective on perceptual, literary, and knowledge-producing processes developed in the first chapter, it certainly cannot be considered an "elementary" structure as it is used in literary analysis or even in Greimas's initial example, cited above. The categories "man" and "woman" appear although that opposition is not a basic, natural category of meaning but one of the most complex constructs of any culture; "marriage," too, functions in many linked systems of meaning. And literary texts take such systems as their raw material, transforming them into new systems—one certainly could not transfer an 'organon' of marriage possibilities wholesale from anthropology to literary analysis. Thus in literary texts we will find not "elementary" structures of signification made up of pure, logical oppositions, ready to be collected like so many geological specimens; rather, we become engaged in a play of meanings that demands our participation in generating structures of signification and a semantic field out of terms that are always already part of semantic fields.

15. Jameson, *The Political Unconscious*, p. 83.

16. This is perhaps the moment to warn that in no case do I give a *comprehensive* account of even a single novel, for many features of a given narrative—while always bound up with genre—are peripheral to discussion of a generic concept, and both my focus and considerations of space preclude attempting such accounts.

17. Since many editions of *Sister Carrie* are available I give chapter references as well as page numbers referring to the most widely available authoritative text, ed. Donald Pizer (New York: W. W. Norton, 1970). The present quotations are from chap. 1, pp. 1 and 8. I use a text based on the first edition, which is the one that had authorial approval and was after all the form in which readers encountered the novel until the 1981 publication of the manuscript. However, I will comment later on issues raised by the manuscript. Clearly, both versions have claims to legitimacy, and we will learn more from analyzing the differences between them than from debating their claims.

18. Alan Trachtenberg, *The Incorporation of America: Culture and Society in the Gilded Age* (New York: Hill and Wang–Farrar, Straus and Giroux, 1982), p. 130.

19. This aspect of *Sister Carrie* is analyzed by Rachel Bowlby in a manuscript in progress.

20. For a discussion of the attitudes toward desire and capitalism revealed in *Sister Carrie* see Walter Benn Michaels, "*Sister Carrie's* Popular Economy," *Critical Inquiry* 7 (1980): 373–90. I find Michaels's analysis provocative and frequently persuasive, but his conclusions are undermined by an excessively abstract use of "capitalism."

21. This is one of the points where one's reading of *Sister Carrie* is affected by the manuscript edition, in which sexual motivations and sexual activities are much more openly described. One can still make this statement about the published text, but it is more clearly true of the manuscript.

22. Donald Pizer, *The Novels of Theodore Dreiser: A Critical Study* (Minneapolis: University of Minnesota Press, 1976), p. 75.

23. Susan Sontag, *Illness as Metaphor* (New York: Farrar, Straus and Giroux, 1978), p. 57.

24. See Martin on the tendency of American thinkers to read determinism optimistically and the Spencerian overtones of such a contention.

25. Sontag, *Illness as Metaphor*, p. 55.

26. The chapter titles of course are not part of the original manuscript, and although Dreiser endorsed them for the first edition, there is evidence that he later regretted their inclusion (see Pizer, *The Novels of Theodore Dreiser*, p. 52, and *Sister Carrie: The Pennsylvania Edition*, ed. Neda M. Westlake, John C. Berkey, Alice M. Winters, and James L. W. West III [Philadelphia: University of Pennsylvania Press, 1981], p. 525). See n. 17 for my comment on the question of the manuscript and the published text of the novel. But in any case the argument does not stand or fall on the basis of this example, which is simply a convenient point at which to begin.

27. Robert H. Wiebe, *The Search for Order, 1877–1920* (New York: Hill and Wang, 1967), p. 145.

28. It underscores the importance of the image of the wolf in London's work to know its importance in his personal symbolic system. As biographer Andrew Sinclair reports, "After 1903, he signed his intimate letters

'Wolf.' He named the house he was to build Wolf House. He kept a husky called Brown Wolf. His bookplate was a wolf's head. He became more and more aware of his correspondence with the wolf—the destroyer and preserver of Norse mythology, the dark force of destruction to the Greeks, and the life-giving inspiration of the Romans who believed that Romulus and Remus were suckled by a she-wolf" (*Jack: A Biography of Jack London* [New York: Harper and Row, 1977], p. 92.)

29. Jack London, *White Fang* (1906; reprint, New York: Macmillan, 1906), p. 3.

30. Claude Lévi-Strauss, *Structural Anthropology*, trans. Claire Jacobson and Brooke Grundfest Schoepf (New York: Basic Books, 1963), p. 225.

31. As I warned earlier, none of my analyses are comprehensive, but I would like to note in passing that *White Fang* suggests a rather bizarre religious allegory: White Fang originally makes a covenant of law with a god (that is, with a man), which after his many trials is replaced with a new covenant with his "love-master," when he is born again into his new life with Scott and becomes the "Blessed Wolf" (p. 328). There is a great deal more to be said about this story, and it deserves more attention than it has so far received from critics of American literature.

32. Jack London, *Martin Eden* (1909), reprinted in *Jack London: Novels and Social Writings*, ed. Donald Pizer (New York: Library of America, 1982), p. 558. Because of difficulty in obtaining a copy of the first edition, I have used this volume, which bases its text on first book publications. Pizer's accessible and reliable editions of London for the Library of America will likely become standard for the works they include.

33. Pizer, *Realism and Naturalism*, pp. 12–13.

34. Frank Norris, *Vandover and the Brute* (1914), vol. 5 of *The Complete Edition of Frank Norris* (Garden City, N.Y.: Doubleday, Doran & Co., 1928), p. 23.

35. Robert W. Schneider, *Five Novelists of the Progressive Era* (New York: Columbia University Press, 1965), p. 133.

36. Becker, "Introduction: Realism as a Literary Movement," p. 32.

Chapter 3

1. Fredric Jameson, "Imaginary and Symbolic in Lacan: Marxism, Psychoanalytic Criticism, and the Problem of the Subject," *Yale French Studies*, no. 55/56 (1977): 393–94.

2. Louis Althusser, *For Marx* (1965), trans. Ben Brewster (New York: Random House, 1969), pp. 233–34. My interpolation reluctantly follows the essay's own use of "men" as equivalent to "human beings."

3. Julia Kristeva, "The Bounded Text," in *Desire in Language: A Semiotic Approach to Literature and Art*, ed. Leon S. Roudiez, trans. Thomas Gora, Alice Jardine, and Leon S. Roudiez (New York: Columbia University Press, 1980), pp. 36–37.

4. Ibid., p. 36; emphasis deleted. The reader wishing to follow this discussion back to its theoretical conditions of possibility might begin by consulting not only the article mentioned but also Fredric Jameson, *The Political Unconscious: Narrative as a Socially Symbolic Act* (Ithaca, N.Y.: Cornell University Press, 1981), Terry Eagleton, *Criticism and Ideology: A*

Study in Marxist Literary Theory (London: New Left Books, 1976), and Tony Bennett, *Formalism and Marxism* (London: Methuen, 1979). I do not claim to reproduce the views of these critics (who in any case differ widely among themselves), but this is the climate of discussion informing the position I take. The relation of these issues to the epistemological questions taken up in Chapter 1 should be readily apparent.

5. Alan Trachtenberg, *The Incorporation of America: Culture and Society in the Gilded Age* (New York: Hill and Wang, 1982), p. 40. My description of the consequences of the depression closely follows his account on the preceding page.

6. Robert H. Wiebe, *The Search for Order, 1877–1920* (New York: Hill and Wang, 1967), pp. 14–15.

7. Lawrence Goodwyn, *The Populist Moment: A Short History of the Agrarian Revolt in America* (New York: Oxford University Press, 1978), pp. xx–xxi. This is an abridged edition of Goodwyn's *Democratic Promise: The Populist Moment in America* (New York: Oxford University Press, 1976).

8. Ibid., p. 86.

9. Ibid., p. 263.

10. "Preamble" to the Omaha platform, by Ignatius Donnelly; quoted in Goodwyn, *The Populist Moment*, p. 168.

11. Maxwell H. Bloomfield, *Alarms and Diversions: The American Mind through American Magazines, 1900–1914* (The Hague: Mouton, 1967), pp. 16–17. He is quoting Finley Peter Dunne, "In the Interpreter's House," *American Magazine* 75 (March 1913): 132–33.

12. Philip S. Foner, *The Great Labor Uprising of 1877* (New York: Monad, 1977), p. 9.

13. J[oseph] A. Dacus, *Annals of the Great Strikes in the United States: A Reliable History and Graphic Description of the Causes and Thrilling Events of the Labor Strikes and Riots of 1877* (Chicago: L. T. Palmer & Co., 1877), pp. iii–v.

14. Henry George, *Progress and Poverty: An Inquiry into the Cause of Industrial Depressions and of Increase of Want with Increase of Wealth . . . The Remedy*, 4th ed. (1880; reprint, New York: Robert Schalkenbach Foundation, 1955), pp. 285–86.

15. Roy Harvey Pearce, *Savagism and Civilization: A Study of the Indian and the American Mind* (1953; reprint, Baltimore: Johns Hopkins University Press, 1965), p. 6.

16. Richard Hofstadter, *Social Darwinism in American Thought*, rev. ed. (Boston: Beacon, 1955), p. 112.

17. Herbert G. Gutman, *Work, Culture and Society in Industrializing America: Essays in American Working-Class and Social History* (1976; reprint, New York: Random House, 1977), pp. 71–72.

18. Melvyn Dubofsky, *Industrialism and the American Worker, 1865–1920* (Arlington Heights, Ill.: AHM Publishing, 1975), p. 24.

19. Hayden White, "The Forms of Wildness: Archaeology of an Idea," in *The Wild Man Within: An Image in Western Thought from the Renaissance to Romanticism*, ed. Edward Dudley and Maximillian E. Novak (Pittsburgh: University of Pittsburgh Press, 1972), p. 4.

20. Jean-Paul Sartre, *Saint Genet: Actor and Martyr*, trans. Bernard Frechtman (New York: George Braziller, 1963), pp. 29–30.

21. John Berger, "Why Look at Animals?," in *About Looking* (New York: Pantheon, 1980), p. 26.

22. John Berger and Jean Mohr, *A Fortunate Man* (1967; reprint, New York: Random House, 1982), p. 110.

23. William Dean Howells, *A Traveller from Altruria* (1894), in *The Altrurian Romances*, ed. Edwin H. Cady et al. (Bloomington: Indiana University Press, 1968), p. 44.

24. John Hay, *The Breadwinners: A Social Study* (1883; reprint, New York: Harper & Brothers, 1911), pp. 74–75.

25. John Higham, *Strangers in the Land: Patterns of American Nativism, 1860–1925* (New Brunswick, N.J.: Rutgers University Press, 1955), p. 30.

26. I adopt the convenient term "general ideology" from Terry Eagleton, *Criticism and Ideology*. See pp. 44–63.

27. Quoted in David M. Fine, *The City, the Immigrant and American Fiction, 1880–1920* (Metuchen, N.J.: Scarecrow Press, 1977), p. 6.

28. Ibid.

29. Mark H. Haller, *Eugenics: Hereditarian Attitudes in American Thought* (New Brunswick, N.J.: Rutgers University Press, 1963), p. 54.

30. Jack London, *The Valley of the Moon* (1913; reprint, Santa Barbara, Calif.: Peregrine Smith, 1975). For the first discussion about the stock of the old Americans see pp. 21–23.

31. Anthony M. Platt, *The Child Savers: The Invention of Delinquency*, 2d ed. (Chicago: University of Chicago Press, 1977), p. 28.

32. Henry M. Boies, *Prisoners and Paupers: A Study of the Abnormal Increase of Criminals, and the Public Burden of Pauperism in the United States; the Causes and Remedies* (New York: G. P. Putnam's Sons, 1893), p. 34.

33. For a polemical statement of this point of view see William Ryan, *Blaming the Victim*, rev. ed. (New York: Random House, Vintage Books, 1976). For a powerful specific study see Stuart Hall et al., *Policing the Crisis: "Mugging," the State and Law and Order* (New York: Macmillan, 1978). I might add in passing that this critique of the ideology of law and order does not necessarily imply that a concern of policymakers should be with criminals as victims and not with the victims of crimes. Rather, it is a diagnosis of the ideological processes that explain crime to us.

34. Robert A. Morace, "The Writer and His Middle Class Audience: Frank Norris, A Case in Point," *Critical Essays on Frank Norris*, ed. Don Graham (Boston: G. K. Hall, 1980), p. 53. Morace also notes that *The Wave*, ironically in view of Norris's later *Octopus*, was founded as a publicity organ for a hotel owned by the Southern Pacific.

35. Frank Norris, "Suggestions: III. Brute" (1897), in vol. 10 of *The Complete Edition of Frank Norris* (Garden City, N.Y.: Doubleday, Doran & Co., 1928), pp. 80–81.

36. Frank Norris, "Man Proposes—No. I" (1896), in vol. 10 of *The Complete Edition of Frank Norris*, p. 58.

37. Frank Norris, "Man Proposes—No. II" (1896), in vol. 10 of *The Complete Edition of Frank Norris*, p. 59.

38. There are five sketches in this series; I analyze only the first two, but the others can easily be placed. The third sketch deals with the danger incurred by a man who does not observe class boundaries carefully enough and gets entangled with a sexually aggressive girl of lower social

class although he is really in love with someone else. Norris describes the situation in a familiar idiom: "There was something in him, some sensual second self, that the girl evoked at moments such as this; something that was of the animal and would not be gainsaid" (p. 68). The fourth is similar to the first; again the proposal is already set in a domestic scene and the girl's love is implied rather than stated directly (clearly Norris sees open consent as putting female purity in doubt). The fifth also deals with the world of the privileged but shows the proposal resulting in a misunderstanding because a catastrophic event (a shipwreck—and the significance of that image will be discussed elsewhere) intervenes. Only the second of these pieces can be considered naturalist; the third and fifth, however, show elements of the naturalist realm disrupting the middle-class domesticity that is unchallenged in the first and fourth.

39. Frank Norris, *McTeague: A Story of San Francisco* (1899), vol. 8 of *The Complete Edition of Frank Norris*, pp. 27–28.

40. Frank Norris, "Outward and Visible Signs: V. Thoroughbred" (1895), in vol. 10 of *The Complete Edition of Frank Norris*, p. 208.

41. Frank Norris, in *The Complete Edition of Frank Norris*, vol. 4. The first two quoted phrases are from p. 43, the third from p. 46, and the long passage from p. 45.

42. Donald Pizer, *The Novels of Frank Norris* (Bloomington: Indiana University Press, 1966). On this point see especially pp. 56–63.

43. See James Richard Giles, "A Study of the Concept of Atavism in the Writings of Rudyard Kipling, Frank Norris, and Jack London" (Ph.D. diss., University of Texas, 1967).

44. Jack London, *Before Adam* (New York: Macmillan, 1907), p. 18.

45. For example, see Stephen Jay Gould, "Fascinating Tails," *Discover* 3, no. 9 (1982): 40–41, for an account of a small contemporary furore over a human infant born with a tail.

46. This analysis suggests a connection between naturalism and a genre to which some of London's fiction has retrospectively been attributed: science fiction. The last chapter provides a model for discussing the way in which different generic strands coexist in a single text.

47. Paddy Chayefsky, *Altered States: A Novel* (1978; reprint, New York: Bantam, 1979), p. 200.

48. Frank Norris, *Vandover and the Brute* (1914), vol. 5 of *The Complete Edition of Frank Norris*, p. 278.

49. Frank Norris, *The Octopus: A Story of California* (1901), vols. 1 and 2 of *The Complete Edition of Frank Norris*, 2:214.

50. This portrait of Derrick as admirable and ethical is not wholly consistent; witness the remark that shocks Presley that he is indifferent to long-term freight rates because "by then we will, all of us, have made our fortunes" (ibid., 2:14). This element of the gambler in Derrick's character manifests a dissonance in Norris's treatment of the profit-seeking rancher.

51. This is not, I should note, a question of whether or not Crane's work "belongs" to naturalism, but a question of a different articulation of materials in different novels. Crane's work is also of course somewhat earlier than the "moment" of naturalism I have taken as my topic.

52. Stephen Crane, *Maggie: A Girl of the Streets* (1893), reprinted in *Bowery Tales*, vol. 1 of *The Works of Stephen Crane*, ed. Fredson Bowers (Charlottesville: University Press of Virginia, 1969), pp. 8, 18.

53. Alan Trachtenberg, "Experiments in Another Country: Stephen Crane's City Sketches," *Southern Review* 10 (1974): 265–85, reprinted in *American Realism: New Essays*, ed. Eric J. Sundquist (Baltimore: Johns Hopkins University Press, 1982), p. 145.

54. Stephen Crane, "An Experiment in Misery" (1894), in *The New York City Sketches of Stephen Crane and Related Pieces*, ed. R. W. Stallman and E. R. Hagemann (New York: New York University Press, 1966), p. 43.

55. Theodore Dreiser, *Sister Carrie*, ed. Donald Pizer (New York: W. W. Norton, 1970), chap. 33, pp. 239 and 244.

56. Ambrose Bierce, *The Devil's Dictionary* (1911; reprint, New York: Albert & Charles Boni, 1925), p. 255. The contents of this volume appeared in newspapers from 1881 to 1906 and were first collected as *The Cynic's Word Book* in 1906.

57. Theodore Dreiser, *The Hand of the Potter* (New York: Boni and Liveright, 1918), p. 169.

58. Theodore Dreiser, *Free and Other Stories* (New York: Boni and Liveright, 1918), p. 101.

59. Although I derive this analysis from the study of naturalist novels themselves, evidence that an opposition between privilege and Otherness fascinated each of these writers is not difficult to find. Robert H. Elias in his biography of Dreiser takes the tension between Dreiser's sense of himself as a spectator and as a vulnerable participant as fundamental to the novelist's character (*Theodore Dreiser: Apostle of Nature*, emended edition [Ithaca, N.Y.: Cornell University Press, 1970]). Warren French finds a similar ambivalence in Norris's college experiences, attributing his "attitude of inherent superiority" and "racial and class snobbery" to the social atmosphere of Norris's fraternity, and his "terrifying self-doubts" to his failure as a student (*Frank Norris* [New York: Twayne, 1962], pp. 20–21). Andrew Sinclair discusses the idiosyncratic determinants of London's fear of the Other: "Jack always said that he had lost his boyhood, but he had never lost his primitive terror of *Them*—the unknown people beating carpets in the yard, the Chinese gamblers of his drunken deliria, the Greek poachers of the Bay and the Italian scabs of the slums who had robbed him of his birthright as a pioneer American, the true heir of the land of California" (*Jack: A Biography of Jack London* [New York: Harper and Row, 1977], p. 220). Each author is different, of course; an analysis of the authorial ideology in each case would be a useful although sizable undertaking.

Chapter 4

1. The first phrase is Jack London's (*Martin Eden* [1909], reprinted in *Jack London: Novels and Social Writings*, ed. Donald Pizer [New York: Library of America, 1982], p. 574); the latter Donald Pizer's (*Realism and Naturalism in Nineteenth-Century American Literature* [Carbondale: Southern Illinois University Press, 1966], p. 13). Both were quoted in the previous chapter.

2. Warren French, "John Steinbeck: A Usable Concept of Naturalism," in *American Literary Naturalism: A Reassessment*, ed. Yoshinobu Hakutani and Lewis Fried (Heidelberg: Carl Winter, 1975), p. 125.

3. Donald Pizer, *The Novels of Theodore Dreiser: A Critical Study* (Minne-

apolis: University of Minnesota Press, 1976), p. 81.

4. Although I bracket the question of the concrete audiences of naturalism and contemporary literary criticism, it is not irrelevant: surely if those readers did not already predominantly think of themselves, or want to think of themselves, as middle class, that position could not be written into and other positions written out of the texts so matter-of-factly. My use of "he" for the reader, although in my case it should be "she," is meant to act as a reminder of the tension between implied and actual readers.

5. Fredric Jameson, "Generic Discontinuities in SF: Brian Aldiss' *Starship,*" *Science-Fiction Studies* 1 (1973): 61.

6. In this comment I disregard as outside my purview modern novels that disrupt "point of view" in various ways and about which these statements would be not so much inaccurate as inappropriate.

7. Stephen Crane, *Maggie: A Girl of the Streets*, in *Bowery Tales*, vol. 1 of *The Works of Stephen Crane*, ed. Fredson Bowers (Charlottesville: University Press of Virginia, 1969), p. 56 and p. 31 respectively.

8. Theodore Dreiser, *Free and Other Stories* (New York: Boni and Liveright, 1918), p. 103. This collection also contains "McEwen of the Shining Slave Makers." Both stories were originally published in *Ainslee's*.

9. The quoted phrase is from the subtitle of Dreiser's *Hey-Rub-A-Dub-Dub* (New York: Boni and Liveright, 1920).

10. Theodore Dreiser, *Sister Carrie*, ed. Donald Pizer (New York: W. W. Norton, 1970), chap. 46, pp. 354–55. The original manuscript is available in *Sister Carrie: The Pennsylvania Edition*, ed. Neda M. Westlake, John C. Berkey, Alice M. Winters, and James L. W. West III (Philadelphia: University of Pennsylvania Press, 1981). Here I quote p. 484. The differences between Ames's role in the manuscript and in the published text are discussed below.

11. All quotations in this paragraph are from Dreiser, *Sister Carrie*, chap. 32, pp. 235–37.

12. I take the image of the ladder from Pizer, *The Novels of Theodore Dreiser*, pp. 66–67.

13. Dreiser, *Sister Carrie*, ed. Westlake et al., p. 482.

14. Charles Child Walcutt, *American Literary Naturalism, A Divided Stream* (1956; reprint, Westport, Conn.: Greenwood Press, 1976), p. 27.

15. Pizer, *The Novels of Theodore Dreiser*, p. 69.

16. Dreiser, *Sister Carrie*, ed. Westlake et al., p. 487.

17. See Alan Trachtenberg, "Experiment in Another Country: Stephen Crane's City Sketches," *Southern Review* 10 (1974): 265–85, reprinted in *American Realism: New Essays*, ed. Eric J. Sundquist (Baltimore: Johns Hopkins University Press, 1982), pp. 138–54 and especially pp. 141 and 148–49 on newspapers of the 1890s. Some of this material becomes part of Trachtenberg's *Incorporation of America*, on which I draw in a more general discussion of newspapers and naturalism in Chapter 5.

18. The difficulties of spectatorship are also central to two interesting recent studies, Mark Seltzer's "*The Princess Casamassima*: Realism and the Fantasy of Surveillance," *Nineteenth-Century Fiction* 35 (1981): 506–34, reprinted in Sundquist, ed., *American Realism*, pp. 95–118; and Carolyn Porter's *Seeing and Being: The Plight of the Participant Observer in Emerson, James, Adams and Faulkner* (Middletown, Conn.: Wesleyan University Press, 1981). There are points of contact between what follows and, in

particular, Seltzer's argument.

19. Jack London, *Before Adam* (New York: Macmillan, 1907), pp. 137–38.

20. Jack London, *The Sea-Wolf* (New York: Macmillan, 1904), p. 3.

21. For examples see ibid., pp. 9, 42, 46, and 311.

22. In a manuscript titled "Repetition and Negligence: Naturalism and London's 'To Build a Fire'" (a portion of which was delivered 29 December 1983 at the MLA convention in New York), Lee Mitchell finds in London's story a related disjunction between spectator and actor; it is only when the protagonist's consciousness is dissociated from his body, when he is on the verge of freezing to death, that he becomes capable of "a certain self-assessment" (p. 30). This is, I should note, only one point in Mitchell's subtle and convincing analysis of how theme and style work together to make the story a narrative enactment of determinism.

23. Naomi Schor, "Introduction," *Yale French Studies*, no. 42 (1969): 6.

24. Leo Braudy, "Zola on Film: the Ambiguities of Naturalism," *Yale French Studies*, no. 42 (1969): 69–70.

25. Phillip Walker, "The Mirror, the Window, and the Eye in Zola's Fiction," *Yale French Studies*, no. 42 (1969): 52, 55.

26. Naomi Schor, "Zola: From Window to Window," *Yale French Studies*, no. 42 (1969): 47, 50–51.

27. Philip Fisher, "Acting, Reading, Fortune's Wheel: *Sister Carrie* and the Life History of Objects," in *American Realism*, ed. Sundquist, p. 261.

28. Franklin Walker, *Frank Norris: A Biography* (Garden City, N.Y.: Doubleday, Doran & Co., 1932), pp. 257–58.

29. See George E. Mowry, *The California Progressives* (1951; reprint, New York: Quadrangle Books, New York Times Book Company, 1963), pp. 11–12, 18, 20.

30. I do not mean to claim that Presley is a consistent spokesman for the author in the sense that he always voices Norris's ideas, an assumption Donald Pizer has persuasively opposed (*The Novels of Frank Norris* [Bloomington: Indiana University Press, 1966], pp. 125 ff.), but I do argue that he has a particularly close relationship with the narrator and reader. Indeed, that is why readers and critics have often assumed that he is a consistent spokesman.

31. Frank Norris, *The Octopus: A Story of California*, vols. 1 and 2 of *The Complete Edition of Frank Norris* (Garden City, N.Y.: Doubleday, Doran & Co., 1928), 1:6.

32. The brute is "red-eyed" with surprising frequency—in *The Octopus* one can cite not only this passage but the description of the locomotive quoted earlier; think also of Maggie's mother with her "inflamed eyes" and of the atavistic brute "Red-Eye" in *Before Adam*. The image is clearly conventional, but it may also be significant that it evokes "seeing red" or anger, violence, and in *The Octopus* quite explicitly (2:85) political radicalism. The spectator's eye is the seat of rational observation, but the brute's is suffused with blood.

33. No one, of course, actually built the P. & S.W.'s fictional tracks, but "the Southern Pacific lines, especially in California, were built almost entirely with Chinese labor" (Elmer Clarence Sandmeyer, *The Anti-Chinese Movement in California* [1939; reprint, Urbana: University of Illinois Press, 1973], p. 15).

34. Richard Hofstadter, *The Age of Reform: From Bryan to F.D.R.* (New

York: Random House, 1955). To define the period thus is of course an act of advocacy as well as analysis, as subsequent historians have noted, and I do not necessarily mean to endorse Hofstadter's views.

35. On populism see the brief discussion in chap. 3 and Lawrence Goodwyn, *The Populist Moment: A Short History of the Agrarian Revolt in America* (New York: Oxford University Press, 1978).

36. David M. Kennedy, "Overview: The Progressive Era," *Historian* 37 (1975): 453. I use "progressivism" to refer not only to the Progressive party (which was not formed until 1912) but to the movement in general.

37. Mowry, *The California Progressives*, p. 91.

38. Both James Weinstein and Gabriel Kolko (see nn. 40 and 41) discuss dissension among business leaders as to what policies will best serve their interests.

39. Mowry, *The California Progressives*, p. 51. The interpolation is Mowry's.

40. James Weinstein, *The Corporate Ideal in the Liberal State, 1900–1918* (Boston: Beacon, 1968), p. 107.

41. Gabriel Kolko, *The Triumph of Conservatism: A Reinterpretation of American History, 1900–1916* (New York: Macmillan, 1963), pp. 2–3.

42. Kennedy, "Overview," p. 458.

43. Jacob A. Riis, *How the Other Half Lives: Studies among the Tenements of New York* (1890; reprint, New York: Dover, 1971), p. 207.

44. Robert H. Wiebe, *The Search for Order, 1877–1920* (New York: Hill and Wang, 1967), p. 169. Anthony Platt argues, however, that, as in the case of other progressive programs, the effect of legal and penal reforms on juvenile justice was not quite what their rhetoric would suggest; his study criticizes "the myth that the child-saving movement was successful in humanizing the criminal justice system, rescuing children from jails and prisons, and developing dignified judicial and penal institutions for juveniles. It argues that, if anything, the child savers helped to create a system that subjected more and more juveniles to arbitrary and degrading punishments" (Anthony M. Platt, *The Child Savers: The Invention of Delinquency*, 2d ed. [Chicago: University of Chicago Press, 1977], p. xvii).

45. Charles Dwight Willard, "The Care of the Unfortunate," *California Outlook* 12, no. 21 (1912): 7.

46. Platt, *The Child Savers*, p. xxviii.

47. Ronald L. Boostrom, "Criminology, Crime Control and the Rise of the Corporate State" (Paper prepared for the annual Conference of the Midwest Sociological Society, Minneapolis, Minnesota, April 15, 1977), p. 15.

48. Platt, *The Child Savers*, pp. xxvi-xxvii.

49. Alan Trachtenberg, *The Incorporation of America: Culture and Society in the Gilded Age* (New York: Hill and Wang, 1982), p. 64.

50. For a general discussion of Taylor see Harry Braverman's classic *Labor and Monopoly Capital: The Degradation of Work in the Twentieth Century* (New York: Monthly Review Press, 1974), pp. 85–123.

51. Frederick Winslow Taylor, *The Principles of Scientific Management* (1911; reprint, New York: W. W. Norton, 1967), p. 10.

52. Thomas L. Haskell, *The Emergence of Professional Social Science: The American Social Science Association and the Nineteenth-Century Crisis of Authority* (Urbana: University of Illinois Press, 1977), p. 26.

53. Burton J. Bledstein, *The Culture of Professionalism: The Middle*

Class and the Development of Higher Education in America (New York: W. W. Norton, 1976), p. ix.

54. The idea of "disabling professions" I take from Ivan Illich et al., *Disabling Professions* (1977; reprint, Boston: Marion Boyars, 1978), without intending to endorse Illich's essentially nostalgic bent.

55. Boostrom, "Criminology," p. 20.

56. Christopher P. Wilson, "American Naturalism and the Problem of Sincerity," *American Literature* 54 (1982): 511.

Chapter 5

1. Theodore Dreiser, "True Art Speaks Plainly" (1903), in George J. Becker, ed., *Documents of Modern Literary Realism* (Princeton, N.J.: Princeton University Press, 1963), p. 156.

2. I hope it is already apparent but let me here explicitly note that I use "genre" and "form" to indicate the same object of study viewed from the slightly different perspectives made available by different critical discussions. "Genre" focuses our attention on the problem of classification, while "form" tends to direct us to the shape or structure of a work. The categories are of course only momentarily separable.

3. Jonathan Culler, *Structuralist Poetics: Structuralism, Linguistics, and the Study of Literature* (Ithaca, N.Y.: Cornell University Press, 1975), pp. 221–22.

4. Sigmund Freud, *Jokes and Their Relation to the Unconscious* (1905), trans. and ed. James Strachey (New York: W. W. Norton, 1960). This easily available volume contains the text of the *Standard Edition*.

5. Fredric Jameson, *Marxism and Form: Twentieth-Century Dialectical Theories of Literature* (Princeton, N.J.: Princeton University Press, 1971), p. 195.

6. I use Austen as an example here precisely because she is not one of Lukács's exemplary realists and to suggest the very different ways in which courtship, marriage, and the family, which are discussed below, are handled in different kinds of novels.

7. See for example Georg Lukács, *Realism in Our Time: Literature and the Class Struggle* (1958), trans. John and Necke Mander (New York: Harper and Row, 1971).

8. My thinking on this point has been influenced by Richard Terdiman, *The Dialectics of Isolation: Self and Society in the French Novel from the Realists to Proust* (New Haven: Yale University Press, 1976).

9. Charles Child Walcutt, *American Literary Naturalism, A Divided Stream* (1956; reprint, Westport, Conn.: Greenwood Press, 1976), p. 22.

10. Georg Lukács, *Writer and Critic and Other Essays*, trans. and ed. Arthur D. Kahn (New York: Grosset & Dunlap, 1971), pp. 115–16.

11. Theodore Dreiser, *Sister Carrie*, ed. Donald Pizer (New York: W. W. Norton, 1970), chap. 27, p. 194.

12. Roland Barthes, *S/Z: An Essay* (1970), trans. Richard Miller (New York: Hill and Wang, 1974), p. 81.

13. Fredric Jameson, "On Goffman's Frame Analysis," *Theory and Society* 3 (1976): 121, 123.

14. John Berger and Jean Mohr, *Another Way of Telling* (New York: Pantheon, 1982), p. 99.

15. Franklin Walker, *Frank Norris: A Biography* (Garden City, N.Y.: Doubleday, Doran & Co., 1932), p. 240.

16. Reprinted in Frank Norris, *The Octopus* (New York: Signet Books, New American Library, 1964), p. vi.

17. Frank Norris, *The Octopus: A Story of California* (1901), vols. 1 and 2 of *The Complete Edition of Frank Norris* (Garden City, N.Y.: Doubleday, Doran & Co., 1928), 2:358–59.

18. Jack London, *The People of the Abyss* (New York: Macmillan, 1903), p. 3.

19. The examples I am thinking of are James Agee and Walker Evans, *Let Us Now Praise Famous Men*; Truman Capote, *In Cold Blood*; Norman Mailer, *The Armies of the Night* and *The Executioner's Song*; Alex Haley, *Roots*; Studs Terkel, *Working*; Ishmael Reed, *Mumbo Jumbo*; E. L. Doctorow, *Ragtime*; Maxine Hong Kingston, *The Woman Warrior*; John Berger, *A Seventh Man* and *Pig Earth*.

20. On this possibility in photography see Allan Sekula, "Dismantling Modernism, Reinventing Documentary (Notes on the Politics of Representation)," *Massachusetts Review* 19 (1978): 859–83. For an important perspective on documentary rather different from the one I take here see Barbara Foley, "History, Fiction, and the Ground Between: The Uses of the Documentary Mode in Black Literature," *PMLA* 95 (1980): 389–403.

21. See *Sister Carrie: The Pennsylvania Edition*, ed. Neda M. Westlake, John C. Berkey, Alice M. Winters, and James L. W. West III (Philadelphia: University of Pennsylvania Press, 1981), p. 525.

22. Ellen Moers, *Two Dreisers* (New York: Viking Press, 1969), p. 67. The full title of the article is "Curious Shifts of the Poor. Strange Ways of Relieving Desperate Poverty.—Last Resources of New York's Most Pitiful Mendicants."

23. Alan Trachtenberg, *The Incorporation of America: Culture and Society in the Gilded Age* (New York: Hill and Wang, 1982), p. 122.

24. Upton Sinclair, *The Jungle* (New York: Doubleday, Page & Co., 1906), p. 38.

25. Upton Sinclair, *The Autobiography of Upton Sinclair* (New York: Harcourt, Brace & World, 1962), p. 109.

26. See Gabriel Kolko, *The Triumph of Conservatism: A Reinterpretation of American History, 1900–1916* (New York: Macmillan, 1963), pp. 98–110.

27. Sinclair quotes his own remark in his *Autobiography*, p. 126.

28. On the failure of *King Coal* see also William A. Bloodworth, Jr., *Upton Sinclair* (Boston: Twayne, 1977), p. 80.

29. Upton Sinclair, *King Coal: A Novel* (New York: Macmillan, 1917), p. 5.

30. The sequel to *King Coal*, dealing directly with the strike, was not published until 1976. Upton Sinclair, *The Coal War: A Sequel to "King Coal"*, introd. John Graham (Boulder: Colorado Associated University Press, 1976).

31. James T. Farrell, *Young Lonigan* (1932), in *Studs Lonigan: A Trilogy* (New York: Random House, 1938), pp. 199–200.

32. Hubert Selby, Jr., *Last Exit to Brooklyn* (New York: Grove Press, 1964), p. 11.

33. John Dos Passos, *U.S.A.* (New York: Random House, 1937), pp. v, vii.

34. John G. Cawelti, *Adventure, Mystery, and Romance: Formula Stories as Art and Popular Culture* (Chicago: University of Chicago Press, 1976), p. 262.

35. Fredric Jameson, "Authentic *Ressentiment*: The 'Experimental' Novels of Gissing," *Nineteenth-Century Fiction* 31 (1976): 130. This essay is an early version of chap. 4 of *The Political Unconscious* (cited in n. 36).

36. I quote Jameson, *The Political Unconscious: Narrative as a Socially Symbolic Act* (Ithaca, N.Y.: Cornell University Press, 1981), p. 141. The argument I make in this section is based partly on Jameson's "Reification and Utopia in Mass Culture," *Social Text*, no. 1 (1979): 130–48.

37. See work in progress by Richard Ohmann and by the collective that produces the journal *Tabloid*. For an example of a study of how mass-culture texts are actually read, see Janice A. Radway, "Women Read the Romance: The Interaction of Text and Context," *Feminist Studies* 9 (1983): 53–78.

38. The word "best-seller" was apparently in use by 1905 to describe the lists published in *The Bookman* beginning in 1895. See James D. Hart, *The Popular Book: A History of America's Literary Taste* (Berkeley: University of California Press, 1963), pp. 184–85.

39. *The Fiction Factory: Or From Pulp Row to Quality Street* is the title of Quentin Reynolds's "Story of 100 Years of Publishing at Street & Smith" (New York: Random House, 1955). The book opens by quoting Dreiser on the need for a history of this publishing house, thus invoking the authority of an author who has been widely accepted in high culture.

40. Christopher Wilson, "American Naturalism and the Problem of Sincerity," *American Literature* 4 (1982): 525.

41. Cawelti, *Adventure, Mystery, and Romance*, p. 261. It is of course not useful to speak of melodrama as "escapist." Cawelti's valuable analysis is often limited by his assumption that wish-fulfillments are universal, that formulas are merely archetypes clothed in specific cultural costumes, thus obscuring the way in which fantasy satisfactions are themselves historically bound and therefore historically significant.

42. Martin Green, *Dreams of Adventure, Deeds of Empire* (New York: Basic Books, 1979), pp. 23, 3.

43. Jack London, *The Sea-Wolf* (New York: Macmillan, 1904), pp. 7, 155.

44. Nina Baym, *Woman's Fiction: A Guide to Novels by and about Women in America, 1820–1870* (Ithaca, N.Y.: Cornell University Press, 1978), p. 27.

45. On the attack on the sentimental and Frederic's relation to realism and naturalism see Everett Carter, *Howells and the Age of Realism* (Philadelphia: J. B. Lippincott, 1954).

46. Harold Frederic, *Seth's Brother's Wife: A Study of Life in the Greater New York* (New York: Charles Scribner's Sons, 1887), pp. 1, 401–2.

47. Cathy N. and Arnold E. Davidson, "Carrie's Sisters: The Popular Prototypes for Dreiser's Heroine," *Modern Fiction Studies* 23 (1977): 395.

48. Frank Norris, *Vandover and the Brute* (1914), vol. 5 of *The Complete Edition of Frank Norris* (Garden City, N.Y.: Doubleday, Doran & Co., 1928), p. 179.

49. Jacob Riis, *How the Other Half Lives* (1890; reprint, Dover, 1971), p. 207; and Finley Peter Dunne, quoted in Maxwell H. Bloomfield, *Alarms and Diversions* (The Hague: Mouton, 1967), p. 17. Both are quoted at greater length in Chapter 3.

Index

Social science, professionalization of, 127, 137–38, 140
Sontag, Susan, 47; *Illness as Metaphor*, 45
Southern Pacific Railroad, 117, 120, 128, 129, 130, 193 (n. 34), 197 (n. 33)
Spectator: in naturalist novels, x, 125–27, 128, 131, 137, 138, 139, 141, 142, 150, 151–52; in Dreiser, 106–11; in London, 111, 114; in Norris, 117–25
Sundquist, Eric, 29

Taylor, Frederick Winslow, 81, 136–37
Tel Quel (journal), 21
Todorov, Tzvetan, 7, 143; *The Fantastic*, 4–6, 183 (n. 1)
Trachtenberg, Alan, 32–33, 42–43, 72, 98, 136, 155–56, 168, 181, 187 (n. 73)

Urbanization. *See* City

Walcutt, Charles Child: on naturalism, 37–38, 39, 40, 69, 99, 109, 131; on art and social change, 116, 125, 126, 140; on naturalist form, 145, 171

Walker, Francis A., 85–86
Walker, Phillip, 114
Watt, Ian: *The Rise of the Novel*, 11
Wave, The (journal), 88, 89, 193 (n. 34)
Weinstein, James, 129–30, 131, 135
White, Hayden, 80; *Metahistory*, 80
Wiebe, Robert, 49, 72–73, 77–78, 79, 133, 135; *The Search for Order, 1877–1920*, 75, 136
Willard, Charles Dwight, 133, 134
Williams, Raymond, 10–11, 12
Wilson, Christopher, 140–41, 170
Window imagery, 114–15, 116
Wolf imagery, 102; in London, 50, 54–57, 59, 112, 190–91 (n. 28); in Norris, 67–68
Workers, stereotypes of, 78–83, 161–63. *See also* Brute imagery

Yale French Studies, 114

Zola, Émile, 12, 18, 19, 22, 26, 37, 76; *Thérèse Raquin*, 11, 62, 114; on naturalism, 13, 16, 146; *Le Roman expérimental*, 17; and American naturalism, 29, 30; window imagery in, 114–15, 116; *Les Rougon-Macquart*, 148